Working on a Dream

Working on a Dream

The Progressive Political Vision of Bruce Springsteen

David Masciotra

continuum

2010

The Continuum International Publishing Group Inc
80 Maiden Lane, New York, NY 10038

The Continuum International Publishing Group Ltd
The Tower Building, 11 York Road, London SE1 7NX

www.continuumbooks.com

Library of Congress Cataloging-in-Publication Data
A catalog record for this book is available from the Library of Congress

ISBN: 978-0-8264-2505-8

Typeset by Pindar NZ, Auckland, New Zealand
Printed in the United States of America

Contents

*This book is dedicated to my mother, Pearl Masciotra,
who every single day teaches me about love, service and
community with the ongoing song that is her life.*

I don't have any delusions about whatever power rock musicians have — I tend to believe it's relatively little. Though it may be little, it is important in its particularness. This first time I recognized the country I lived in, the truest version I ever heard, was when I put on Bob Dylan's *Highway 61 Revisited*. I went, "That's it. That's what it feels like." . . . All you want is for your voice to be part of the record, at a particular time and place. You try to be on the right side of history. And maybe some other kid will hear that and go, "Oh, yeah, that sounds like the place I live."

— Bruce Springsteen

Listen to people's stories. You want to help the world? Read the poetry of the people we're bombing. Write poetry for them. Sing songs for them, and for us.

— Sherman Alexie

Song Lyric Permissions

Introduction

We learned more from a three minute record than we ever learned
in school

— "No Surrender," 1984

The power of my first memory of Bruce Springsteen's music is difficult to explain to someone who has not undergone a similar moment of transformation initiated by the artistic production of a total stranger. Yet when I determine the origin of my own real education, mobilization of my creative energy, and expansion of my social conscience, I begin with the day I rented *Bruce Springsteen: Video Anthology 1978–1988*.

I was 13 years old and I had already grown to appreciate and admire the music of John Mellencamp — a towering songwriter in his own right, with an impressive catalogue of work and a social conscience to match. One day my middle-school principal caught a glimpse of Mellencamp's *Scarecrow* between my notebooks as I was attempting to conceal it, so I would not be punished for listening to music during school hours. Instead of reprimanding me, Mr. Helming expressed his approval of my newly formed musical tastes and casually said, "If you like Mellencamp, you should check out Springsteen."

Curiosity, along with admiration for Helming, motivated me to follow his advice and rent the video anthology I remembered seeing on the shelf at the local video store. That night, I hardly knew that by pressing the play button on my duct tape-repaired remote control that I was signing the release for my own intellectual emancipation. The small world that I lived in, while enjoyable and congruent to a happy life, was busted open and entire worlds began to appear when I closed my eyes and heard the soulful serenade of Springsteen's harmonica opening "Thunder Road" or ending "The Promised Land."

I enjoyed Springsteen's music on a variety of levels. His deep and raspy voice, while not traditionally strong, sounded soulful and honest — like a prophet painting a dreadfully grim portrait of the future and in the middle of it stopping and shouting, "This is the way it is and if you want hope, damn it, you better listen." I appreciated his style — the cowboy boots, blue jeans, and tough, but not humorously macho, demeanor. The most obviously appealing aspect of Springsteen was the music he made with the phenomenal E Street Band. It offered a provocative and electrifying hybridization of 1960s soul, 1950s rock, and timeless folk.

However, what kept me coming back and back to the Springsteen catalogue, eventually collecting bootlegs, and attempting to gain a greater understanding of his words and music, was the profound and shattering impact it had upon my life. I was more moved by those songs than by anything I had ever previously encountered — including the religion that I was told by family and teachers would make me feel reborn. I did not believe that I needed redemption or existential reawakening at such a young age — but I found it and what seemed to be the "key to the universe," not in the "engine of an old parked car," but in those Springsteen songs.

The non-traditional and secular hymns, filled with emotive melodies and contemplative lyrics, both famous — "Born to Run," "Born in the U.S.A.," "Badlands" — and obscure — "Racing in the Street," "The Promise," "The Ghost of Tom Joad" — catalyzed my political awakening, philosophical development, and commitment to understanding what it means to be an American, and what it means to be human.

In the years since I discovered Springsteen, I have gone to plenty of diverse sources to deepen my understanding of American and human identities. Fyodor Dostoevsky, Karl Marx, Herman Melville, Cormac McCarthy, Cornel West, Noam Chomsky and Gore Vidal have played pivotal roles in my intellectual life, but it all started with a screen door slamming on the streets of a runaway American Dream.

On September 27, 1999, I rode with Principal Scott Helming to the United Center in Chicago to see Bruce Springsteen and the E Street Band in concert for the very first time. Helming had not seen Springsteen perform in decades. As the band walked out on to the stage, followed by Bruce, I felt an overwhelming wave of emotion engulf me and was unable to come up for air throughout the rest of the night as we marveled at the guitar solo on "Prove It All Night," sang along with "Out in the Street," were asked to suffer with "The Ghost of Tom Joad," and danced while "Working on the Highway." The band opened that night with "The Ties That Bind," a song about the love, human solidarity and communitarian possibilities that bind us all together if we embrace them, and which we reject at our own peril. That night, the tie that bound Helming and me together was our deep love and admiration for

Springsteen, and when the opening chords of "Jungleland" lifted through the arena, I saw a tear in Helming's eye. This man that was 30 years my senior, and a prominent authority figure in my life, was no different than me that night. The music of Bruce Springsteen had not only connected the singer to his audience, but members of the audience to each other.

This is the promising and powerful capability of Springsteen's music that is duplicated in city after city throughout the world. His ability to make people feel transformed and connected is what allows him to get away with a sincerity and resistance of irony and outright rebellion that is otherwise mocked in rock and roll. Springsteen has observed that he has "never really fit in" to the music scene at any point in his career. In the 1970s, his music was romantic and contained a sense of innocence, which contrasted with the popular rock of that decade. In the 1980s, there were few nods to commercialism, narcissism, or trendiness on his albums. Instead he told stories of people immobilized by heartbreak and despair, either due to their own personal failures or the consequences of political and social decision-making processes that were out of their control. Although he never again reached the popularity he had with *Born in the U.S.A.*, he was never punished for his passion and commitment to making emotionally real, and socially and politically honest music. His ability to remain true to the artistic integrity of his own vision unscathed is a testament to his musical brilliance and his ability to remain maladjusted to the mainstream. He has not been subjected to an artistic ghetto of limited visibility, but he has also refused to be exploited and manipulated for agendas that strengthen and solidify the status quo — whether they come from Ronald Reagan or Corporate America. By doing this he has effectively empathized with the victims of America's marketplace politics and imperial hubris — the despised minorities made invisible on the margins of society — and provoked his audience to recognize that bitter alienation and existential emptiness that afflicts the working class of a country and culture controlled by profit utility-obsessed corporate capitalists who neglect the public interest and common good. To rise from the ashes of the "darkness on the edge of town" throughout this nation, Springsteen has advocated a return to community, solidarity and assistance for others rooted in our common humanity. The values that guide these processes are difficult to miss, as they are constantly returned to in Springsteen's work: empathy, democracy, and most of all, love. Love for the working class, love for the subjects of his songs, and love for all peoples is the centerpiece to his dissent, which offers a crucial lesson for the preachers of the gospel of greed on the right and the too often patronizing, condescending and elitist left. His ability to propagate this radical message within the mainstream institutions and media forums dedicated to undermining it has been agile and acrobatic.

The negative consequence of Springsteen walking this political and musical tightrope is confusion among a significant amount of his fan base. His tendency to couch powerful commentary in storytelling narratives with poetic terminology has also provided an excuse for casual fans to miss or deliberately ignore the points as well. Some of Springsteen's peers who have taken a more straightforward approach to social and political commentary in music like that of Steve Earle, Neil Young and Mellencamp have not enjoyed the same success as Springsteen (with the possible exception of Young), but have also not had the core message of their music so often confused.

Of course, the confusion among many of Springsteen's fans is evident at any Springsteen concert. For every fan that displays comprehension of the multifaceted psychological, sociological and political importance of Bruce's music, there are three or four who seem to have, at least partially, missed the point. They can be seen drunkenly stumbling into the bathroom while Springsteen plays a new or philosophically relevant song, whining about not hearing "Glory Days," which has a strong feeling of regret and disappoint-ment that is also probably lost on them.

They were also quite vocal when Springsteen decided to actively campaign for John Kerry during the 2004 Presidential race. Only someone not paying close attention could listen to Springsteen for several years and be surprised that his politics lean left. Using Springsteen's own music and previous record of activism to measure radical progressivism, the John Kerry endorsement, while it was his first foray into electoral politics, was politically mild.

To be sure, there are plenty of reasons to listen to Springsteen's music: The epic qualities of "Jungleland" and "New York City Serenade," the danceable rhythms of "Ramrod" and "Cadillac Ranch," the soulfulness of "Tenth Avenue Freeze-Out" and "Mary's Place," or the devastating rock of "Badlands" and "Murder Incorporated." However, to substantively allow Springsteen's music into one's life, one must confront the radical vision the songwriter presents to America, which includes both a diagnosis of the disease created by America's corporately controlled marketplace politics and culture, and a progressive prescription to heal its often self-inflicted wounds.

In recent years this vision, or at least an intentionally misunderstood version of it, has been tackled by a host of right-wing critics who react to his anti-war and anti-Bush criticism by calling him one of two preferred totalitarian terms, "unpatriotic" or "anti-American." This style of language has been used before in places like the Soviet Union and Nazi Germany where dissidents, before being imprisoned or executed, would be labeled "anti-Soviet" or "anti-German." The current popularity of this line of attack in America is indicative of how distorted many pundits' and politicians' concept of democracy is, and the perversion of their political priorities. The same people who serve as apologists for growing inequality, disgraceful public schools and abysmal social conditions in poor and expanding parts of America arbitrate staggering amounts of outrage when someone commits the unforgivable sin of expressing dissent. Favorite right-wing targets who illicit the most hatred and scorn, from popular filmmakers (Michael Moore, Sean Penn) to little-known ethnic studies professors (Ward Churchill), have all been guilty only of saying things that offend the delicate sensibilities and sentimentality of jingoistic and depoliticized reactionaries.

Springsteen was correct to respond to such attacks by saying, "That's just the language of the day — the modus operandi for anybody who doesn't like somebody criticizing where we've been or where we're going. It's unpatriotic at any given moment to sit back and let things pass that are damaging to some place that you love so dearly and that has given you so much."[1]

His idea of democracy is in favor with Frederick Douglass and Thomas Jefferson, who both placed dissent at its heart.

The other criticism often levied against Springsteen is that because he is rich, he cannot possibly empathize with the oppressed and downtrodden. Critics who accept this platform fail to recognize that empathy and political sympathy are not exclusive to any race or class. There are a large number of working-class voters who continually vote against their own economic interests for social and religious reasons, just as there are many in the middle class who, although closer in proximity and financial situation to the poor than Springsteen, are the first to object to proposals of universal health care or increased funds for the vital public institutions and support centers that grant opportunity, security and dignity to American citizens. On the flip side of the same coin, there are wealthy people throughout the world dedicated to progressive politics and philanthropy — just as there are selfish rich people and compassionate poor and middle-class people.

One can only judge a person by his work, which demonstrates a love or indifference to people, and the consistency of his courage to stand for causes of service. Springsteen has shown a capacity for empathy and service to others that is rare in popular music, and while the right often reminds people that "one should not be punished for success," they attempt to use the success of Springsteen and others like him to silence political expression from the arts and entertainment community.

While the right wing of American politics continues to display their own ignorance and narrow-mindedness by dishing out these smelly canards about dissenters, the left celebrates certain aspects of Springsteen's music but reveals its weakness and ineffectiveness by failing to apply its message to activist outreach programs that could have great potential. The failure to recognize the power of Springsteen's music may be small by comparison to other liberal political failures but it is symbolic of a general inability of liberal politics to meaningfully and persuasively express itself in tough and smart terms. The left and right sort out their own misgivings and deficiencies while a vast amount of Middle Americans, both in the financial and political senses of the word, enjoy Bruce Springsteen's creative output while missing its prophetic, progressive and powerful message.

Therefore, the goal of this book is three-fold.

First, it is to reveal that Springsteen's music, vastly varied in style and scope, provides listeners with a "danceable education" (to quote Cornel West in a different context), which presents crucial insights into the American psyche, sociology and political reality. Its analysis of poverty, community, race, and the usage of American power cannot be ignored. Nor can its ability to provide hope, meaning, purpose and renewal in the harshest of conditions be dismissed. In recent decades, America has embraced Springsteen as its poet laureate without fully grasping his willingness to wrestle with the tragic. This wrestling demonstrates an understanding of where human drama and public policy meet that is sorely lacking in America. This book aims to reverse that indifference and apathy by revealing the important and confrontational challenge of Springsteen's vision so that readers and listeners gain the ability and willingness to self-apply it in a critical fashion, which promotes understanding and reflection on consequential issues. Familiarity with Springsteen's music will not cause the elevation of political consciousness alone but it can be used as a predicate for exploration of topics and subjects pivotal to social justice.

Second, this book is written to make Springsteen's message accessible to activists. An introduction to Springsteen would assist the cause of activists because it may provide them with another tool of recruitment. But, more likely and more importantly, it will speak to their spirit and inspire them to hope and keep moving "further on up the road." Progressive political activism can often be characterized by depressing and fruitless labor. Hope comes in short supply, and the vision of self-respect, solidarity and self-actualization found in Springsteen's best work would be entirely useful to beleaguered activists. Truth and hope have been found in art throughout the course of human history and an understanding of Springsteen may have the power to reintroduce people to the vocation and invocation of the artist. This will be especially important after the promising and inspiring victory of electing Barack Obama president. It will also be necessary for the left to mobilize with greater commitment, energy, vision and hope when dealing with an administration that will be more sympathetic to their needs, concerns and goals. Adding a Springsteen flare to the American left could provide it with a taste of the energy, positivity and ability to remain maladjusted to the mainstream, while engaging the mainstream, that it has lacked for decades.

Finally, this book is my way of performing the same invaluable service my former principal, Scott Helming, performed for me by saying, "you should check out Springsteen." If after reading this book readers are inspired to tap into the hope and vitality offered by Springsteen's music, then this service will be rendered. This means, more than anything, that one must dive head first and deep into the music. The best way to feel the power, purpose and transcendence of Springsteen's music is to listen to it.

One hopes this book does not neglect to emphasize the "danceable" while speaking of the "danceable education" of Springsteen. "Born to Run" would not mean much without its wall-of-sound exuberance that moves from the ground up and sings directly to the soul. The sadness of "Streets of Philadelphia" would not be nearly as palpable without the ominous, dull hum of a melancholy synthesizer riff or the dread repeating of a defeated "li, li, li, li, li, li, li" chorus. Reflection upon how the music interacts with the words and vice-versa to create such a grand and great expression of vision will be required.

So, while we begin the journey through the wilderness and darkness inhabited by Springsteen's characters, the communities of hope and fulfill-ment mapped out by the singer, and the political and sociological landmarks containing crucial windows into American society, the best way to start may be the most familiar.

"Ah 1, 2, ah 1, 2, 3, 4!"

Chapter 1

Open to Pain and Crossed by the Rain

A Biographical Sketch

Bruce Frederick Joseph Springsteen was born on September 29, 1949, to Douglas and Adele, and would eventually have two sisters — Virginia and Pamela. The Springsteen family lived in a working-class section of Freehold, New Jersey, called "Texas" because of the high amount of Southern Americans who migrated to Freehold in a rarely discussed migration. Around the time of the great migration north, there was much prediction of an economic boom in Freehold, but none of the promise turned out to be bankable. Freehold never found prosperity and was destined to be permanently blue collar. The most steady and stable source of work in Freehold during the 1950s and '60s was a rug mill on the edge of town where Springsteen's father was employed for several years before working as a bus driver and prison guard. The rug mill was considered by many to be not only the economic center of the town but the "spiritual center" as well — a "brick reminder" of the town's hopes and past.

Socially and politically, Springsteen has described the Freehold he grew up in as a "redneck town." During his youth, it was extremely segregated with whites and blacks living on literally opposite sides of a railroad track. Race relations were tense and bitter, and Springsteen classifies the overall mentality of Freehold as "small, narrow-minded, very conservative, and stagnating."

Springsteen attended Catholic grade school and usually applied the same description to the nuns and priests who taught, but perhaps more often scolded, him. Highlights of his middle-school experience include being stuffed in a trash can by a nun and being punched by a student on a different nun's order.

Unsurprisingly, Springsteen chose not to continue Catholic education and instead enroll in Freehold's public high school which, due to its high number of black students, was despised and looked-down upon by the community. In high school, Springsteen dealt first hand with the contradicting treatment one receives when hated — the polar opposite kinds of visibility. In some moments, because of his long hair and detached attitude (he participated in no school activities) he was glared at, mocked, and given the form of special attention that is never wanted. In the next moment, he would be invisible and the entire school community would barely acknowledge his existence. Springsteen put it simply, "there was the wall, then me."

He began attending class at Ocean County Community College in Jersey but abruptly quit when a counselor called him into his office and interrogated him about his long hair and leather jacket, and told him to stop thinking about rock 'n' roll. Springsteen asked him, "What's your problem?" and walked off campus, never to return. If it were not for the one liberating force in Springsteen's life, rock 'n' roll, he probably would have ended up at that rug mill — a prospect which terrified him. But, at the age of nine when he saw Elvis Presley perform on the *The Ed Sullivan Show*, he knew what his life was supposed to be about. Bob Dylan said the first time he saw Elvis it felt like he was "busting out of jail." Springsteen would most likely share that characterization.

Rock 'n' roll gave him hope, meaning and strength. It provided him with a "community of people, brothers and sisters, who I don't know, but know are out there," and a "home where my spirit could wander." There is no exaggerating the power that music had in Springsteen's life — as the man himself has said on more than one occasion, "It gave me a reason to live."

It also established a great divide in the already divided relationship he had with his father, who Springsteen described as "embittered" and "dark," and without a single friend. Springsteen still contends that in 20 years not one person came to their house to visit him. He was a menacing authority figure in the Springsteen household, prone to staying awake, sitting in the pitch-black kitchen, slugging booze and smoking, waiting for Bruce to return so he could violently yell at him about his hair, his obsession with rock 'n' roll and casual attitude. Physical confrontations were commonly broken up by Springsteen's mother. Douglas Springsteen was a brooding figure who could not muster any support for his son's musical ambitions. He referred to Bruce's practicing exclusively in these terms, "Turn down that goddamn guitar!" and would sometimes resort to turning on the gas jets on the stove and directing them into the heating ducts in an attempt to smoke Bruce out of the house.

Springsteen joked that his father may have believed that "Goddamn" was actually a guitar manufacturer, and was not really trying to belittle his passion. The guitar was not produced by "Goddamn," but actually made by Kent in Japan. It was purchased for him by his mother, Adele, in a moment that has been immortalized, along with his abiding love for her, in the song "The Wish." Although Adele was a legal secretary who worked for minimum wage, she took out a $60 loan to buy her son the one thing he wanted more than anything in the world.

Springsteen has often spoken of his mother's act of love and generosity: "Sixty dollars was more money than I had ever seen in one place in my life. It was a very defining moment, standing in front of the music store with someone who's going to do everything she can to give you what you needed that day, and having the faith that you were going to make sense of it."

This contrast between his mother — a loving, optimistic and sweet-hearted woman — and his father — a dark, brooding and nearly oppressive figure — makes some of the contradictions in his music more understandable. His home life hosted a battle between the dark and the light, just as America has done throughout its history, and every individual must do at some point in his or her own life. Juxtaposing Springsteen's mother and father, one parent willing to take a loan out to support her son when working for minimum wage while the family drives a car that will not go in reverse, and another parent only willing to scream and berate his son's interests and dreams, reveals a stunning disposition that the young Springsteen had to sort out, accept and attempt to psychologically rectify. Springsteen sang about this juxtaposition in "The Wish": "If pa's eyes were windows into a world so deadly and true / You couldn't stop me from looking but you kept me from crawlin' through."

The paradigm of Springsteen's relationship with his parents is best symbolized by his guitar, which was a gift of love and support from one parent and source of resentment and anger to the other. That guitar became an obsession of Springsteen's, for purposes of wealth, work and self-respect. He said that one of the first times he could stand looking in the mirror was when he was holding his guitar. He played night and day and got into his first band, "The Castilles," after learning how to play five songs in one night in response to the band leader telling him that he would have to be able to play lead on at least five songs to be welcomed into the band. They played at any venue that would accept them, from the local roller-dome to an insane asylum, but never found much success or popularity.

It was not until he formed the band "Steel Mill" that he would begin to get a taste of what music stardom could be like. It featured future members of the E Street Band, including Steven Van Zandt and Dan Federici, and took after the hard rock riff-oriented music of Led Zeppelin and Cream. They quickly developed a large following around the Jersey Shore, and even earned themselves a few opening gigs in San Francisco at well-known music clubs.

Despite all of this, the band failed to garner a record contract, which motivated most members to quit and get "real jobs." Springsteen, however, took a bus up to Greenwich Village and played shows at the folk clubs and coffee houses, which paid him just enough to eat and sleep in a bed.

His next band, while talented and musically exciting, was more of a carnival-style representation of performance art than a real attempt to earn a living making rock music. "Dr. Zoom and the Sonic Boom" featured 30 members, including the soon-to-be Jersey Shore favorite Southside Johnny, most of whom did not play instruments but depicted the stories being told in the songs or engaged in random acts of maintenance like engine repair. Eventually "Dr. Zoom" downsized into the less confusingly titled "Bruce Springsteen Band," which was composed entirely of future E Street Band members in the late 1960s and early 1970s.

Still bigger than what became the E Street Band, it featured an entire horn section and three female backup singers. This was the first band Springsteen led that was dedicated to performing his original work, which was growing ever more popular in the Jersey clubs, most especially Asbury Park.

Springsteen's heart found peace and comfort in Asbury, along with a significant audience for its holder's music. He also traces his appreciation for community back to his days playing the Uptown in Asbury Park — a now lionized club where young musicians "looking for that million dollar sound" would gather on the weekends. Springsteen wrote that the young people at the club were "a living spirit of what rock 'n' roll is all about. It was music as survival, and they lived it down in their souls. The guys were their own heroes and they never forgot." Springsteen continues to call the Uptown a "community of ideas and values."

After being crowned the king of Asbury Park and dominating the vibrant Jersey Shore music scene, Mr. Springsteen was offered a record deal by Mike Appel at the ripe age of 23. The deal was financially unfair, denying him ownership of his songs and most of the revenues from future sales, but Appel worked harder than imaginable to find opportunities for his budding young star. He earned Springsteen an audition for John Hammond at Columbia Records, who was responsible for signing and promoting Billie Holiday, Aretha Franklin and Bob Dylan.

Springsteen played songs that would eventually be recorded and released on his first album, *Greetings from Asbury Park, N.J.* Upon release in 1972 it received mixed reviews and to this day does not hold up as strongly as most of his other work. It contains classics such as "Growin' Up," "Spirit in the Night," "For You," and "Blinded By the Light," but is slowed down and somewhat tarnished by the presence of songs like "Mary Queen of Arkansas" and "The Angel."

His second album, *The Wild, the Innocent and the E Street Shuffle*, is now perceived as a masterpiece, despite being a commercial failure following its release. All of the songs were too long and eccentric to be played on radio. However, they demonstrated Springsteen's first flirtation with singing about community. The songs contained youthful characters in a circus-like atmosphere guided by music and camaraderie. The narratives often seemed like fantasy, perhaps out of necessity. The music is wild, loose and unpredictable. Solos, chants and changes in tempo come so quickly it is difficult for the listener to keep pace.

Springsteen's next release, *Born to Run*, came in 1975 and is always mentioned during any discussion of the greatest rock 'n' roll albums of all time. It put him on the cover of *Time* and *Newsweek* during the same week, and made his name known internationally. After three years battling for the intellectual property rights to his music, he wrote, recorded, and released *Darkness on the Edge of Town* — another major figure in Bruce's pantheon.

Throughout the '80s, Bruce enjoyed great success and became a major superstar, first with the release of *The River* and in 1984 with *Born in the U.S.A.* The album that came in between, *Nebraska*, was an acoustic departure from rock that contains some of Springsteen's most haunting songs, and his first, and arguably best, attempt to tackle a major social crisis that exists throughout America. He also got married to Julianne Philips in the '80s and later divorced. The album written about his marital problems, *Tunnel of Love*, remains one of his crowning achievements of musical emotionality and lyrical complexity.

In the 1990s, Springsteen married backup singer Patti Scialfa (a Jersey girl), and had three children before moving to Los Angeles and, after a few years, moving back to New Jersey. He released two rock albums without the E Street Band, another acoustic folk record, and reunited with the E Street army in 2002 to record and release *The Rising* — a musical response to the events of 9/11 but written about universal themes of loss and loneliness. He released another album with the band in 2007, the highly political *Magic*, and in between formed a glorious folk revue called the "Seeger Sessions Band" which toured the world and released one studio and one live album. He also recorded another folk record with the help of a few musician friends, and launched a worldwide solo tour. In 2008, Danny Federici, an original member of the E Street Band who played organ and accordion, lost a battle with melanoma and died. The next year Springsteen released another album with the E Street Band, *Working on a Dream*.

It is important to note that while Springsteen was beginning in the music industry he stayed in New Jersey when insiders were telling him that his career may hinge upon his moving to New York. He decided to stay on the Jersey Shore and remain connected to the community that he found solace and comfort in. His clarity of vision to make a life of rock 'n' roll was impressive and unwavering, but he would not move to New York City — a mere 60 miles away from Asbury. The meaning of this decision was not lost on the residents of the Jersey Shore; neither was the title and cover of Springsteen's debut album, which colorfully announced *Greetings from Asbury Park, N.J.*

Music writer Robert Santelli, who is from the Jersey Shore, explained that after being the butt of so many jokes it was indescribably encouraging and prideful to be able to hold up that record made by a rock 'n' roll star unafraid to say, "I'm from here." This was especially striking since it came after the Asbury Park race riots, which essentially destroyed the town's financial base and reputation. Families began avoiding Asbury and one writer has said that "Crime, drugs, and the accoutrements of urban decay eventually replaced the disappearing vacationers."

Springsteen's loyalty to place and community was without limit and his decision to stay along the shore — spending his weekends in Asbury and writing "Born to Run" in his home in Long Branch — epitomizes it.

Through this admittedly brief and unoriginal biographical sketch of Bruce Springsteen, one can already see his values taking form and get a strong sense of his priorities. His emphasis on community becomes entirely understandable and admirable when considering his deep and steadfast appreciation for Asbury Park. His fearful warning against isolation and his ability to write about the darkness of lost dreams and diminished hopes can be assumed to be rooted in his childhood experiences with his father. The most plentiful source of hope, besides community, for Springsteen was music, which makes his sincerity and belief in renewal through music and community more meaningful.

The Springsteen house was full of ominous dread and Springsteen's second home (Asbury Park) underwent a transformation from a bright, cultured and exciting world of possibility to an impoverished center of crime and drugs where hope and dreams were unwelcome. These tough encounters with disappointment and despair inform much of Springsteen's best work, and cannot be ignored when interpreting the origins of his unique vision.

While Springsteen dealt with the loss of the American Dream by realizing that it is just that for many — a fantasy that is tangibly unattainable — he suffered through the loneliness and isolation that is born after the burial of a mythic promise once clutched as a hopeful embodiment of the future. But he found redemption through hope, gathered from music, and imbued with a familiarity of the darkness and understanding of the odds. This existential synthesis was played out when his solitary father would greet him in a dark kitchen, when his mother walked to the bank to take out a $60 loan to pay for his first guitar, and when he found friendship, companionship and solidarity in Asbury, even while it slipped into its own American nightmare. His suffering of the loss of large dreams — for America and for Asbury — did not cast him in a role of bereavement and defeatism but provided him with additional incentive for cherishing a personal dream of rock 'n' roll creative expression that could save his life and, in the process, connect him with that community of "brothers and sisters" he knew existed somewhere "out there." This story is repeated throughout his music in intelligent, uplifting and painfully honest terms, over the inspiring, energizing and seemingly life-giving melodies. Therefore, it is important to place the music within the context of the life of its maker. Postmodern literary critics claim that the author of any particular form of "text" (in which they would include music) is irrelevant, because once the "text" is made available for consumption it exists independently of the author and is therefore open to most any interpretation. Postmodern pronouncements of the "death of the author" not withstanding, Springsteen's own life is not only important when examining the origins of his vision but also useful when determining the courage and constancy of his positions and service. His coming of age is particularly important because it allows listeners to gain a deeper understanding of where the man they are trusting, and putting belief in, comes from and what traditions, transformative moments and essential experiences imbue his artistic production.

Just as important is a reading of Springsteen's political work — in the non-musical world. The questions of what causes he has identified with, what approaches to public policy he has advocated, and what people he has prioritized for assistance and solidarity must be answered when evaluating the political relevancy of his body of work. One must know whether or not there has been action behind the music, which strengthens or denigrates it. One must be able to rest comfortably knowing that Springsteen has made a conscious effort to apply his message to a variety of events with real social consequences — that he has taken his vision from the pathos to the pavement.

This will not only lend a certain credibility to Springsteen's amplified public voice but also energize any examination of Springsteen's work, which is shot through with issues that are pivotal in the everyday lives of everyday people. Before examining Springsteen's personal responses to various political patterns developing throughout his life, it is necessary to get a general idea of those political developments. Ironically, Springsteen's increased success throughout his career coincided with a rise of narrow marketplace visions that overwhelmed politics, effectively transforming the United States from a nation into a marketplace.

Robert Reich, the former Secretary of Labor for Bill Clinton, makes the case in his most recent book, *Supercapitalism*, that Capitol Hill is overwhelmed by lobbyists and corporate jackals that not only influence legislation, but often write the bills.

Former *Wall Street Journal* senior reporter Jeffrey Birnbaum wrote that campaign money "has flooded over the gunwales of the ship and threatens to sink the entire vessel. Political donations determine the course of and speed of many government actions that — though we often forget — will deeply affect our daily lives."

The fact that a former Clinton cabinet member, and a senior writer from the world's leading financial paper have regarded "how a bill becomes a law" as legalized bribery does not interest most members of the two major parties, which mainly enlist sycophantic corporate suck-ups who neglect the public interest in order to serve the rich interests that fund their campaigns. While everyday Americans struggle with health bills, sift through a dwindling job market for decent work, witness the folding of unions, and question if their children will attend a functional school, the richest Americans and corporations, up until the current financial crisis, acquired wealth at rates unprecedented since the New Deal. Even in the midst of the great recession, the bailouts — the majority of which have been governed by a Democratic President — have benefited massive, multinational corporate interests.

The New Deal, conceived during the last period of widespread economic misery, pushed America in the direction of a more equitable society, and significantly humanized prevailing political philosophy. Truman increased funding for FDR's programs, Lyndon Johnson raised the stakes with his Great Society, and even the reptilian Nixon remained partially loyal to the vision of domestic fairness and compassion by increasing funding for public education programs and signing the Environmental Protection Agency into law. It was not until the "saintly" presidency of Ronald Reagan, a man now revered at a level somewhere between Santa Claus and Jesus, that politics became repackaged to exclusively complement the marketplace and placate its greedy designers. Reagan's union-busting, trickle-down economics and cutting of social programs, along with his fostering of a new alliance between the corporate right and religious right, reshaped American politics for the worse. The dominance of the corporate right, which fetishizes the unregulated market, has continued pretty much without a break since 1980. The Clinton administration represented a slow-down period and was responsible for exceptional economically sound and compassionate initiatives such as increases in college aid and children's health-care programs. But market critics should not be too nostalgic for the 1990s, considering it was Clinton who engineered welfare reform that has devastated single mothers, and the North American Free Trade Agreement, which is responsible for the exportation of American jobs and the increased exploitation of Latin America.

Meanwhile, marketplace politics have not only ignored the needs of everyday people but also showcased fawning favor towards the rich. The most obvious example to illustrate this case is the consistent changing of the tax code. Warren Buffet has famously condemned the fact that his secretary pays almost the same tax rate that he does. Of course, the George W. Bush tax cuts, which were packaged like a Christmas present to the wealthy, only exacerbated this problem of inequality. His other programs shined the shoes of the rich in every conceivable way, while those very shoes kicked everyone else in the face. Contrary to the message promulgated among hysterical hoopla and lunatic convulsions on talk radio and at "tea parties" over Obama's proposed rearranging of the tax code, his slight increase on the rate the richest Americans pay would still place it below that which existed under Reagan, Carter, Ford and Nixon.

In a market the people with the most money have every advantage. They can go on a delightful shopping spree and satisfy the most minor consumer cravings. Those without fat wallets and deep pockets are forced to leave empty-handed, and that is fair. Businesses have to produce a profit; otherwise society will cease to function. However, to apply these cold principles to the governance and organization of society is perverse, demented, and far outside the moral universe.

> Hey there mister can you tell me
> What happened to the seeds I've sown?
> — "This Hard Land," 1995

Bruce Springsteen, most likely due to his myopic focus on rock music, did not participate in any of the activism that dramatically changed the country in the 1960s and 1970s. Despite his spectator role, the lesson of the activist movements in the '60s was not lost on him. In the middle of Reagan's reign in the 1980s Springsteen expressed great discontentment with national politics. He refused to call Reagan a "bad man," but feared that "there are people whose dreams don't mean much to him." Springsteen also believed that much of Reagan's sloganeering and sunny optimism, including his infamous mention of Springsteen during a speech in New Jersey, were shallow attempts to manipulate the voting public. However, Springsteen's most adamant objection was delivered to the American shift in priorities and values that he observed from the 1960s to the '80s. "The difficult thing out there right now is that the social consciousness that was a part of the 1960s has become old-fashioned. You go out, you get your job, and try to make as much money as you can and have a good time on the weekend. And that's considered okay."

Despite his anger with Reagan and disappointment in the American people, he distanced himself from processes that the media traditionally and narrowly defines as politics — chiefly, endorsing candidates and participating in activities organized by one of the two major political parties.

Springsteen outlined this position clearly and it could be used as the blueprint for analyzing his political involvement up until 2004: "I want to try and just work more directly with people; try to find some way that my band can tie into the communities that we come into. I guess that's a political action, a way to just bypass that whole electoral thing. Human politics. People on their own can do a lot. That is what I'm trying to figure out now: where do the aesthetic issues that I write about intersect with some sort of concrete action, some direct involvement, in the communities that my audience comes from?"

This form of "human politics" — issue advocacy combined with charitable/political organization support — began with Springsteen in 1979 when he agreed to perform at a series of concerts in New York organized by Musicians United for Safe Energy. The concert series, titled "No Nukes," was performed in protest of nuclear energy and the continuing construction of nuclear weaponry. Although his presence meant a great deal, given his exploding popularity at the time, his demeanor expressed a form of detachment from the event's political cause. Unlike other musicians at the concerts — James Taylor, Crosby, Stills and Nash, Bonnie Raitt, Jackson Browne and several others — he did not give a political speech or play politically charged music. He certainly supported the purpose of the evening, and it showed through the labor he put into his performance, but his hesitance to address the audience in political terms perhaps demonstrated an uneasiness or uncertainty about being there.

That began to change in 1982 when he released *Nebraska*, a haunting portrait of America containing images of hopelessness and restlessness sung by a ghost-like voice floating through the tour of destruction left in inner-cities by Reaganism. Two years later, when *Born in the U.S.A.* made Springsteen a larger-than-life mega-star, there were several conservative and corporate attempts to co-opt his message and image.

Republican columnist George Will praised Springsteen's message in a stunning display of artistic illiteracy and mind-numbing nationalism that believes any evocation of the flag and America must be positive: "I have not got a clue about Springsteen's politics, if any, but flags get waved at his concerts while he sings songs about hard times. He is no whiner, and the recitation of closed factories and other problems always seem punctuated by a grand, cheerful affirmation: 'Born in the U.S.A.!'"

The song to which Will refers to is inspired by Bobby Muller — the Vietnam vet turned anti-war activist and veteran advocate after returning home from Southeast Asia in a wheelchair — and tells the story of a man who fought in Vietnam, lost his brother to the war, and when back in the U.S.A. could not find suitable employment or an American institution offering assistance or structural support. Muller's organization, "Vietnam Veterans for America," received direct assistance from Springsteen in the 1980s when the rock singer organized two benefit shows for the struggling advocacy and peace group. Although its inspiration is not accessible through the song's narrative, its meaning can be gained from the often ignored verses of the song, which place the chorus in an entirely different context than the one Will imagines. It is a cry of anger, bitterness and despair. Springsteen has to place a little of the blame on himself for the common misreading of "Born in the U.S.A." as a patriotic anthem. Although it was the fans and media that chose to ignore almost all of the song's words, Springsteen's posing next to the flag with his fist raised in the air — physically resembling Rambo — certainly did not help matters.

Ronald Reagan most famously misinterpreted Springsteen's music by saying the following at a campaign stop in New Jersey: "America's future rests in a thousand dreams inside your hearts; it rests in the message of hope in songs so many young Americans admire: New Jersey's own Bruce Springsteen. And helping you make those dreams come true is what this job of mine is all about." Although it can be safely assumed that Reagan could not separate a Springsteen song from a Bob Dylan tune, this speech captured the extent of admiration that existed for Springsteen, along with the intensity of the desire to enlist him in the conservative revolution cadre.

The title track of *Born in the U.S.A.* is its opening song. Its closing song, "My Hometown," about a small town struggling with poverty and racial tension, is much more difficult to misinterpret, and Springsteen punctuated its message on the road by introducing it with a heartfelt speech about poverty, homelessness, and working-class difficulties. During the speech he would announce that representatives from a local food bank will be waiting in the lobby after the show hoping for either donations or volunteer commitments. A portion of the proceeds raised at every Springsteen concert since 1985 has gone to an area food bank or homeless shelter.

Springsteen's road show in the mid-80s presented a stark contrast to Reagan's "morning in America" rhetoric and imagery. Springsteen sang of American struggles often ignored by the mainstream media, and certainly ignored by the Reagan administration. It not only presented a challenge to his audience but a strong response to Reagan's attempt to enlist Springsteen as one of his ideological allies. The symbolic nature of Springsteen's activities and music was more than enough to indicate his political position. His only direct mention of Reagan from the stage came in Pittsburgh when Springsteen introduced "Johnny 99" — a song about a man who goes on a crime spree after his factory closes and he cannot find a suitable employment substitute — by remarking, "The President mentioned my name the other day, and that got me wondering what his favorite album might be. I don't think it's the *Nebraska* album. I don't think he's been listening to this one."

If Reagan toured and governed the country while operating under the perpetuation of a myth founded upon the clichés of "work hard and you can make it no matter your socio-economic conditions" and "America is a classless society," then Springsteen presented the truthful alternative — a land torn by inequality, social division and conflict but still containing room to dream big and hope large if its people are willing to work at it.

Springsteen's next public political move was to headline an international tour for Amnesty International — one of the world's largest and most active human rights organizations — in 1988. Supporting acts on the tour included Sting, Tracy Chapman, Peter Gabriel and Youssou N'Dour. Concerts in the developing world were ticket-admission only, with all proceeds benefiting Amnesty, while concerts in the Third World, such as Africa and India, were free of charge. This represented an important stage in Springsteen's political evolution. He had come to be personified by Americana and ran the risk of being forever cast as an all-American archetype. However, this international tour that focused on global issues of human rights violations, coupled with *Tunnel of Love*, Springsteen's latest album that featured mature songs about relationships and self-doubt, introduced a Springsteen much larger than the mold branded for him by the American media and public.

A few years later Springsteen headlined another series of benefit concerts, this time for the Christic Institute — a law firm famous for representing Karen Silkwood in a case against the Kerr-McGee Nuclear Power Company, which has been depicted in the motion picture *Silkwood*, starring Meryl Streep. The firm also won a verdict against the Ku Klux Klan and members of the Greensboro, North Carolina Police Department for conspiring to murder five civil rights activists. Its most controversial case was in defense of two journalists in Nicaragua working to expose CIA involvement in atrocities committed against the Nicaraguan people. This small benefit had large implications, because it was Springsteen's first flirtation with radical politics. The American media bitterly condemned the Christic Institute after the Nicaragua case, and supporters were few and far between. Springsteen still possessed a wholesome image, but did not hesitate to support a struggling law firm committed to preventing injustice, even if it was politically unpopular.

Springsteen's form of "human politics" continued on throughout the 1990s. He began writing more blatantly political songs, including 1992's "Souls of the Departed" which sang of death in Iraq and America's inner-cities met with indifference by elites. During his tour in the early 1990s, "57 Channels (And Nothin' On)" — a social satire that appears on *Human Touch* — became a centerpiece of the show used as a predicate for commenting upon the L.A. race riots, poverty, and media shallowness and simplicity when reporting on important issues.

In 1994, Springsteen won an Oscar and Emmy for the song "Streets of Philadelphia," which was written about the same subject that the film for which it provides the opening song on its soundtrack addresses — a gay man dying of AIDS. Springsteen, often viewed as the epitome of American machismo, was quick to sing in the voice of a gay character and express strong support for gay rights in interviews with gay publications, such as the *Advocate*: "People felt safe with me [challenging their notions of heterosexism and homophobia] because I knew where their fear came from. I was brought up in a small town, and I received nothing but negative images about homosexuality — very bad. Anybody who was different in any fashion was castigated and ostracized, if not physically threatened . . . The bonus I got out of writing 'Streets of Philadelphia' was that all of a sudden I could go out and meet some gay man and he wouldn't be afraid to talk to me and say, 'Hey, that song really means something to me.' My image had always been very heterosexual, very straight. So it was a good experience for me, a chance to clarify my own feelings about gay and lesbian civil rights."

Springsteen reached a new level of political aggression with the 1995 release of *The Ghost of Tom Joad* and its subsequent tour. The songs on the album and featured during the live set focused mainly on the lives of Latino immigrants in the southwest, but could be projected onto a national screen of increasing poverty, displacement and inequality. Taking the total opposite approach to the silence he showcased at the "No Nukes" concert in 1979, Springsteen spoke often from the stage during the "Tom Joad" tour, sometimes making audiences uncomfortable by condemning the treatment of migrant workers and insulting the potentially naïve sensibilities of audiences in both Republican and Democratic cities: "If you believe that America has metamorphosized into a race-and-gender-blind society, you also believe in Santa Claus."

Throughout the tour, which lasted until 1997, Springsteen frequently met with people on the "front lines" — legal advocates and social workers from homeless shelters, advocacy groups for the poor and subjugated racial classes, and veterans' groups — and would work with organizations providing immediate care for people in distress and attempting to have an impact on local policy. Bruce attempted to affect Los Angeles politics at the end of his tour by performing at an L.A. rally, hosted by Jesse Jackson, and organized labor to protest a California proposition to sharply reduce affirmative action programs across the state.

When Springsteen first began depicting American hardship, existential emptiness and class struggle it was from the perspective of a white, straight male, and sung in the voice of characters with the same race and sexual orientation. His moving demand for empathy was an important tribute to the democratic spirit of inclusiveness and community, and the call for ecumenical change sweeping across private psyches and public policies, but it was mutually referential between the singer and his audience. Listeners were being asked to empathize with people that looked like them and shared their lifestyles and traditions. Springsteen's more radical demand to identify with poor migrant workers, neglected African-Americans, and gays and lesbians, affirms his conceptions of love, democracy and service, which cannot exist independently from one another, but also challenges his audience in much deeper and profound ways.

Springsteen's radical politics of identification continued in 2000, when he wrote the song "American Skin (41 Shots)" about Amadou Diallo, a Guinean immigrant who was murdered by four police officers who fired 41 shots at him when he reached for his wallet after being stopped because he resembled a suspect for whom the officers were searching. They were tried for murder, and acquitted on all charges. The song debuted in Atlanta and by the time the E Street Band rolled into New York City, the press was running wild with innuendo, outrage and cries of controversy. Police officers promised to protest Springsteen's concerts and scores of media commentators were berating Bruce for being "anti-cop." Springsteen responded only by playing the song to a tension-filled Madison Square Garden with Diallo's mother in the audience — there by special invitation from Springsteen. Springsteen won an NAACP Image Award for the song.

In 2002, Bruce Springsteen and the E Street Band toured in support of *The Rising* and Bruce made "public service announcements" near the end of every show. These announcements called for "vigilance" in response to civil liberty violations of the Bush administration and later focused on anti-war commentary. When asked about fans who do not want to hear a political speech at a concert Springsteen said, "I usually make that speech at the end of the show. I think after three hours of playing music, people can give me two minutes." Prior to the tour Springsteen performed at two benefits for families of victims of 9/11 — one dedicated to a national fund, and the other going towards residents of New Jersey communities.

In the middle of the tour, Springsteen performed two benefit shows in Massachusetts to save *Double Take*, a struggling literary magazine with left-ist political sensibilities, from bankruptcy. The shows were a success, and brought Springsteen high acclaim from concert reviewers, but their effect was only temporary. *Double Take* ceased publication in January of 2008.

Springsteen finally broke his vow to refrain from electoral politics in 2004 when he performed at several rallies for the Democratic nominee John Kerry, and organized the "Vote for Change" tour, which benefited political action committees working in support of the Democratic Party. The tour featured a long and impressive list of performers, from James Taylor to Jurassic 5, and from John Mellencamp to Pearl Jam, which helped it sell out venues across the United States.

Springsteen candidly discussed his decision to change political policy and step into the hyper-partisan world of electoral politics: "I always liked being involved actively more at a grass-roots level, to act as a partisan for a set of ideals: civil rights, economic justice, a humane foreign policy, democracy. That was the position I felt comfortable coming from." But because of the stakes of this election and the extremeness of the Bush administration he felt that "Sitting on the sidelines would be a betrayal of the ideas I'd written about for a long time. Not getting involved, just sort of maintaining my silence or being coy about it in some way, just wasn't going to work this time out. I felt that it was a very clear historical moment."

Despite Kerry's disappointing loss, Springsteen maintained participation in political activity. He once again raised the banner of migrant workers with 2005's *Devils & Dust*, another fine album of Western songs, à la *The Ghost of Tom Joad*, while saving room for songs about soldiers in Iraq and serious philosophical issues that every person must confront.

His next project was *We Shall Overcome: A Tribute to Pete Seeger*, which invoked great folk anthems of protest and dissent but also of joy, spirituality and hope. The tour focused on American cruelty and incompetence in New Orleans after Hurricane Katrina, poverty and the war in Iraq. His attempt to reconnect America with its great folk traditions of working-class protest, Negro spirituals and immigrant song and dance mapped out a seemingly mythic "one nation indivisible" where all peoples and parties are endowed with the rights to life, liberty and the pursuit of happiness. It also served as a healthy reminder of past American struggles with injustice that could be applied to the fatal consequences of Bush's policies.

In 2007, Springsteen organized the E Street Band to record *Magic*, an album containing anti-war themes and a call for reunion with violated American constitutional values, and toured the world following its release. The shows during the *Magic* tour resembled those from *The Rising*, complete with "public service announcements" about the dangers of political apathy and praise of local food banks and homeless shelters.

The next year Springsteen returned to traditional electoral politics to campaign passionately and energetically for Barack Obama. Their similar visions of hope and community complemented each other greatly, and Springsteen speaking from the stage at a rally in Cleveland said, "I spent most of my life as a musician measuring the distance between the American Dream and American reality. For many Americans who are today losing their jobs, their homes, seeing their retirement funds disappear, who have no health care, or who have been abandoned in our inner-cities, the distance between that dream and their reality has never been greater or more painful. I believe Senator Obama has taken the measure of that distance in his own life and work. I believe he understands in his heart the cost of that distance in blood and suffering in the lives of everyday Americans. I believe as president he would work to bring that dream back to life, and into the lives of many of our fellow Americans, who have justifiably lost faith in its meaning."

Springsteen's political evolution from quiet objection to Reagan policies through narrative-based folk songs and encouragement of organizations alleviating the poverty, displacement and hopelessness that was intensified by Reagan, to a creative spokesperson for progressive ideals — speaking from the stage, endorsing candidates and working directly with protest groups — demonstrates the maturity, elevation of social consciousness, and familiarity with the intersection formed by social misery and political failure that is expressed in his music.

Bob Dylan, despite having been chosen as the voice of the '60s protest movements, did practically all he could to distance himself from political activity. After participating in a few demonstrations, including the 1963 March on Washington, he determined that the best role for him to fill was one of politically, spiritually and morally prophetic song while adopting an apolitical lifestyle. An artist's level of commitment to the social and political causes they write or sing about cannot be used as a criterion for judging the quality of their creative output. Dylan's protest anthems are timeless musical expressions that capture the heart, spirit and issues of an important era of American history better than nearly any other work of art. The quality of Dylan's music remains unaffected by his refusal to participate in the struggles he lionized.

However, when examining the importance of one's vision in an attempt to offer hope in hopeless times and make it accessible to activists, it is useful to determine the priorities of the visionary. Springsteen has demonstrated not only willingness, but a need to take his message from the pathos to the pavement by making tangible connections with the people that he sings about. He has not cowered from crises of social consequence because of possible popular backlash or personal immunity from their effects. On local, state and national levels he has consistently engaged the populace and the powerful by bringing his radical, prophetic and progressive vision to bear on social, economic and political injustices perpetuated throughout the country that he was born, raised and made in.

Springsteen's resistance to political apathy and social indifference is a prominent example of how one can effectively reject the temptations and seductions of the mainstream consumer culture that rewards narcissism, uninterrupted hedonism and relentless commodification. Within recent decades it has become fashionable in America not to care about the suffering of others. While Springsteen has been given the option of counting his money and insulating himself from the problems of American society, he has chosen to use his financial and cultural capital to invest in those that are attempting to address economic inequality and social misery. In doing so he has become an impressive voice for progressive politics, guided by values of community, solidarity and assistance for others. His love for the people and his service to them should be exemplified as a positive example of meaningful engagement by those operating within the struggles he sings about and supports.

It should also provide the bedrock for an examination of the political implications and importance of Springsteen's music. The knowledge of Springsteen's activist work does not have to be constantly referenced throughout a discussion of his creative work, but it should be remembered that the vision promulgated in his songs rests upon a firm foundation of "human politics," courageous political speech and the prioritization of service over coolness and commercialization.

It will be helpful to some when seeking enlightenment and "danceable education" in Springsteen's music to know that the artist has complemented his creativity with consequential action. It will also lend an undeniable credibility to Springsteen's perspective and positions. Others may choose to follow the advice of Springsteen himself, who once said, "Trust the art, not the artist." Either route is fine as long as it leads to the same place — the destination built for analysis and reflection in the face of the life-and-death questions asked in Springsteen's music — questions that must be answered not only for individual growth and personal fulfillment but also for the sake of our ever-weakening and decelerating republic.

Chapter 2

On a Downbound Train

The Politics of Isolation

Isolation is the most dangerous thing on Earth.

— Bruce Springsteen, 1987

Tragic lovelessness, hopelessness and emptiness have swept across America. It is visible on the streets of mostly black, mostly brown, all poor, opportunity-deficient centers of poverty and dread in the inner-cities: politically neglected slums where crime, drugs, alcohol and mindless hedonism grapple for attention, while education, upward mobility and meaningful self-actualization are seemingly impossible.

The severely weakened American middle class does its best to remain insulated from the lower class, and it is usually driven by fear at the mere mention of poverty's name. Wealthy elites of American society are further cut off from the rest of America due to unseemly rising rates of inequality which are without precedent since the Great Depression. For decades the United States has been transforming from a nation into a marketplace, pitting citizen against citizen in the process. Unlike other developed nations where social services and collective responsibility are emphasized through universal health care, excellent public schools, subsidized higher education and publicly funded child care, America has applied social Darwinism to its societal management. A consumer culture, fed by $150 billion spent per year on advertising, reinforces this meaningless and purposeless lifestyle.[1] The message delivered is that one must maximize profit and accumulate obscene amounts of commodities to achieve happiness. Empathetic connections and sympathetic concerns for other people are discouraged and disabled.

While groups of Americans separate themselves from each other and live disparate lives, many individuals retreat into self-made cocoons, eschewing social responsibilities and avoiding collective involvement. Political scientist Robert D. Putnam famously issued an indictment against American individual isolationism in his classic best seller, *Bowling Alone: The Collapse and Revival of American Community.*

In this groundbreaking text Putnam argues that America is suffering a decline in "social capital" that may very well become perilous. With incisive analysis and penetrating research he proves that Americans are voting less, joining civic and political organizations in fewer numbers, and even socializing less frequently. If fewer citizens are participating in the political process, it becomes much easier for a democratic republic to transform into an oligarchy. An informed and organized citizenry must provide essential balance to the wealth and power of corporate giants. If it fails to do so, the public interest and common good get lost in the money count.

Isolation and the "breakdown of community and social capital" also go a long way in explaining the mental health afflictions that are spreading throughout America. During a conversation with Dr. Jim Nelson, Director of the Psychology Department at Valparaiso University in Valparaiso, Indiana, I learned that "every single mental health problem in this country is getting worse." When I asked Nelson for an explanation, he spoke of how people are more "fragmented" than ever, and referenced an American Sociological Association study showing that the number of people Americans say they can "talk to about a personal crisis" has been declining for decades.[2] When people have nowhere to turn in moments of doubt, discomfort and pain, they are vulnerable to pernicious influences, such as drugs, alcohol and crime, which will only exacerbate their problems. Others will attempt to find solace in the prizes of a commercial-obsessed and consumer-driven culture, which will result in temporary pleasure but fail to bring lasting joy and meaning to one's life.

Regardless of where Americans go, they cannot escape marketing campaigns to get them to spend their money on items, services and commodities they may or may not need. These advertisements are the most visible infection of the marketplace disease poisoning the culture at large. Walking through a sports arena is like taking a tour of these shallow, attention-grabbing billboards. Television, newspapers, radio and most of the internet rely upon advertisement revenue to make a profit, which not only makes their respective electronic landscapes dominated by marketing tactics, but also subscribes their loyalty to those that dish out the advertisement dollar.

The amount of money spent on public relations firms — the same ones that represent companies that sell toothpaste and lifestyle drugs — is unprecedented in American politics. Candidates have become dependent upon imagery masters and gimmick inventors who subvert serious discussions about serious issues by encouraging candidates to run on qualities, i.e.

"good Christian," "nice guy," "just one of the boys," etc., instead of political positions.³ The *New York Times* reported that Creative Response Concepts, the PR firm most infamous for representing Swift Boat Veterans for Truth, handled the Supreme Court Justice Samuel Alito during his nomination process — exalting his finer qualities and undermining criticism before the Senate Judiciary Committee hearings even began.⁴ From baseball to politics to judicial appointments, nothing functions outside of the realm of consumer culture.

One cannot produce a 30-second ad for democracy, civic values or community involvement to air between competing commercials for *Girls Gone Wild* and State Farm Insurance. Civic traditions, political participation and social activism have no place in a nation turned marketplace because they do not produce a profit. Therefore, even if Robert Putnam has difficulty identifying the single cause of decline in community, a rational observer can notice that the one thread that runs through all the political, social and cultural fabrics that make up Americans' disconnection is consumer culture.

America has become a cultural wasteland where serious creative production lies on the side of a superhighway like road kill, while behemoth gas guzzlers drive to the epicenters of American politics and cultural export — Wal-Mart and small business-killing corporate chains that make the landscape, market and financial opportunity of every town identical — and blow their horns in mockery of the dissenters poking the road kill with a stick in hopes for survival.

FROM ELVIS TO RADIO NOWHERE: "57 CHANNELS (AND NOTHIN' ON)"

The highway that provides an intersection for marketplace madness, constant consumerism and intense isolation is acutely mapped out in Bruce Springsteen's 1992 song from *Human Touch*, "57 Channels (And Nothin' On)." The song has gone through three incarnations. The live debut version sounded like a humorous folktale sung with a twang and played with whimsical picking of the acoustic guitar. The album-released version features Springsteen performing the song in a talk-sing style over a lone bass line. A live version, which is documented on the DVD *Plugged* is unlike either of the two previous incarnations. It begins with a mini-choir of backup singers chanting "No justice, no peace," while sound bites from television news talk programs are played in rhythm with the chant. We hear President George H.W. Bush claiming he wants a "kinder, gentler nation." Joan Rivers tells us that the best way to start each morning is with "gossip, gossip, gossip!" An unidentifiable voice either assures us or warns us that "American history says none of this will happen." All of these thoughtless platitudes are uttered against the "No justice, no peace" rhythmic cry, reminding people of the Los Angeles riots that occurred shortly before the concert, until the chant and the sound bites reach their culmination in a repeated shout, "57 channels and nothin' on!"

The shallowness, simplicity and cheapness of public discussions started by the media is rightfully revealed and condemned. Whether these meaningless statements come from the President, a comedian talk show host or an armchair analyst, they do not inspire confidence or comfort. They are to be ignored and dismissed as distractive sentimentality or absurdity, intended only to massage the marketplace managers who create the conditions that create upset and discontent. It is impossible for them to provide forums welcoming of justice and peace. The staggering increase of media consolidation makes these inanities more dominant and less challenged. Rupert Murdoch's News Corporation owns an estimated 35–50 percent of the media, while the remainder is owned by four other corporate conglomerates which are operated by men who probably shop at the same clothing store.[5] By the time Bruce Springsteen begins singing in a deep growl that expresses the character of the song's bitterness and dissonance, the scene of an America where struggling people are failing to be heard over the white noise of media manipulation has already been established.

> I bought a bourgeois house in the Hollywood hills
> With a truckload of hundred thousand dollar bills
> Man came by to hook up my cable TV
> We settled in for the night my baby and me
> We switched 'round and 'round 'til half-past dawn
> There was fifty-seven channels and nothin' on
>
> Well now home entertainment was my baby's wish
> So I hopped into town for a satellite dish
> I tied it to the top of my Japanese car
> I came home and I pointed it out into the stars
> A message came back from the great beyond
> There's fifty-seven channels and nothin' on

The character is more than telling a story. He is offering an anecdotal indictment of a pervasive consumer culture that has had a powerful influence over his behavior. He attempted to find solace and happiness in the rewards of the American doctrine of wealth. He bought a mansion, a souped-up Japanese car, and sat down for an evening of detachment with his "baby." Instead of strengthening the connection they already have and exercising it in a fulfilling fashion, they sit down in front of the glow of the screen — cold and paradoxically isolated while together. The emptiness of the experience, along with its inability to please, becomes clear as the character protests in a high-pitched hellcat scream which captures rage and disbelief: "Fifty-seven channels and nothin' on!"

The most obvious criticism of the consumer culture that dominates the American mentality is that there is no way to satisfy the hunger of the beast. One can continue to feed it with more goods, commodities and technological updates but it will continue to crave more until it eventually devours its master by swallowing his identity and creative potential. This is illustrated in verse two of the character's lament when he describes purchasing a satellite dish after viewing cable was unsatisfying. But, the message he receives is more of the same: "There's fifty-seven channels and nothin' on." It is not only flirtation with consumer culture that causes impotence, but also disengaged spectating, as opposed to personal involvement with community and the woman sitting next to him on the couch. His immersion into consumer-driven, technologically enhanced passivity has caused a troubling isolation, which is evident in the singer's angry and urgent tone of voice, and also the repetition of the chorus: There's so much to choose from yet nothing is working because it is a false choice. Regardless of where one stops the clicker, one is still making a conceited choice to be apathetic, uninvolved and inactive.

As the song moves to the bridge, the band picks up the pace. The beat moves quicker, and the guitars are played in a chaotic fury. The singer begins spitting faster and louder, almost as if he were shouting at his girlfriend, but we quickly learn that she is gone, leaving him there all alone, screaming at the wall in anger, regret and loneliness.

> Well we might'a made some friends with some billionaires
> We might'a got all nice and friendly
> If we'd made it upstairs
> All I got was a note that said "Bye-bye John
> Our love is fifty-seven channels and nothin' on"

The singer's screaming at the wall is done entirely in denial and delusion. By his own admission, the upgrade from cable to satellite television, while living in a mansion and driving a fancy foreign car, was not enough to provide happiness or meaning. However, he is still holding on to the false promise of the marketplace-created consumer culture: "If I had just gotten a little more, I would have been happy."

The original version of the song contained the lyrics "We might'a got all hot and horny, if we'd made it upstairs," which placed an increased emphasis on the singer's point. He has fetishized commodity and status, making them a sexual idol that can give pleasure, power and prestige, even after it has failed to do so — twice. His delusion and denial has alienated him from the one that he loves and desires. Instead of trying to make her happy by being there for her when she is in need of love, emotional support and friendship, he attempted to satisfy the basest of her urges for "home entertainment." Now that she feels disappointed and neglected, he is confused. He cannot comprehend how his love is as empty and meaningless as his consumer cravings because he still has not come to terms with the truth of consumerism. He has become isolated by turning off those around him in order to turn on the temporarily satisfying energies of the market.

He soon undergoes a violent, enraged and impulsive moment of transformation, in which he is unable to channel his boiling energy into a positive outlet.

> So I bought a .44 magnum, it was solid steel cast
> And in the blessed name of Elvis, well I just let it blast
> 'Til my TV lay in pieces there at my feet
> And they busted me for disturbin' the almighty peace
> Judge said "What you got in your defense son?"
> "Fifty-seven channels and nothin' on"

The singer's invoking of Elvis is telling, beyond the obvious reason that he had a penchant for shooting television screens when he did not approve of the programming. Elvis was described by those who loved him and knew him best as the loneliest person in the world, effectively cut off from life outside of his inner circle in Graceland and Las Vegas. Even those around him offered fleeting connections to outside communities, as they functioned as mere jesters and jacks for "The King." If Elvis wished to go to an amusement park or movie theater, he would rent out the entire park or building. After thrilling audiences on stage he would quickly retreat to his limousine, digest an extreme amount of pills, and allow not only his body to leave the world but also his mind. Elvis eventually became delusional and deranged — asking his bodyguard to kill the man his wife Priscilla left him for, performing long-winded and incoherent sermons or karate demonstrations to his employees at Graceland, and riding on the Memphis highway on a golf cart at three in the morning in his pajamas. Elvis's isolation is what tragically did him in. His talent and charm never failed him. All one has to do is watch him perform his 1977 operatic takes on "Hurt" or "Unchained Melody" to understand that the power of his voice and the charisma of his personality were present until his last days. It was his inability to stay connected to the outside world, and listen to perspectives other than his own, that killed him. Very few people tried to tell him that his drug habit was out of control and that he was systematically killing himself. The circumstances surrounding Elvis's death are tragic not only because of his young age of 42 and his ability to give hope and inspiration to diverse people all over the world, but also because they were Shakespearian. He self-destructed. It was self-imposed isolation and insulation that killed Elvis, and it is the same thing that has caused the character in "57 Channels (And Nothin' On)" to lose his mind.[6]

When he shoots his television screen, the character invokes the "blessed name of Elvis" to suggest a kinship with and an honoring of Elvis's solitary spirit. When the television set lays in pieces at his feet, he may or may not feel vindicated. But he has engaged in a personal act of protest against the mindlessness, shallowness and depressing advocacy of the self-absorbed consumerist living celebrated in mainstream culture. He feels alone and trapped in a country where people are disconnected and social services, such as health, education, child care, etc. are absent or increasingly privatized. His protest of "Fifty-seven channels and nothin' on" within the criminal justice system makes it clear that he is not referring merely to television programming but to social structure, public policy and societal organization. Due to his isolation, or "atomization" as Noam Chomsky would call it, he is unaware of a productive or effective way to voice his discontent and express his dissent. Therefore he "disturbs the peace." While being prosecuted the judge demands an explanation, a legal defense, and the singer releases the familiar cry of "Fifty-seven channels and nothin' on." Brilliantly, the question is then raised, should the peace remain undisturbed? Is peace even possible in this culture, where people are isolated, cut off from each other and the institutions that guide and regulate their lives? "No justice, no peace."

Fifteen years later, Springsteen introduces his audience to a new character in the same predicament. A loud, distorted and dark guitar riff, which resembles the destructive noise of a jackhammer, begins grinding before a thunderous drumbeat begins, creating room for the singer.

> I was tryin' to find my way home
> But all I heard was a drone
> Bouncing off a satellite
> Crushin' the last lone American night
> This is radio nowhere, is there anybody alive out there?

"Radio Nowhere," from the 2007 release *Magic*, is full of apocalyptic imagery evoking desperation and externally enforced solitude. Instead of television, it uses radio as a symbol for the distorting of meaningful communication throughout society. The quality of commercial radio has suffered along with the quality of television. Clear Channel Communications owns and operates over 1,200 radio stations across America and, like television, most of the remaining stations are owned by similar companies with similar agendas. Local coverage and DJs are disappearing as stations are turned over to satellite programming.[7] Political discussion operates within such a narrow framework that only the most right-wing voice of the Republican Party is amplified over the airwaves. Music has become increasingly homogenized, while corporate radio programming is all derivative of each other, refusing to take risks and play anything outside of the already established "hit making" mainstream. Despite all of this, one can be confident that within the context of "Radio Nowhere," radio is applied to the character's struggle to be heard and addressed, and is emblematic of a larger failure of America to overcome its own isolation.

This character, wandering through a concrete jungle, is searching for "home" — a place of happiness and security. English is one of the few languages to give different words to distinguish the concepts of "house" and "home" from each other. A "house" is interpreted to mean a residency in its most basic sense. A place, as George Carlin put it, "to keep your stuff." While "home" is inseparable from belonging, community and the comfort and stability that are only possible in a loving, nurturing environment. On this character's search, he becomes distracted and led off course by a "drone" that is "bouncing off a satellite." This impersonal, non-human entity has caused the character to wallow in his solitude and become trapped in an endless quest for community. This entity embodies the cultural forces that separate Americans from each other, keeping groups disparate and individuals atomized, thereby wrecking the foundation for communal construction.

The singer's vocals are distorted, which muddies some of the lyrics, making him just out of reach from the listener of the song and those attempting to hear the voice of the character. However, the singer's desperate plea, "is there anybody alive out there?" is heard loud and clear following the dread announcement of the "crushing of the last lone American night" — a now defunct setting that once belonged to a nation with a linked populace and clear purpose. The character is broadcasting his program from nowhere, a place without a name, without a population, and without a tangible method for joining with other places and people. "Is there anybody alive out there?" is sung in a low voice, totally devoid of the urgency and rage of "57 Channels (And Nothin' On)." This character is not deluded; he asks his question and files his protest in vain. He is all too aware that no one is waking up to hear his cry for connection. During the second verse, in the same distant voice, he sings of being "Just another lost number in a file." His very humanity — the core of his existence — is up for question in this dreadful world of destruction, where methods of communication have been broken down and mechanisms to find affirmation of a common humanity are dysfunctional.

The singer continues to drawl in a dull voice over a combination of a grinding guitar, hyperactive drumbeat and doubled saxophone and guitar solo that sounds similar to a soundtrack of a science fiction story, in which the world has become a technologically thriving but spiritually dead war zone, hosting battles between isolated in-groups fighting for the precious little resources and opportunities for hope that still exist. Think *Blade Runner* or *Brave New World*. Through the ashes of deceased dreams and the dust of obsolete machinery, the singer comes alive to urgently scream in panic, "I just want to hear some rhythm! . . . I just want to feel your rhythm!"

This man is aching for a connection. He is so alone in a world where ways to defeat loneliness and despair no longer exist that his spiritual and emotional desires have manifested into a physical need. But it remains unclear who he is talking to. The subject of "you" and "your" is never identified. Perhaps this character cannot even answer that himself. He is shouting in the dark, talking to the air, "tryin' to find [his] way home." He is the lost child in the woods screaming for help as the hours go by and the days get longer. He begins to sense that no one is coming, but continues to yell and cry.

RACING IN THE STREET WITH A STOLEN CAR: FROM *COP LAND* TO THE NIGHTHAWKS' CAFÉ

As Robert Putnam shows in *Bowling Alone*, there is a rational dimension to the need for community and group involvement. People are healthier and happier when they participate in some form of organized recreational or socially beneficial activity. However, the most painful aspect of the community-craving is irrational. It is the feeling down in one's gut that comes from being emotionally imprisoned, and thereby forcefully cut off from the people and institutions beyond the bars that can provide emancipation. This indefinable urge for connectivity is expressed in the primal screams of "Fifty-seven channels and nothin' on" and "I just want to feel your rhythm." But what happens when those screams are ignored or dismissed? When the "powers that be" in whatever sense — political, social, economic or even romantic — choose to summarily reject them as inarticulate noise and unimportant nonsense? Springsteen deals with these questions boldly and brilliantly.

In 1980 Springsteen released the double album, *The River*, which includes the haunting and disturbing track "Stolen Car." On the surface of things, this song is about a character's lament over lost love, and the sorrow that results from it. Heartache, as country music so often calls it, can be lonely enough, but a deeper examination of and reflection on the Springsteen song reveals a pain much more intense, and an existential emptiness much more encompassing than the breakup blues.

I met a little girl and I settled down
In a little house out on the edge of town
We got married, and swore we'd never part
Then little by little we drifted from each other's heart

At first I thought it was just restlessness
That would fade as time went by and our love grew deep
In the end it was something more I guess
That tore us apart and made us weep

And I'm driving a stolen car
Down on Eldridge Avenue
Each night I wait to get caught
But I never do

The man driving the stolen car summarizes the story of his marriage and reminisces on how he and his wife swore they would never separate, but "little by little we drifted from each other's heart." This lyric demonstrates how isolation goes beyond being alone. It is deep despair and a longing for tangible connections with other people who are in sight, but feel miles away. He and his wife live together, sleep in the same bed, and wake up side by side. But they cannot see each other beyond the shadows and doubts left in the wake of a disparate relationship darkened and cracked. They have not physically moved apart, but they have drifted from each other in vastly more important and consequential ways — emotionally and spiritually. It is "something more" indeed.

The song begins with a light strumming of a guitar, while high notes on the piano are played that would otherwise evoke happiness and lightheartedness. The whimsicality of the notes is undermined and subverted by the way they are played — slowly and with deep breaths in between. As the singer goes on with the story, it becomes clear that the lighthearted beginning will not be complemented by a happy ending. The piano notes, which operate as musical indicators of hope over a dark and melancholy melody, become softer and more separate. The hope fades with the character's sense of belonging and purpose. Only someone lacking both those essentials would steal a car with the self-destructive hope of getting caught.

In the second verse of the song, the character's depression and separation are articulated in even starker and more dread terms.

She asked if I remembered the letters I wrote
When our love was young and bold
She said last night she read those letters
And they made her feel one hundred years old

At this point the singer is describing the alienation of emotionally positive and mutually reassuring feelings. The way this couple felt when exchanging letters is so distant that to revisit them makes the woman feel ancient. Feelings of isolation can result from mapping the distance between hope and reality. A publicly painful consequence of this disparity is the detached political apathy that engulfs many Americans when they consider their disappointment with the political system. They believe, with good reason, that the powerful political and social structures are no longer working with them in mind.

Journalists and former insiders, such as the already mentioned Jeffrey Birnbaum and Robert Reich, report that Washington D.C. has welcomed an invasion from lobbyists that do the bidding for billionaire industries with agendas that are harmful to the majority of the American public. Examples abound — from the health-care industry remaining privatized even though it continues to fail to provide adequate care for millions of Americans, to the failure of the United States to implement an economically beneficial and environmentally friendly energy policy, one can smell the toxic stench of corporate cash. Instead of protesting, picketing, and inspiring democratic resistance, the majority of attentive citizens throw up their hands and remain immobilized and inactive, due to being overcome by isolation and emptiness. The ideal that they imagine seems so removed from the reality on the ground that they cannot bring themselves to do something about the problems they very often rightfully identify. Their detachment from American politics runs parallel with the "Stolen Car" driver's detachment from his relationship. Just as much of the American public has found a source of pride in the hateful process of scapegoating — whether it be of blacks, immigrants or gays — the singer has found solace in self-destructive and distractive behavior. In the final chorus, we learn the nature and origin of this behavior.

> And I'm driving a stolen car
> On a pitch black night
> And I'm telling myself I'm gonna be alright
> But I ride by night and I travel in fear
> That in this darkness I will disappear

The character's unimaginable fear of becoming indistinguishable from the darkness is overpowering. He feels that his humanity will be lost because the only thing keeping him human was his connection with others and now that those connections have been broken, he is no longer able to maintain a strong identity. Therefore, his desire to be arrested for grand theft auto is a protective measure against disappearance, which demonstrates the irrationality that isolation causes. He feels that by being pulled over and apprehended, the police will be acknowledging his existence, which will affirm his humanity. His angst is similar to all of those inner-city youth who choose to join street gangs after being abandoned by their families, cities and country. They live in neighborhoods devoid of social services and institutional efficiency. Oftentimes their family lives are miserable, so they begin to behave self-destructively and sadistically, preying on the weak and vulnerable, while risking their lives for the drug profits of a higher-up gangster. Measuring this nihilistic behavior with instruments of reason from the rational world, one can only call it self-destructive. But in the eyes of many of the gang members it is protective, because it is giving them identity, pride and community in a wasteland lacking clearly visible opportunities for all three. Even in cases where the consequences are not so extreme, the debilitating effects of isolation are powerfully obstructive to upward mobility and personal growth.

"Stolen Car" is wisely and strongly used in the 1997 film *Cop Land* to capture the isolation of its main character Sheriff Freddy Heflin, played by Sylvester Stallone. The film takes place in the fictional town of Garrison, New Jersey — a small town where a significant amount of residents are New York Police Department officers. Although nominally the sheriff, Freddy has no real power in the town; its affairs are mainly handled by corrupt NYPD officers who use the town as a headquarters for criminal planning. Heflin both admires and envies his police officer friends. He dreamed of being on the NYPD, but failed the physical due to a hearing impairment he obtained while saving the life of a young girl he loved in high school, Liz Randone (played by Annabella Sciorra). Freddy continues to love her into adulthood and is single because of it. He interacts with her and her husband often and maintains a friendly relationship with the NYPD cops who live in town. However, he is essentially isolated from everyone. He cannot develop the relationship he craves with Liz because she is married and he is not truly accepted into the cop circle because he is not a New York policeman. His life is one defined by loneliness, regret and lost dreams. None of his hopes, wishes or aspirations have materialized. He is shown drinking too much, being disrespected by corrupt police officers, and blankly staring into his television screen late at night similar to the bitterly detached protagonist of "57 Channels (And Nothin' On)." Though he suspects several police officers of corruption, he refuses to investigate or go to the proper authorities, even after he is given an opportunity to do so by an Internal Affairs officer played by Robert De Niro. His courage and ability to express his own value and potential are severely stunted by the disconnect he struggles with on a daily basis. Without what Putnam calls "mutual reciprocity" found in the respect and love of others, people decline into perpetual negativity, moral constipation and overall listlessness — what Chomsky calls the "atomization" of the American public. Sheriff Freddy Heflin is a prime example found in cinematic fiction.

In a profoundly moving scene, Liz visits Freddy after having a violent argument with her degenerate husband. When Freddy answers the door he is already listening to "Stolen Car" on vinyl, which leads Liz to say, "You know you can get this on CD, it would be stereo," to which Freddy replies, "It wouldn't matter to me." Liz pauses and gets a look in her that expresses her understanding that Freddy listens to this sad song for purely emotional reasons, whispers, "All right" and sits down on the couch. Freddy soon joins her. They painfully stare at each other until Liz breaks the tension by tearfully remarking, "You know it's a funny thing when you owe someone your life." Freddy tilts his head up and reveals a melancholy smile that people transparently wear when trying to appear content and gracious while dying inside. Still teared-up, Liz, with an aching sadness as if she already knows the answer to her question, asks, "Why is it you never got married, Freddy?" Freddy looks into her eyes, while his appear empty, rocks a little back and forth, looks away as if he can no longer bear to put his soul on display, tilts the side of his lips and softly says, "All the best girls are taken."

Liz extends her hand and places it over Freddy's mouth. He closes his eyes and holds it there for a few seconds before leaning forward. She expects a kiss and leans her face forward with a downward slant of her head, her hair falling into his face. She appears shocked, like her heart has just been sliced in half, when Freddy continues to lean forward and holds his cheek on hers to feel the life-giving touch of her skin, while his head rests on her shoulder and she runs her soft fingers through his hair. Although Freddy loves her like only a man can love a woman, his momentary need was not sexual. It was to have his humanity affirmed by the connective interaction and sensual touch of Liz. Before he could consider arousal, his heart and soul needed to be reawakened by the love, security and companionship he longed for in Liz's arms. He suspends himself there for a moment, producing an image that more closely resembles a mother holding a child than two lovers preparing to act on their mutual attraction. The purest form of love is presented in this scene, and it is exactly what Freddy needed. The placement of "Stolen Car" in it is perfect, as the character speaking in that song is undergoing the same heartbreak and despair, which can only be healed by the same kind of transformative love.

Freddy is seen throughout the rest of the movie walking down the streets of Garrison surrounded by laughing children, white fences and freshly manicured lawns. This seemingly idyllic setting starkly contrasts Freddy's inner turmoil. His knowledge of police corruption casts a shadow across the landscape of the American Dream. His inability to become a part of that dream, because of his hearing impairment but also an even more severe handicap — an isolationist instinct that prevents him from behaving with conviction and courage — makes his picturesque town look ugly, distorted and threatening.

In this sense Freddy is much like a character ripped from the canvas of an Edward Hopper painting. The twentieth-century American painter captured the dread and loneliness of American life better than possibly any other visual artist.

Hopper was reticent in speaking about his own work, and went so far as to self-deprecatingly imply that all he ever desired to do was paint the rays of a sunset bouncing off the roof of a New England house. Like the narratives in his paintings, his "artist statement" is ambiguous, mysterious and vulnerable to diversely varying interpretations. In an importantly symbolic sense, Hopper's refusal to speak freely about his work provides a more clear and potent insight than any words could muster.

His silence is complementary to and indicative of the unnerving silence of his characters. The most commonly used word by Hopper's admirers and critics is "isolation," and any viewer of Hopper's art can understand why. A sense of dread, despair and dejected sensibility can be seen on the young woman's downward-looking face in *Automat* (1927). Feelings of detachment and loneliness, and the uneasy boredom that accompanies them, are projected onto the onlooker of the usherette staring at the spot where the floor and wall meet in *New York Movie* (1939).

The greatest and most discomfiting presentation of isolation can be found in Hopper's paintings that include more than one person. *Cape Cod Evening* (1939) presents two people who appear to be lovers, or at least live in the same house, sitting in their backyard with their dog. There is no eye contact between any of the characters — both the man and woman look out on to the grass, and the dog stares into the landscape. The young man places his hand onto a few spikes of grass to feel the wind blow them against his palm, reaching out for something on his skin even if it is as disloyal and restless as the wind, while another human being stands right next to him. In *Office at Night* (1940) a woman appears to be longing for her co-worker's attention and affection, while leering over his shoulder and pretending to file through a cabinet. He is focused on his desk, oblivious of her company.

Desolation, isolation and separation are evoked and emoted most famously in *Nighthawks* (1942), the classic and perhaps definitive work of American realism. Four people, presumably strangers, sit in an all-night diner. One employee, in a white uniform and paper hat, reaches for something underneath the counter while affixing his eyes straight ahead out the window. The three customers — two men and one woman — appear utterly depressed as they seem to make a strong effort not to look at each other.

Nighthawks has become part of the American iconography and a central part of Americana — reproduced on television, movie screens, book covers and album artwork; referenced in film noir, *The Simpsons* and Tom Waits records. It seems to simultaneously capture and destroy the American myth of self-made strength through "rugged individualism" by presenting its underbelly — its social consequences that manifest in personal and national insomnia. This is the night side of America.

The superpower is tossing and turning, listening to the dull hum of the ceiling fan, glancing at the blood-red digital clock, desperately wishing to fall back asleep to visit American dreamland. The "Nighthawks", with their grim outlooks, chipped shoulders, and discouraged demeanors are those that have come to realize that the American Dream is just that: a dream. It is not tangibly attainable. It is fleeting. It is a fantasy.

The Nighthawks mourn, along with the Cape Cod family and the New York usherette, as Hopper mourns, for something that never really existed. They grieve for a myth that they once believed in and in the absence of such a belief they find their loneliness. Unable to find comfort in others, they become isolated.[8]

When Springsteen sings of a girl staring into the night with "the eyes of one who hates for just being born" in "Racing in the Street" (1978) or a small-town drifter watching idealized America but longing for a connection as "girls in their summer clothes" pass him by ("Girls in Their Summer Clothes", 2007), is he not presenting the same burnt-out, passed-over and betrayed individuals that are visible in Hopper's painting?

The woman in "Racing" is described to the listener by the song's male protagonist — a small-town racer who, devoid of another reason to live a proud and self-respecting life, races cars along the shore. He reminisces about meeting his lover in an exciting scene of speed and sexuality. He remembers her there with another man who drove a Camaro, and leaving him sitting in his hot rod staring at his bumper as he won the race in thrilling fashion. In the heat of celebration, he swept the girl off her feet and took her home. After retelling this story the fate of their relationship immediately turns to heartache and emptiness, leaving the impression that it peaked on its first night.

> I met her on the strip three years ago
> In a Camaro with this dude from L.A.
> I blew that Camaro off my back and drove that little girl away
> But now there's wrinkles around my baby's eyes
> And she cries herself to sleep at night
> When I come home the house is dark
> She sighs "Baby did you make it all right"
> She sits on the porch of her daddy's house

But all her pretty dreams are torn
She stares off alone into the night
With the eyes of one who hates for just being born
For all the shut down strangers and hot rod angels
Rumbling through this promised land
Tonight my baby and me we're gonna ride to the sea
And wash these sins off our hands

Following a brief chorus — a pronouncement that "Summer's here and the time is right / For goin' racin' in the street" — a long coda begins taking the listener on a ride as emotionally wild as the physical thrill of racing. As the piano plays melancholy notes that represent the singer's past torment, regret and resentment, they soon become overwhelmed by quickening drums, winding guitars and the triumphant rise of an organ — the sound of redemption and renewal. One can actually hear the battle of emotion that is waged when a human being becomes restless enough to break out of a solitary cell that has kept him in bondage, and desperately searches for a meaningful connection that provides a positive appraisal of the value of his own individual existence. The appraisal will never occur when one is alone.

This is the same lesson that the Hopperesque character in "Girls in Their Summer Clothes" learns. He is placed right square in the middle of an idealized America that is not only depicted in the song's lyrics but is also portrayed by its music — 1960s beach pop that encourages dancing, long rides along the shore, and confidence that "everything is gonna be all right." The protagonist begins by simply describing what he sees — children playing, couples walking along Main Street, the town's bright lights — but soon describes his own separation from this scene of happiness, and the resulting pain by answering a waitress's simple question with an unexpected proposition.

Frankie's diner, an old friend on the edge of town
The neon sign spinning round
Like a cross over the lost and found
The fluorescent lights flick over Pop's Grill
Shaniqua brings the coffee and asks "Fill?"
And says "Penny for your thoughts now my boy, Bill"

She went away, she cut me like a knife
Hello beautiful thing, maybe you could save my life
In just a glance, down here on magic street
Love's a fool's dance
And I ain't got much sense, but I still got my feet

The expectation that Shaniqua can save this man's life may seem hyperbolic, but how else could he feel when alone, losing to debilitating depression, while watching everyone around him walk by in an almost non-human, never-ending joy? More importantly, he has gotten to the point which will no longer allow him to wallow in self-pity and loneliness. He has extended his hand to feel another's skin and another's love. Whether he gets it or not, his act of emotional bravery demonstrates a risk-taking capacity that is exactly what he needs to overcome his isolationist dread. It is also a lesson in outreach and self-expression that should not be lost on America.

The transformation of America from nation to market where social programs and services are consistently cut, labor unions are devastated, and civic traditions (voting, running for local offices, political participation) are weakened with each passing year has coincided with a rise in consumer culture that advocates shopping over service and commodity over community. Respectable forums of public engagement in the media are either being dismantled by new media, which is good because of its great accessibility, but worrisome because of its vulnerability to hyper-selectivity of users only looking for information that validates their own opinions, or systematically cheapened and simplified by uncivil and undemocratic screaming matches that include more invective than insight.

Technology that was supposed to alleviate the worst calamities of Americans' creeping isolation has either not gone as far as previously hoped or ironically made problems worse. While the internet has allowed people to more easily maintain long-distance relationships, it has also provided a means for people to stay inside all day, only communicating via the pixels on an electronic screen, and has increased the superficiality of social interaction with "social networking" websites.

Public policy changes will have to be made in order to adequately address the problem, as will reversals in current media and education policy. Public funding of campaigns, reforming the school-funding scheme to achieve equity and diversity, and attempting to encourage media forums that intellectually challenge and stimulate the citizenry would be good places to start. Labor unions — the one vital institution connecting workers to each other — must also be strengthened. There are also important psychological and sociological solutions to consider.

However, it all begins with what Springsteen captured with the words "Tonight my baby and me, we're gonna ride to the sea / And wash these sins off our hands." This is the commitment to renewal through togetherness. The sins that must be absolved are those that are made when alone, when under the insulation of fear and deceptively protective coating that obstructs meaningful and lasting human connection. By simply being together — riding together in the machinery that conceived their relationship — they will tap into the life, energy and love that have the potential to save them. By employing a baptismal metaphor Springsteen emphasizes this simple and collective action's power to provide rebirth. The transcendent and redemptive rise of the musical coda that follows the lyric contains a deep and profound insight into the joy and hope that is possible when one breaks the chains of isolation and demands transformative communal life.

America finds itself at the crossroads where the male racer and male drifter meet in "Racing in the Street" and "Girls in Their Summer Clothes." It must choose between isolation — cutting its citizens off from each other, polarizing them based on class, race, gender and sexual orientation, selling devotion to consumption while unilaterally violating international law — and democratic and dignified community. Clues and indicators of what will occur if America stays the course have already been gathered in the work of activists, journalists, politicians and, as demonstrated, Bruce Springsteen. One of America's other leading social critics and public intellectuals, Cornel West, has laid out the condition that currently afflicts America and will only intensify if events continue to unfold without a reversal of national policy. He calls it nihilism.

> What is most terrifying (in America) is the insidious growth of deadening nihilisms across political lines, nihilisms that have been suffocating the deep democratic energies in America . . . Psychic depression, personal worthlessness, and social despair are widespread in America as a whole. The vast majority of citizens — struggling to preserve a livelihood, raise children, and live decent lives — are disillusioned with social forces that seem beyond their control. The saturation of market forces in American life generates a market morality that undermines a sense of meaning and larger purpose . . . The oppressive effect of the prevailing market moralities leads to a form of sleepwalking from womb to tomb, with the majority of citizens content to focus on private careers and be distracted with stimulating amusements. They have given up any real hope of shaping the collective destiny of the nation. Sour cynicism, political apathy, and cultural escapism become the pervasive options.[9]

The unattractive combination of "deadening nihilisms" that result from corporate dominance over public affairs, social divides that continue to disrupt efforts aimed at harmonizing America, and private citizen isolation produce a myriad of consequences ranging from unpleasant to deadly. Progressive politics are constantly undermined because they rely upon collective organization and mentalities that view other groups of people as allies, brothers and sisters — not enemies vying for the precious few financial resources that remain (observe popular right-wing-written narratives about affirmative action and illegal immigration for relevant examples). Progressive politics also require a gravitational pull of attention from self-interest to communal need. A progressive is willing to pay higher taxes if it means the schools will improve, thereby strengthening the lives of local children and future of the neighborhood. A progressive is happy to pay for social security knowing that not only will she be giving elderly assistance, but also disabled people and widows. A progressive cannot rest easy knowing that millions of people, many of them children, do not have access to health care, even if he is able to afford all the medicine he needs.

It is difficult for a person disconnected from the outside world to make this jump from private pleasure to compassion, charity and justice. For many, politics does not become a priority until it is personal, and if a citizen does not know someone affected by poverty or structural mistreatment and neglect, it will be hard for that citizen to abstractly empathize with victims that remain theoretical to him. Progressive politics will continue to decline in popularity as Americans become more separated and desolated.

DELIVER ME FROM NOWHERE: POLITICAL REGRESSION, DOSTOEVSKY, RAND AND *NEBRASKA*

The politics that rise from the devastated heap of aborted progressivism will be defined by intolerance, selfishness and regression. One obvious example is the growth in power and influence of the religious right. Christian forces on the right overwhelm those on the left, leaving the country with a bizarre version of Christianity that demands successive wars, cutting social services to lower taxes, and dislike for people whose lives its proponents know nothing about. The late Arthur Miller said that this "powerful and vocal minority is aching for an ayatollah."[10]

This unfortunate development should not be treated as a shock, because it has coincided with the breakdown of secular community in the United States. When people cannot politically or socially organize to find lasting association with meaningful entities in their own lives, they are not just going to give up. They will go to the source of sustenance and solidarity that remains, which in this case is right-wing religion.

A recent rise of "superpatriotism," which projects communal association onto nationalistic symbols, is also evidentiary of dark social capital. Dissent is demonized, and skepticism levied against supposedly pious national motives is akin to blasphemy.[11] The only way to defeat a socially negative community is to speak to the same isolation that draws people into it by offering a positive alternative. This must be on the left's most-attended missions in American politics.

If the left fails to accept this mission, the political consequences will continue to intensify and compound, while individuals will continue to slip into one of the "deadening nihilisms" that West so eloquently and urgently describes. The existential effects of deadening nihilism are told in the most disturbing detail in the real-life events of school shootings, inner-city gang wars, and rising mental health problems. They are also depicted brilliantly in classic works of literature.

Fyodor Dostoevsky in *Crime and Punishment* employs Raskolnikov, a young, ex-law student living in extreme poverty in St. Petersburg, as the book's protagonist. He is a handsome and intelligent man who is socially impotent and psychically depressed. He objects to the social misery that epitomizes his surroundings but does not know how to express his objection meaningfully. He falls into a pattern of extreme acts of altruism followed by paralyzing apathy. Unable to observe results of his charity, and failing to envision a brighter future, he becomes consumed with his own insanity and "genius." He begins rambling to himself, becomes terribly neurotic, and afraid of crowded places, until he theorizes that people can be categorized as "ordinary" or "extraordinary." After deciding to act on this theory, he murders a cruel shopkeeper and takes her money, promising himself to invest it in helpful social causes. Raskolnikov panics when exiting the shop upon realizing that the shopkeeper's mentally slow sister has witnessed the entire event. He kills her, and because he cannot justify her homicide, begins to hate himself more with each passing day. His derangement that led him to such an unspeakable crime, and to formulate an absurd theory that motivated it, was very much due to his pervasive isolation. It is not until he falls in love with Sonia, a pious and ethical prostitute who sells her body to provide for her family, that he begins to recover from all-encompassing dread and despair. He proclaims his love in spiritual ecstasy, and she convinces him to confess his crimes. He is sentenced to exile in Siberia, where he begins mental and spiritual rehabilitation. Truth, love and goodness saved him from depression, nihilism and insanity, and this was only possible once he made a meaningful connection with the outside world.

In *The Fountainhead*, Ayn Rand tells the story of Howard Roark, a brilliant architect who is just as deranged as Raskolnikov, only Rand does not know it. His architectural inventiveness is ridiculed by mainstream society to effectively show America's resistance to creative innovation. However, Roark is also socially desolate, preferring to live in isolation with his genius as his only companion. He meets a woman he lusts after and forces himself on her sexually. The woman claims to have enjoyed it, but does not find comfort in Roark's uncompromisingly distant attitude. He is offensive to friends and condescending to everyone else. His failures in compassion, kindness and connectivity, set against his professional brilliance, reveal the contradictions of capitalism that manifest themselves in a laboratory of social ills. Rand celebrates Roark and her capitalist model, but fair and ethical readers should see it for what it is — a cold machine that has great productive potential but, being a machine, is unable to feel, empathize and morally evolve. Roark is the personification of this machine — a talented person cut off from society, unable to make meaningful connections and positive social contributions.

Springsteen introduces his listeners to characters similar to Raskolnikov and Roark in his darkest work. *Nebraska*, greatly inspired by Flannery O'Connor's dark and despondent characters in search of grace, was released smack-dab in the middle of Reagan's sunny optimism. It is a tour de force through broken promises, dying dreams and hopeless people with dejected sensibilities, discouraged demeanors and depressed psyches. The title song is based on the life of Charles Starkweather, a young man who took his girlfriend on a road trip from Nebraska to Wyoming. During the trip, they murdered 11 innocent people. Starkweather was a thoughtless killer who lacked any respect for life and fully embraced a nihilistic worldview, saying, "Shooting people was, I guess, a kind of thrill. Dead people are all on the same level."[12] Springsteen, in true artistic form, attempts to get in Starkweather's head and sing in his voice, refusing to apologize for the brutal murders and even referring to them with similar phrasing. The final verse of the song is the most chilling, and can cause deep psychological deliberation upon listening.

> They declared me unfit to live said into that great void my soul'd be hurled
> They wanted to know why I did what I did
> Well sir I guess there's just a meanness in this world

How does one declare another human being "unfit to live?" This question is especially relevant in the case of Starkweather, who was most likely unfit to live long before he was sentenced to death in the court of law. Starkweather's separation from the world transformed into a derangement luckily uncommon even among the most isolated and tormented people. His explanation for his brutality is hauntingly vague. One cannot deny the existence of an unnamable meanness in the world, and Springsteen's protagonist's reference of it (Starkweather has never been quoted saying as such) is quite disconcerting when considering that he embraced, lived for, and found a home within it. Whatever meanness he felt lost in and embattled by, he chose to turn it on other people in the most extreme and vicious form. Springsteen's impressive resistance to editorialize in the song or cast judgment on Starkweather or capital punishment forces the listener to wrestle with the uncomfortable and dark issues that are at the center of the song. Its bleak and whining harmonica, which resembles the sound of a dying animal calling for help in a vast space of emptiness, provides the perfect soundtrack.

"State Trooper," which appears on the same album, is an even sparser and more restless portrayal of a creeping isolation and derangement that permeates into every iota of a person's being. Springsteen's playing of the acoustic guitar sounds like a building of energy that never culminates into a crescendo. Its refusal to go anywhere gives listeners a sense of the disappointment, broken connections and lost opportunities that haunt the protagonist. He is whispering a desperate yet seemingly half-sincere plea to a state trooper, pausing only to describe his setting in unsatisfied terms.

> New Jersey Turnpike ridin' on a wet night
> 'Neath the refinery's glow, out where the great black rivers flow
> License, registration, I ain't got none but I got a clear conscience
> 'Bout the things that I done
> Mister state trooper, please don't stop me
> Please don't stop me, please don't stop me
>
> Maybe you got a kid, maybe you got a pretty wife
> The only thing that I got's been both'rin' me my whole life
> Mister state trooper, please don't stop me
> Please don't stop me, please don't stop me
>
> In the wee wee hours your mind gets hazy, radio relay towers lead me to
>   my baby
> Radio's jammed up with talk show stations
> It's just talk, talk, talk, talk, till you lose your patience
> Mister state trooper, please don't stop me
>
> Hey, somebody out there, listen to my last prayer
> Hiho silver-o, deliver me from nowhere

The character's depression, desolation and dejected sensibility are evident in such extreme lines as "Maybe you got a kid, maybe you got a pretty wife / The only thing that I got's been both'rin' me my whole life." The most troubling part of the song is its conclusion, in which the isolated character prays to a non-deity as unreceptive and unaddressed as "somebody out there" for deliverance "from nowhere." Nowhere is typically thought of as nothingness, as a non-existent non-place devoid of anything that defines a real setting. However, this is where this character lives. He may be physically surrounded by people, activity and noise, but emotionally and psychologically he is in a place where absolutely nothing happens. There are no relationships, common humanity or meaningful purposes. He is nowhere and seeks deliverance from an unnamed source likely to let him down. After he sings, the music finally opens up and makes just enough room for a high-pitched scream from the singer which provides little insight into the character's future but further disturbs the consciousness of the listener. It is unclear if this scream signifies an act of personal or social destruction, *à la* Raskolnikov, Starkweather and "57 Channels (And Nothin' On)," or if it expresses one last attempt to connect to a life-giving and vitality-providing force. The protagonist's course of action remains a mystery, but the choice presented to him is very clear.

The same choice was presented to a jail guard in Birmingham in 1963 by Dr. Martin Luther King Jr., while he was locked up for acts of civil disobedience. After being harassed and insulted by a white, working-class jail guard, King decided to engage the man with the love, humanity and empathy he utilized to lead an entire movement of equality and democracy. He asked the guard why he could not understand that he has more in common with him, despite their different shades of skin color, than the elite managers of racial discrimination and marketplace politics that use divide-and-conquer tactics to solidify the oppression of two under-classes — black people and working-class whites. King called upon the man to search inside himself to find who was truly benefiting from his hate.

This story serves as a microcosm for America's historically existent and still prevailing dilemma. Will it, and its people, continue to isolate and find comfort and pseudo-meaning in the consumption of commodities, or will it extend and project itself into unexplored territory that has the potential to uplift, invigorate and inspire? Will America, and its people, continue to cash "bad social capital" that invests in division, intolerance and fear, or will it build reserves of good social capital that invests in loving, giving and democratic communities?

Springsteen has wrestled with these life-and-death questions throughout his career and provides a useful template for analyzing the painful consequences of isolation and the vast benefits of community. It is a good place for a study of his music to begin, as well as an appropriate topic for America to self-critically examine in its search for renewed democracy, revitalized community and economic recovery.

Chapter 3

Up to My Neck in Hock

The Politics of Alienation

T he image of a vacationing American has become a near cliché, reserved for jokes from Europeans and others who have difficulty understanding what has unfortunately become the American way of life. There he is, lugging a laptop on to the airplane so he can regularly check back with the office through e-mail and keeping a cell phone attached to his hip like a gun in a holster which enables him to rapidly fire back with directions, orders or requests at the sound of a high-pitch ring or muffled and muddied pop song that obnoxiously infiltrates his surroundings through a tiny phone speaker. Technology, despite all of its benefits and conveniences, has facilitated a lifestyle for Americans that is perpetually occupation-driven. The typical American middle-class worker is bordering on monolithic in his approach to life, operating according to the functionality of a machine that is programmed to work and spend the earnings on commodities. Add this to the lack of leisure Americans enjoy as they work longer hours, often without overtime compensation, and what Bruce Springsteen once called "the saddest line I've ever written," becomes even sadder: "I've been workin' all week, I'm up to my neck in hock" ("Ramrod," 1980).[1]

The lyric that immediately follows that melancholy denunciation of joyless living, sung in a celebratory tone — "Come Saturday night I let my ramrod rock" — has now become questionable. The average worker may be tied to work on Saturday night — completing homework similar to a high-school student by collecting faxes, studying numbers, making calls and writing e-mails — or he might be too tired to let much rock but the remote control. Suffering from paralyzing fatigue accumulated from overworking and under-resting throughout the week, he may only have the energy and desire to vegetate in front of a flashing screen. This debilitated mode of existence contributes to an overwhelming sense of isolation that permeates throughout society, and also induces a static state of routine meaninglessness which cannot address the holistic person or offer sustained enrichment or fulfillment. If one does muster the strength to leave the home on the weekend, it is usually motivated by an urge to consume large amounts of alcohol, which on its own merits is not condemnable and can be quite fun, but is unfortunate considering the circumstances and psychology that often accompany and initiate that urge. The need for drinking comes from an experiential desire to be transported into another world, one in which work is not a concern and office-inflicted pressures can be momentarily loosened. In almost encouraging induced psychosis, overworked people grant themselves a few hours of freedom to satisfy themselves but rarely fill their leisure with activity that is more permanently rewarding. Drinking, dancing and sexual excitement on the weekend are all recommendable categories for anyone hoping to relax and enjoy a few hours of unmonitored, unrestricted and autonomous behavior. Party rituals not only possess a physical value but also a psychological and spiritual value, as they enable people to thrive under a nocturnal identity which is often much more satisfying than the half-charged version of themselves they embody during the work week. The desire to escape the work world, and enhance that escape with alcohol is understandable, as long as it is done responsibly and safely. However, if consuming massive amounts of booze is the constant focal point of a person's leisurely weekend activity, it may be indicative of an overall lack of imagination, energy and communal belonging within the psyche of the average worker.

The condition that is being summarized is one that goes far beyond isolation, which contains a plethora of problems, and mutates into alienation. Karl Marx famously theorized that alienation is a common result of capitalist labor, because workers are separated from the product, which is privately owned by economic superiors. They are treated as commodities themselves on the market, because labor is viewed as something to be bought and sold, which undermines its social capacity, and most depressingly, the worker is alienated from her own humanity, especially when she does not feel a connection to her labor and cannot find a clearly visible communal value to her productive output. Devoid of intrinsic satisfaction, alienation sets in, and existential emptiness, social debilitation and psychological regression are entirely symptomatic.[2] Needless to say, this affliction affects the working class with far worse severity than the middle class, due to the destruction of labor unions, stagnation of wages, and lack of respect that is afforded to them in an increasingly status-based society.

In 1978, greatly influenced by his father, who held a string of unfulfilling jobs and lived an observably unhappy life, Springsteen wrote, recorded and released a song titled "Factory." It brilliantly captures the unsatisfying routine of an individual suffering from labor alienation. Its country-music-style melody, plodding drumbeat and darkened, almost lifeless, vocal delivery dramatize the despair and angst that characterize this mode of living. The first verse summons the simple imagery of a worker reporting to the job but, sung over a sad melody, it leads the listener to contemplate what goes unsaid and unseen in this common scene.

> Early in the morning factory whistle blows,
> Man rises from bed and puts on his clothes,
> Man takes his lunch, walks out in the morning light,
> It's the working, the working, just the working life.

The story of countless people is relatable to this brief verse. Those who occupy every morning with identical routine can be enveloped by a boredom which can often transform into dread. Although "Factory" is sonically similar to country music, its sentimentality differs entirely. From Merle Haggard to Brooks & Dunn, great country singers have often paid tribute to their listeners by glorifying the routine of the worker, instead of wrestling with the complex and often disturbing implications of the "working life." This glorification is respectable and admirable because it reminds working-class listeners that their jobs and lives have great value which is deserving of recognition. However, if it is done without balance, or consideration of the societal neglect of the laborer, it falls into the one-sided trap of unrealistic idealization. Springsteen refuses to do this, and instead takes a more nuanced and confrontational approach to the capital-obsessed society he inhabits by relating his father's story — which was nearly free of glory. Even his insistence on repeating the word "working" demonstrates an understanding of the repetition of the worker. As writer Jim Harrison once said, "Repetition can be damaging to the soul."[3] However, certain forms of labor can also be physically destructive. Sadly, many are forced to write-off bodily losses and find the strength to report to duty again for the millionth time.

> Through the mansions of fear, through the mansions of pain,
> I see my daddy walking through them factory gates in the rain,
> Factory takes his hearing, factory gives him life,
> The working, the working, just the working life.

The continuance of the imagery of the first verse has now taken a darker tone and shape. As the worker struggles through the inequality, hardship and systematic injustice of the society that demands his physical sacrifice, and is reminded of it every day with the sight of residential and manufacturing mansions, he continues onward to those factory gates. The cold, hard rain peppers him — an unpleasant introduction from a day of unpleasant work. With the morning's chores, the worker may be slowed down by his weakening physical state, which is marked by a loss of hearing. His intensifying disability — a symptom of the "working life" — follows him home, and makes all activities, both work- and non-work-related, tougher than before. Every time he needs words repeated or turns the volume on the television set just a little higher than the last time he watched, he is reminded of his labor, and may either consciously or unconsciously be forced to personally reckon with the cost of his occupational devotion. Given these wounds, both physical and emotional, and how the inhabitants of the towering mansions that cast a discoloring shadow on him while he stumbles to work ignore his toil and struggle and deny his dignity, it is easy to wonder: What reward does he receive for his sacrifice?

He has a family, and is obligated to take care of them. He nobly reports to the job and slogs through day after day of unsatisfying, alienating labor for the sake of others. As the "Factory takes his hearing," the factory "gives him life." He is dependent upon this mechanization that has robbed him of his senses and psychic joy. This cyclical state of depression is without an escape hatch, meaning that even if he changes jobs or takes a short vacation he will find himself in the same state. He will become withdrawn, embittered and purposelessly angry. Political apathy and social stasis will characterize his citizen output, while he becomes more and more isolated from those closest to him. His capabilities for contributing to his community will remain unknown and elusive. When the day ends, nothing feels gained, and escapism seems to be one's only friend.

> End of the day, factory whistle cries,
> Men walk through these gates with death in their eyes.
> And you just better believe, boy,
> Somebody's gonna get hurt tonight,
> It's the working, the working, just the working life.

The men pass through those same gates they did eight or nine hours earlier, and are hauntingly and brutally depicted as having "death in their eyes." The physical difficulties of manual labor combined with the mental paralysis of the nature of the work make these men unreachable. They typify Marx's alienated worker. Hostility builds inside of them, and their resentment for their structural surroundings breeds unhealthy behavioral repercussions. The song's warning that "Somebody's gonna get hurt tonight" captures the desire for "induced psychosis" and recklessness that follows. These men are not looking for positive fulfillment to balance the hopelessness they battle 40 hours a week. They search out a fleeting escape. Damage is done to the self, the family and the community. But, for them, that is all part of the "working life."

The song ends with a sweeping coda which, similar to other Springsteen songs, evokes passions and emotions of mourning. The alienated worker's suffering and struggles are to be mourned, as is what communities lose when workers are objectified in this particular fashion. Most of all, they are to be remembered — in art, life and politics.

Far from exclusively glorifying the worker's continual lull in life, Springsteen honestly wrestles with its tragic implications in grim and provocative artistry. Although it bears similarities to Marx's theory of labor alienation, its impetus is not derived from a philosophical text but from his own household. He witnessed the real-life effects of theoretical diagnosis in his father's eyes, and felt it in the air of his working-class home. Springsteen would go on to write more songs about his father, but none of them focused on the condition created by his work as precisely and powerfully as "Factory." He nearly navigated the same territory in 1984 with the *Born in the U.S.A.* hit "Glory Days," but for unknown reasons eliminated a significant portion of the song's lyrics, which would have made the impact of the song much stronger and would have provided a clearer picture of the America he described in that album's misunderstood title track. The "lost" verse was published in a collection of Springsteen lyrics titled *Songs*, and is worth examining in the context of labor alienation and unfulfilling work.

> My old man worked 20 years on the line and they let him go
> Now everywhere he goes out looking for work they just tell him that he's
>   too old
> I was 9 years old when he was working at the Metuchen Ford plant
>   assembly line
> Now he just sits on a stool down at the Legion Hall, but I can tell what's
>   on his mind
>
> Glory days
> Yeah gone bad, glory days
> Oh he ain't never had, glory days
> Glory days

The dichotomous predicament of "Factory takes his hearing, factory gives him life" is demonstrated clearly in the "lost verse" and altered chorus of "Glory Days." As stultifying, unrewarding and alienating as some work can be, without a proper substitute it becomes misapplied to life, and misinterpreted as the central source of purpose. Once that source of purpose is sealed, deep depression and feelings of worthlessness can multiply. The expendability of the worker in modern America is also indicted in this verse. As corporatized globalization becomes an assumed, unquestionable part of everyday existence, job outsourcing becomes more and more common. Suddenly, people who learned a trade or cultivated a skill can no longer find decent work because they are competing with people in the Third World who, without any other viable options, are willing to work for pennies a day. The worker in "Glory Days" has suffered through a lifetime of cyclical heartache and psychic scarring — wandering from unsatisfying labor to unemployment lines to smoky bars, and back again.

The working class of America has largely been relegated to unfulfilling work to supply purpose in their lives — with the significant and sustaining exception of family, which provides them with essential and reliable love, comfort and support. Their towns have been transformed into corporately homogenized centers of behemoth box stores and faceless chain businesses. Their government has mutated from political representation into exploitative, manipulative employment headquarters for those same companies that own the box stores, chains, oil companies and insurance agencies. In many instances, they feel disconnected from American institutions, communities and industry. Spending the overwhelming majority of their time punching away at a clock without gaining something besides a paycheck cannot be healthy.

The middle class, while on shaky but less threatening financial ground, becomes more and more work obsessed. The already described vacationing American cliché aggravates countless people abroad, but becomes less common as vacations are becoming a grander and more fantastical luxury for the average American family. The majority of middle-class workers, who do not have the time or finances necessary for travel, spend more hours at the office and less time with their families or participating in intellectually stimulating and emotionally satisfying activity. They also seem to be more driven by consumption and fantasies of riches than the working class, which prevent them from finding joy in life's more open-ended and potentially liberating moments. Working-class Americans may suffer from a lack of acknowledgment and inclusion in the main polity of America but, through an understanding of that inclusion, take a soulful approach to leisure, which encourages the enjoyment of party rituals that are often lacking among the middle class, whose education and slightly elevated status teaches them to toil further.

From the beginning of life in America, young people are molded into work-obsessed consumers of products or producers of goods. In high school, "hard work" — not intellectual innovation or creative achievement — is rewarded. Many young people have internalized these values by the time they reach college, as they invest large amounts of time and energy into obtaining the perfect grade but simultaneously ignore the value of a liberal arts education by paying no attention to the vast lessons to be gained from literature, philosophy and the natural and social sciences. Everything must have a utilitarian function, and unless an activity or idea can be demonstrated to clearly assist someone in the quest to make more money or earn a better job, it is to be mocked, chided or summarily eliminated from one's own personal priorities.

As Springsteen makes clear, this methodology and philosophy of life is destined for trauma, boredom and questions of self-worth. Those who accept it for themselves will eventually share the quality of those workers marching through the factory gates, being pelted with rain, all sharing "death in their eyes" and prepared to behave recklessly, risking physical health, mental stability and social reputation just to feel something . . . anything.

The misplaced priorities of Americans can be analyzed from many angles. However, it is perhaps most revealing to view them with a scope that places work at the center. America is a work-driven society, and in many ways still grasps tightly on to the Protestant work ethic, but is more closely connected to other people's oppositional work than ever before. As retirement plans have shifted from traditional pensions to market-dependent 401K plans and other investment packages, middle-class Americans have developed an emotional and financial bond to Wall Street, and have been given a strong incentive to offer political support to those who work tirelessly to placate the agenda of Wall Street, which ironically often harms the typical middle-class family. During the financial crisis, the media has reported on workers losing retirement funds that were tied into the stock market without questioning why pensions are not more dependable, instead of riding on the speculation and instrumentation of the unregulated elite.

As Springsteen does with so many other kinds of people, he attempts to offer an understanding of the worker through empathy. Whether it be the spiritually dead factory worker, mentally absent shoe salesman ("Highway 29"), or dreadfully depressed railroad worker ("Downbound Train"), the listener is presented with an opportunity to consider their suffering, whether it be socially induced or self-inflicted (or a combination of both), by imagining how one would react, behave and struggle in a similarly undesirable situation.

In the case of alienated labor and the workers that live with it on a daily basis, it may be best to begin with an examination of the political and economic reasons why swelling amounts of people feel the need to work to the point of exhaustion, even when they do not particularly like what they do.

"TOTALLY SPENT": ECONOMIC DECLINE AND JUSTIFICATION FOR WORK OBSESSION

In February of 2008, Robert Reich wrote an article of monumental importance for the *New York Times*, which presciently began with the sentence "We're sliding into a recession or worse." Under the headline "Totally Spent," Reich concisely and brilliantly summarized the woes of the American economy, how increases in wealth at the top fail to "trickle down," and how the increasingly agitated, anxious and asphyxiated working and middle classes are coping with economic developments and public policy changes that undermine their financial, emotional and familial stability. He also thoroughly explained why Americans, despite being stricken by the awful condition of alienated labor, devote unseemly amounts of time and energy to work.

Stagnating wages have caused American workers to stretch themselves to the limit, in a variety of ways, to keep up with inflation, rising health-care costs, and the demands of parenthood. First, women found jobs and eased financial tension by bringing a second income to the family budget. When that effort became inadequate, workers turned to credit cards, and began borrowing at a greater cost. Once credit-card bills became insurmountable, work hours had to increase, even when it adversely affected familial life and psychic stability. In the words of Reich, "Americans became veritable workaholics, putting in 350 more hours a year than the average European, more even than the notoriously industrious Japanese."[4]

After comprehensively, yet succinctly, summarizing the reasons why Americans must overextend themselves at the job, and punch in more hours than citizens of other developed nations, Reich lays some key steps to assisting Americans who are "totally spent" — namely creating a more livable economy, which would alleviate much of the burden bearing down on working- and middle-class shoulders. Sensible solutions such as expanding the earned income tax credit for low-income families, making health care more affordable (the cost of which is the number-one cause of bankruptcy in the United States), strengthening unions, and repairing damaged public schools so as to ensure educational equality are recommended to pad Americans' thinning wallets and put a halt to rising inequality. However, what Reich fails to dive in to — he merely hints at it in the beginning of the article, saying that consumers have been "spending beyond their means" — is that even though American governmental institutions have failed miserably in regulating elite managers of the market who are driven by greed and self-interest, Americans themselves are also partially to blame for their current financial and psychological woes.[5]

By allowing themselves to be baptized as members of the consumerist cult, which is at the heart of American life, many citizens have also neglected their non-working, non-spending lives by acting as if leisure is a dangerous habit to be avoided, rather than an elemental part of a fulfilling life. The World Tourism Organization released a report in 2000 that placed Americans in last place among the developed world for vacation time. While the average Italian takes 42 vacation days a year, and the average Canadian takes 26, the typical American vacations only 13 days out of the entire year.[6]

Lack of leisure and abundance of labor is especially calamitous when much of America's work fits Marx's painful description of "alienated labor," and produces a plethora of political, sociological and psychological consequences. Springsteen has brilliantly, starkly and dreadfully described the routines and fates of countless workers who hear a whistle, slog through gates in the rain only to hear a whistle in the afternoon, slog through those same gates, and wait to rinse and repeat in the morning — all the while carrying that mean, ominous and apocalyptic look of death in their eyes. His dark portrait may be inspired by his father, who underwent this lifestyle and, as in the lost verse of "Glory Days," only found solace in cheap beer and the company of similarly dejected, debased, down-and-out types in a smelly and smoky room.

As Springsteen has sounded a warning alarm against allowing oneself to slip into a life governed by alienated labor, he has also promoted the rewards — psychical and psychological, sexual and spiritual — of wisely and wildly spent leisure.

I'M HOME, I'M OUT OF MY WORK CLOTHES: THE GLORIES AND IDEALISM OF LEISURE

"Out in the Street" has become a staple of E Street Band concerts. Typically preceded by Springsteen's primal scream of "Is there anybody alive out there?," which is always answered with a deafening roar from the capacity crowd, it has become a celebratory anthem for a live Springsteen event. Its opening chords transmit a signal of rejuvenation, redemption and recreation for the thousands in attendance and the millions around the world whose weekly hopes, fantasies and dreams it represents. The power chords of dueling guitars create space for a light piano riff which eventually opens to reveal the fractured, grounded, and not ambitious idealism of the tired but eager and excited protagonist. For casual listeners, idealism may seem like an odd philosophy to associate with this fun rocker from *The River*. But, its writer has claimed on more than one occasion that it was almost cut from that 1980 double album because it seemed "too idealistic" and "too much like a fantasy." The idealistic and fantastical elements of the song become clear after examining the lyrics, while appreciating the exuberant and bouncy melody that supports them. This live anthem, which always draws ritualistic audience participation on the chorus and coda, sanctifies the vaguely addressed "street" as a destination where anything is possible and life-altering blessings are bestowed upon its visitors like the rain that darts against the faces of the cold and dissatisfied factory worker. Freedom, dignity, respect, romance and love are within grasp.

> Put on your best dress baby
> And darlin', fix your hair up right
> Cause there's a party, honey
> Way down beneath the neon lights
> All day you've been working that hard line
> Now tonight you're gonna have a good time
>
> I work five days a week girl
> Loading crates down on the dock
> I take my hard earned money
> And meet my girl down on the block
> And Monday when the foreman calls time
> I've already got Friday on my mind
>
> When that whistle blows
> Girl, I'm down the street
> I'm home, I'm out of my work clothes
> When I'm out in the street
> I walk the way I wanna walk
> When I'm out in the street
> I talk the way I wanna talk

Beginning with an invitation to a beloved woman, the singer instructs her to make an effort to present herself in an aesthetically pleasing way — with beauty, class and sex appeal. Cosmetics are important "out in the street," because as this benevolent destination provides freedom, it also gives its visitors an opportunity to cultivate a self-made image — unlike the workplace setting which at a minimum requires a dress code and for many, including the character singing this song, a head-to-toe uniform. The combination of freedom, individuality and autonomy during one's leisure on the street affords the worker a sense of dignity, belonging and indeed "home" that is not possible on the job. Instead of being viewed as a tool to be utilized for operations necessary for profit, he is viewed according to his own terms. He defines his identity, purpose and agenda — rather than some unsympathetic boss demanding obedience. This promise of autonomy and self-stated identity maintains the worker's endurance throughout the week, and he is fully aware that it also sustains his girlfriend who, despite "working that hard line" all week, can be rejuvenated by the announcement "tonight, you're gonna have a good time."

The second verse does not significantly differ from the first. The listener learns that in the street the worker "never feels alone," and is again reminded of the communal belonging he feels when his feet hit the ground of this seemingly sacred pavement. He makes us aware of police presence but is confident that they will not obstruct his vital pursuit of pleasure. Authority does not pose a threat on the street, as it does on the job. This, after all, is a different world entirely where rules, bylaws and guidelines do not have the same meaning or importance. Within this world, he can replace the monotony of occupational diligence with the unpredictable adventure of sexuality which is invigorating, energizing and exciting.

As the lyrics become a bit repetitive, the melody grows more jubilant and provokes sing-alongs and dancing from the crowd. It bounces along with celebratory purpose which underscores the lyrical content and demonstrates the value of lyrical repetition. The predictability of the comforts, excitement and sustenance of the street may be all this worker can depend on. It gives him strength, purpose and motivation to labor on through an unsatisfying job to which he feels no connection and can assign no value beyond the paycheck. Roy Bittan's ebullient piano riff, Max's steady drum, and triumphant trading of vocals between Bruce, Steve and other members of the band serve as evidence for the awesome power of the "street" — a fantastical place of unlimited reward.

One can understand why Springsteen has labeled it "too idealistic." Everyone can find home and joy somewhere, but it may be difficult, even for the happiest of souls, to imagine a place possessing the perfection described in "Out in the Street."

Springsteen himself undoubtedly realized that perfection of that sort (of any sort) is unattainable. Five years prior to the release of "Out in the Street" on *The River*, the masterpiece *Born to Run* burst on to the radio and soared throughout theaters and arenas. One of the few obscure songs on that album is the three-minute, all-engines-firing-full-speed rapturous rocker "Night." Similarly to "Out in the Street," the singer grants transformative power to a setting and suggests that when one is within it, he or she will find redemption, resurgence and an unimaginable quality of life. It also offers a joyful alternative to alienated labor, and through that alternative all of the humanistic needs unattained through work can be had.

> You get up every morning at the sound of the bell
> You get to work late and the boss man's giving you hell

Till you're out on a midnight run
Losing your heart to a beautiful one
And it feels right as you lock up the house
Turn out the lights and step out into the night

And the world is busting at its seams
And you're just a prisoner of your dreams
Holding on for your life 'cause you work all day
To blow 'em away in the night

The opening of the song resembles a rapid-fire machine gun created by crushing drums and fire-shooting guitars. When the firing line ends, Clarence Clemons's saxophone enters the space to create the sense of transcending triumph. The lift it provides symbolizes the simultaneous escape and sanctuary one can find in the night. The monotony and malignity of his workplace conditions are attacked by the seemingly endless possibilities of the leisure-induced, activity-fueled night, which explains the military-like assault on the senses that the E Street Band launches from the opening chords of "Night" to its final notes. However, the assault will never be entirely successful.

Despite the award of being "in love with all the wonder it brings / And every muscle in your body sings as the highway ignites," after one works "nine to five to survive till the night," and despite the same promise that the street holds of self-defined identity — "All day they're busting you up on the outside / But tonight you're gonna break on through to the inside" — the night is not paradise, and will fail to bring its visitor more than temporal joy. Emotional fulfillment and spiritual security require much more than a few hours of freedom on the weekend. This is a reality with which the narrator of "Night" is all too aware: "Somewhere tonight you run sad and free / Until all you can see is the night."

Sadness accompanies freedom because its condition is fleeting. Eventually the worker must return to his alienation, and suffer through the grind of intellectually stultifying and emotionally stunting labor. Springsteen's music, from "Factory" to "Out in the Street," honestly grapples with the severe consequences of labor alienation. It also preaches the benefits and rewards of leisure by attempting to capture, even at times too idealistically, the way certain characters feel when enjoying it. But very few people are able to live a life of total leisure. Meaningful work is essential to the health of the individual and society, and it does not appear that Upton Sinclair's communes are coming back any time soon. However, one can hardly doubt the power of leisure to fulfill and grant meaning, nor can one fairly argue with a good policy that would increase the amount of leisure time available to Americans, especially given the damage that stress and work obsession has done to the collective American psyche.

TAKING A DEEP BREATH: RELAXATION, RECREATION AND LEGISLATION

British writer Tom Hodgkinson has written two books and created a journal, *The Idler*, to reveal how Westerners not only work more and vacation less in the literal sense but also, while actually on vacation, have their cell phone in their pocket and their laptop at their side, unable to see the irony of dealing with business in Barbados. With wit and research he demonstrates the predictable consequences of this — stress and discontentment rise while the intellect and pursuit of happiness suffer. People no longer have the time or energy to learn for the sake of learning, participate in civic activities or enjoy hobbies because periods of inactivity that should be dedicated to leisure time are transformed in zombie time. Leisure time is about balancing the pressures of one's life with soulful conversation, strengthening of the intellect through studying topics of interest, creativity and authentically fun activities like travel, social gathering and the attendance of appealing events.[7]

The overdriven, underpaid worker not only lives a lifestyle that sacrifices his soul on a silver platter, soon to be swallowed by the mouth of self-imposed responsibility, but also witnesses her loved ones eventually become collateral damage in the war zone of modern American life. The typically overworked, overstressed family person does not have sufficient time or energy to devote to playing with children, counseling them, or giving the spouse sufficient attention. Perhaps the biggest buzz phrase for applause in all of politics is "family values," yet we have constructed a society which does not give families enough valuable time to spend together.

The worst part of all of this is that Americans seem to have become believers in their own suffering. They haven taken vows of martyrdom and allowed themselves to be crucified on a cross constructed of one board marked "wealth" and another "efficiency." Many of them associate enjoyment of leisure with laziness which is a standard, but foolishly simple, comparison. Successfully spent leisure may include laziness, but it also might mean cooking a meal instead of picking up fast food, gardening, writing, making a stained glass lamp or playing sports. All of those activities are laborious and require a significant amount of physical exertion, mental exercise or a combination of both. This point is lost or forgotten by many who grow up to raise their children in a world of play dates, where even their time for fun is given management and deadlines. The ultimate punishment for these children is a "time out" — a brief period of isolation and inactivity. As toddlers,

American citizens are now being trained to dread downtime and solitude. The lessons remain embedded in the young mind, which allows toilers to accept their filled schedules and overextended duties without question.

While it may be difficult to reform the inner workings of the American mind after such thorough indoctrination, which begins when they are children and is uniformly practiced at home and in the schools, public policy changes can be made to not only relieve the pressures of working- and middle-class people who feel they must work non-stop, but also encourage leisure and vacation for those who consciously choose to devote their lives to work. The psychological, social and political rewards would be as immense as the mental afflictions, social fragmentation and political apathy that result from alienated labor.

Robert Reich correctly identifies the public policy reforms that should be made to alleviate people's financial suffering: establish universal health care, make the tax code more progressive, strengthen public schools, and undertake a considerable effort to increase wages, chiefly by supporting labor unions. Organized labor not only protects the safety of the worker, ensures higher wages, and bargains for better benefits, but it also provides workers with the solidarity that is sorely lacking when people view each other as job competition rather than occupational allies. The solidarity, camaraderie and community that can result from union membership can strike a serious blow against labor alienation. If Americans were guaranteed health care, consistently given pay raises, and could depend upon a body of organized labor to work on their behalf for protection, fairness and security, they may feel more comfortable leaving work for an extended period of time. This dreamlike scenario could easily be made reality but it seems like an alternate universe compared with contemporary America, where not only do Americans who are suffering from stagnating wages and unaffordable health care feel they can never take time off from a dissatisfying job but, when given the opportunity, refuse it. In 2005, American workers failed to use 421 million vacation days.[8]

One does not need to board a spaceship to visit an alternate universe where people actually enjoy vacationing regularly throughout the year. One need only step into such science fiction vehicles as the car or airplane. In Western Europe, Canada, Japan and parts of South America laws have been made that require businesses and organizations to give their employees mandatory vacation time. The United States, with its increasingly work-obsessed way of life and decreasingly happy citizenry, is one of the only developed nations without a mandatory vacation law, which goes a long way in explaining why the average Western European worker enjoys at least five weeks of vacation, and both the average Canadian and Japanese worker takes, at the minimum, two weeks off for relaxation and recuperation.[9]

By instituting the economic reforms recommended by Reich and others, and also establishing a mandatory vacation law, the United States would move significantly in the direction of a progressive society, where people are treated as human beings, encouraged to live humanistic lives, and not viewed merely as tools for expanding and operating the marketplace.

Bruce Springsteen, with some inspiration from his childhood and a few strokes of his imagination, has provided listeners with a highly usable outline for measuring the dangers of alienated labor and unbending occupational devotion, as well as the pleasures, benefits and rewards of leisure. He has also taken an empathetic and supportive approach to the working class that many on the left, especially the Democratic Party establishment, fail to express. It is telling and damning of the Democratic Party that the only person on the ballot from the two major parties in the 2008 presidential election to consistently utter the phrase "working class" was Sarah Palin.

In a 1980s anthem, "Seeds," which has a ZZ Top-style guitar riff, tough backbeat, and muscular saxophone solo, Springsteen sings in the voice of an unemployed oil worker who desperately longs to provide his family with a decent life. Sadly, they spend most nights sleeping in his car or in a tent pitched along the highway. Hard-working people like him have been ignored by corporate, financial and political institutions of power, and better-off citizens have made them feel like social pariahs, while suffering daily indig-nities such as hearing his child helplessly cough and being reprimanded for sleeping in a parked car by a police officer. One day after frustration has built, while moving along the freeway, the singer sees a "long, shiny and black" limousine whose passenger doesn't "look ahead and don't look back." He swears that if he could "spare the spit," he'd "lay one on your shiny chrome / And send you on your way back home." This rightful anger and contempt speaks to the condition many Americans suffer from when their dignity has been denied by the power managers of society. The working class suffers in silence to provide meaning and opportunity for their children and in doing so can make claim to a quiet heroism. That heroism is unacknowledged throughout the dominant culture, and political proposals to assist its efforts have little support. The needs of the middle class, which are growing dur-ing harder and harder times, are given political lip service, and sometimes substantive legislation. The working class has been rendered invisible.

When considering such Americans who have been exiled to the mar-gins of society, and who face obstructions and obstacles wherever they go in search of stability, security and dignity, it is immensely beneficial to use Springsteen's words and music as an artistic navigator for exploration through the night side of the superpower, where far too many unseen victims of marketplace politics reside.

Chapter 4

Saw My Reflection in the Window

The Politics of Invisibility

On February 4, 1999, Amadou Diallo, a Guinean immigrant who had traveled to the United States to study biochemistry and scrapped by on money he earned selling gloves and socks on the streets of New York City, was approached by four plain clothes police officers who believed he matched the description of a serial rapist. They claim that after identifying themselves as police officers, Diallo, who was not proficient in English, ran up a flight of stairs outside his apartment building, ignoring their orders to stop. At that point he turned around, and reached into his pocket. Diallo's version of the story will never be told because he was killed after being shot 19 times by the four policemen, who fired a total of 41 shots. Upon inspection of Diallo's body, they discovered that he was not reaching for a gun, as the officers fatally assumed, but his wallet. Unable to fully understand the officer's orders, he believed the right thing to do was to identify himself, which would have corrected the case of mistaken identity. For that simple action — reaching into his pocket — he lost his life in the most brutal, vicious and frightening fashion.

His death incited a large movement across New York City for civil rights, punishment of the officers responsible for Diallo's death, and increased monitoring and prevention of police brutality. Then mayor of New York City, Rudy Giuliani, strongly sided with the New York Police Department, offering sympathy to Diallo's family but refusing to admit that there was any wrongdoing on the part of the four officers involved. According to him, they followed the proper protocol, and therefore should not face criminal charges. Giuliani's cruel indifference and moral idiocy motivated more protests and civil disobedience, in which several people were arrested. Charges of second degree murder and reckless endangerment were filed against the officers, and the trial was set to take place in Albany after receiving a change of venue, made in response to the unending media coverage of the trial which the judge believed impeded the court's ability to act fairly.

On February 25, 2000 — just over a year from the day that Diallo's life ended in a blaze of bullets, the jury brought back a verdict of not guilty, acquitting the officers of all charges. Outrage, confusion and despair ensued. Black people, especially the poor, were forced into yet another moment of painful questioning of their own self-worth. They were compelled to wrestle with the idea of a socially imposed status of deprived humanity, diminished value, and denied American identity. The inquiry of value judgments on poor, African-American worth was intensified in 2001 when the Justice Department determined that the four police officers, who sprayed 41 shots at Diallo after an obvious case of racial profiling, did not violate his civil rights. Kadiatou Diallo, Amadou's mother, sued the police department for $61 million ($20 million plus a million dollars for every shot) and received only $3 million. Despite the case being over, and the protests dying down, New York's blood was still boiling and this diverse city, often rife with racial tension, intensified further into a concrete jungle smoldering with paranoia, distrust and resentment.

The ashes left from such unextinguished smoldering looked familiar to the few that were willing to examine them — destroyed remnants of attempts at democratic and egalitarian society. The quiet smoldering of chances for harmonious and equitable race policy, along with tangible opportunities for meaningful expression from oppressed and marginalized people, was met by uniform silence from both the New York and Federal governments, and the elite opinion brokers of the media. Alternative rap artists and voices of dissent continued to draw attention to the Diallo case, but they operated out of cultural ghettos and were therefore easily ignored.

On June 4, 2000 Bruce Springsteen and the E Street Band performed a concert in Atlanta — a city with a high black population and an important role in the civil rights movement. Seven songs into the performance, the lights went down, leaving only an eerie blue spotlight on Springsteen, as he softly sang over a synth riff, repeating in mantra-like manner, "41 shots." That phrase is repeated a total of 28 times throughout the song he would go on to perform, forcing the listener to reflect on the sheer number of bullets fired at an innocent man. There is something so obscene about the amount of shots fired, something so offensive to any notion of common humanity that by merely repeating those words Springsteen makes a powerful commentary on the tragic killing of Diallo. Needless to say, the song, "American Skin (41 Shots)," includes many more words, which offer a great opportunity for moral deliberation.

Such opportunities were largely missed and rejected before the lyrics even became public. The *New York Post*, which is the flagship print publication of Rupert Murdoch's dominant right-wing media empire, put Springsteen on the front page calling him anti-cop and questioning if he would play "American Skin (41 Shots)" at his next concert, which was scheduled to take place at Madison Square Garden in New York City. A Police Union Captain called Springsteen a "floating fag," (a term with a definition that remains mysterious) while an Internal Affairs leader referred to the songwriter as a "dirtbag." Several police unions and organizations called for a boycott of all future Springsteen concerts. The more extreme boycott advocates demanded that NYPD officers that provided security during Springsteen's entrance and exit of the arena, and the performance itself, go on strike, leaving the singer and band vulnerable to any form of threat. The usual slew of television and radio commentators debated the song, still without hearing it, with typical simplicity and shallowness.[1] A few narrow thinkers accused Springsteen of "cashing in" on the controversy without mentioning that the song was not available for sale, and that all ten of his upcoming Madison Square Garden concerts were already sold out. Talking heads with little knowledge of Springsteen's music and performance history made predictions on whether or not he would play the song in New York, which would open him up to another round of attacks and possible threats from armed and angry men. Some critics claimed he lacked the courage, while others expected him to play the song after a lengthy spoken introduction. Those that knew his music best were pretty confident in their idea of Springsteen's response to the "scandal" — he would play the song without additional commentary, and allow the music to speak strongly for itself. That is exactly what he did, on June 9, 2000. Springsteen remembers that night well.

> The air was thick in the Garden that night. The band gathered in the back a few feet from the stage as the house lights came down. We put our hands together as we often do before a show. I said, "This is what we were built for, let's go!"[2]

The band, and Springsteen's music, were built to offer hope, joy and meaning to struggling peoples — in this case those who were forced out of sight from the structural institutions of power in America, those whose struggles were deemed unimportant and thereby made invisible. The controversy of "American Skin (41 Shots)" soon died down, but for a moment the issue that inspired the song could not be ignored because Springsteen, an acclaimed musical poet crowned "Mr. America," disturbed mainstream comfort by summoning his creativity and empathy to ignite a conversation that Giuliani, the NYPD, and the American media did not want to host — an open-eyed look into "what systematic racial injustice, fear, and paranoia do to our children, our loved ones, ourselves. The price in blood," as Springsteen summarized it.³

The conversation was averted by distractive tactics commonly used by the media when attempting to avoid a painful or potentially outrageous subject. They ignored the song's power, and chose to frame any discussion of "American Skin (41 Shots)" with an unenlightening and narrowly framed "Is Springsteen anti-cop?" debate. Had they decided to focus on the music, with its open quality of ominous brooding that eventually culminates into a guitar solo and gospel-like vocals to inspire redemptive hope, along with contemplative and morally philosophical lyrics, they would have taken advantage of a great opportunity for consideration of democracy expansion, enlargement of the mind, and a resuscitation of America's promise for equality. This opportunity would have been shot through with a sense of the tragic and problematic in American democracy: "The price in blood."

> 41 shots
> 41 shots
> 41 shots
> 41 shots
> 41 shots
> 41 shots
> 41 shots
> 41 shots . . .
> and we'll take that ride
> 'cross this bloody river
> to the other side
> 41 shots . . . cut through the night
> You're kneeling over his body in the vestibule
> Praying for his life
>
> Is it a gun, is it a knife
> Is it a wallet, this is your life
> It ain't no secret
> It ain't no secret
> No secret my friend
> You can get killed just for living
> In your American skin
>
> 41 shots
> Lena gets her son ready for school
> She says "on these streets, Charles

You've got to understand the rules
If an officer stops you
Promise you'll always be polite,
that you'll never ever run away
Promise Mama you'll keep your hands in sight"

Is it a gun, is it a knife
Is it a wallet, this is your life
It ain't no secret
It ain't no secret
No secret my friend
You can get killed just for living
In your American skin

Is it a gun, is it a knife
Is it in your heart, is it in your eyes
It ain't no secret

41 shots . . . and we'll take that ride
'Cross this bloody river
To the other side
41 shots . . . got my boots caked in this mud
We're baptized in these waters and in each other's blood

Is it a gun, is it a knife
Is it a wallet, this is your life
It ain't no secret
It ain't no secret
No secret my friend
You can get killed just for living
In your American skin

"American Skin (41 Shots)" begins with the police officer perspective in such a way that evokes possible sympathy for their predicament; or points to their cynicism. The listener is left to decide whether or not their prayer is motivated by self-interest or real compassion and remorse — either of which would provide an incredibly strong incentive for hoping for his survival. But even before the question of police intention — while operating under a program of plain clothes stop-and-search street patrol implemented by Giuliani — can be asked, all citizens must "cross the bloody river to the other side." We must break down our walls of division; look into each other's eyes without prejudices of inferiority, distrust or a "veil of criminality" (the phrase Springsteen used to describe how most white Americans look at people of color).[4]

The social consequences of viewing racial minorities with a long history of brutal victimization at the hands of white-supremacist thinking and policy through a "veil of criminality" are dreadful and devastating. Fear of black people drives much of the collective polity and action of the United States. One cannot overemphasize the misery created by "white flight," — a clever, but flippant term to describe the mass exit that white people take from neighborhoods when black people move in, even if those blacks are middle-class professionals. Research by Kyle Crowder, a sociologist at Western Washington University; Kevin Kruse, author of *White Flight: Atlanta and the Making of Modern Conservatism*; and *The Chicago Reporter* prove that sociological airports are still in full operation in white suburbs across the country, and that the canards served for the in-flight meal have not changed.[5] This is not only problematic because of sociological reasons but also because property values descend when panicked whites quickly sell their homes, and businesses respond by leaving town with them. The loss of revenue to the town results in a shrinking base of job opportunity which in turn leads to more crime. The hurtful combination of these factors has a dreadful impact on the schools because when property taxes are lowered the school's funding is severely decreased, which not only leads to a loss of educational resources but also to pedagogical problems that result from overcrowding and teacher shortages.

White flight, along with political indifference to social misery in black neighborhoods, encapsulates the bipolar treatment of racial minorities in American life. In some instances, they are viewed with hyper-sensitivity, which results from over-visibility. Black over-visibility influences white flight, stereotyping, and de facto segregation. The white tendency to view black people with a sense of hyper-visibility also contributes to their unhealthy and irrational fear of blacks. This is the "veil of criminality" which, in contradiction to the metaphor, makes blacks even more visible than whites. This condition manifests itself in media coverage of crime, and black responsibility. Despite the fact that the murder rate for black men is double that of American soldiers in World War II and that they are 18 times more likely to fall victim to homicide than white women, and that black and Latino people are more likely to be victims of crime than whites, the media focuses with laser precision on crimes in which the victims are white and the perpetrators are black.[6] Caryl Rivers, professor of journalism at Boston University, described television depiction of crime quite simply: "night after night, black men rob, rape, loot, and pillage in the living room."[7]

Unsurprisingly, the economic consequences of white paranoia and prejudice continue to be destructive, especially in the wake of hundreds of years of institutionalized inequality and structural racism. A recent Princeton study called "Discrimination in Low-Wage Labor Markets" sent white and black men to over 3,000 job interviews in New York City in fields varying from manufacturing to food service. The results were predictable: Employers are more likely to hire a white man than a black man, even if the black applicant is more qualified for the job. Most stunning about the study was the finding that employers are more likely to hire a white convict than a black male without a criminal record. This experiment was also conducted in Milwaukee by Northwestern University with the same results. It is worth mentioning that both of these experiments were performed in large, Northern and progressive cities. Whites in denial about the persistence of racism in the United States, even in the age of Obama, should take a thorough look at the important work done by scholars at Princeton and Northwestern.[8]

The flip side of the visibility coin invested in white-supremacist legacies in America is invisibility. While over-visibility is defined by intense concentration on demonized qualities of a seemingly monolithic (if we are to believe popular portrayals) black populace; black concerns, struggles and narratives that run counter to the stereotyping scripts are ostracized into cultural, social and political ghettos, which accounts for the way that poor black people are made invisible to the power structure. Absence of black struggles in the mainline political debate, coupled with cultural commodification that emphasizes the lowest form of hip-hop but ignores other creative black output, casts African-Americans into second-class roles in which suffering is to be expected and met with cruel indifference.

Nothing illustrated this more than Hurricane Katrina. The already poor and already neglected city of New Orleans was left helpless for five days after its broken-down levees finally broke for good. In a shocking display of incompetence and wickedness, the Bush administration responded to the destruction of one of America's great cities and the pain of its people with an oblivious and insulting flyover, while people died in the Super Dome or stood on the rooftops of their homes waiting for assistance in the world's richest nation. The unforgettable images from the storm's aftermath sent shivers down the spine and tears to the eyes of any moral person. The death, disease and despair of poor, mostly black people in New Orleans were deemed irrelevant. Springsteen captured this condition well in a song he performed with the Sessions Band in 2006 called "How Can a Poor Man Stand Such Times and Live?" In a lyrically updated version of the Blind Alfred Reed song, he lends voice to the New Orleans struggle:

> "Me and my old school pals had some mighty high times down here
> And what happened to you poor black folks, well it just ain't fair"

He took a look around, gave a little pep talk, said "I'm with you" then he
    took a little walk
Tell me how can a poor man stand such times and live

There's bodies floatin' on the canal and the levee's gone to Hell
Martha, get me my sixteen gauge and some dry shells
Them who's got got out of town and them who ain't got left to drown
Tell me how can a poor man stand such times and live

Got family scattered from Texas all the way to Baltimore
Yeah and I ain't got no home in this world no more
Gonna be a judgment that's a fact, a righteous train rollin' down this
    track
Tell me how can a poor man stand such times and live

By updating the old folk song, and placing it within the tradition of prophetic folk music which the Seeger Sessions paid tribute to, Springsteen informed the audience how the difficulties and oppression of the Bayou's residents have parity with those of black people during the civil rights movement. The insincere superficiality of presidential gestures — giving "pep talks" — set against the real-life suffering of people — bodies floating in the canal; being named a refugee in one's own country — gives listeners a starting point to understand how the consequences of viewing certain segments of the population as invisible bear out. This is what rapper Kanye West meant when he famously said on national television, "George Bush does not care about black people." As Professor Michael Eric Dyson explains:

> First of all he's [West] not speaking about George Bush the individual. Not the person. Not the private person. But the public persona, the institutional identity of the face of the American government, and the representative of democracy of our culture. In that sense, we're speaking about George Bush, the President. And care is not measured in terms of personal sentiments of compassion. They are measured by if you are willing in politics to deliver resources in a timely fashion to vulnerable communities who are under need and crisis. And in that sense, George Bush, the face of the government, did not care to deliver resources in a timely fashion to vulnerable communities that were disadvantaged in a way that helped them.[9]

Dyson brilliantly measures care in political terms, not personal feelings, and therefore defines the state of invisibility as being victim to political blindness. Certain "scandals" that would have been shrugged off decades ago, such as the outrage over radio shock-jock Don Imus referring to the

Rutgers women's basketball team as "nappy-headed hos," reveal a progression in sensibility, but not a maturation of racial intelligence (which understands the complexity and interdependence of racial relations, institutional legacies, and public policy) or growth in compassionate demand for justice. As idiotic and offensive as Imus's remarks were, they were not responsible for public-school misery, joblessness and criminal justice biases that afflict the black community. Until democratic energies are mobilized to address those injustices, America cannot pretend to be an egalitarian society. In order to summon these energies, the philosophy of white normalcy must also end. Currently, white behavior is viewed as positive and universal, while non-white attributes are determined to be negative and particular. Therefore, anything that deviates from white-established and white-dictated norms is automatically suspect. Stereotypes, prejudice and racist political policies and social conventions follow suit.

The obvious and hopeful contradiction to all this information and analysis is Barack Obama's inspirational presidential victory in 2008. His authoritative defeat of John McCain demonstrated that a majority of Americans have evolved beyond overt bigotry, and that white America may finally recognize the great potentiality of African-Americans. It was a historic moment of triumph for the American republic which has already expanded the imagination of youth — black, white and the world over. Barack Obama not only became president, but a symbol of the possibility of reconciliation and progress that is achievable in the United States. However, he is not endowed with magic powers, and therefore will not single-handedly be able to eradicate hiring-discrimination, white flight, and other remnants of institutionally biased legacies which still persist in varying forms. How then does one proceed bearing this American contradiction in mind that many white Americans will welcome a black man in the White House but may get nervous at the prospect of a black man in the next house? Will visibility be granted to everyday African-Americans who do not have the resume, talents and inspirational power of Obama?

Returning to "American Skin (41 Shots)," it is not necessary to understand all of this information and wrestle with these questions to enjoy or be moved by the song, but it is required knowledge for placing the song within its proper social and political contexts. It is important to think about what may have been in the minds of those officers as they approached a black man on the streets of the Bronx, and why they believed, driving through a dark street, that this barely visible black man matched the description of a serial rapist. The hyper-visibility/invisibility contrast explains why Giuliani instituted a program of plain clothes stop-and-search, placed upon the ever-weakening shelf of a "war on drugs," but ignored the social and economic struggles of those neighborhoods.

It also helps explain the feeling of fear and insecurity that nearly paralyzes families in poor, black communities. Consider Lena's admonition of her son Charles, in the second verse of "American Skin (41 Shots)," to "always keep his hands in sight" when in the company of police officers. She understands that in her neighborhood, most likely dragged down by joblessness, lack of educational resources and low hopes for emotional uplift or financial stimulus, people have somehow been stripped of part of their identity. They are no longer viewed as fully human. To the police, her son is just another threatening body wandering the street, no different from a serial rapist. His body is visible; his humanity *in*visible. This is how they saw Diallo, amazingly on a poorly lit street, driving by in a car, and Lena painfully realizes that that is how they will see her son. Therefore, she implores him to never give them that moment of confirmation they need to escalate the confrontation with violence. Springsteen's amplification of the voices of millions of mothers — whose pain, worries and tragedies are too often ignored or relegated to superficial sentimentality — followed by his dread warning that one can "get killed just for living / In your American skin," gives a powerful means of expression to the oppressed invisibles of American society. That is why it was met with such harsh attack and invective. It was too deep and catastrophic for an America which Gore Vidal calls the "United States of Amnesia" to wrestle with because, through that wrestling, America would soon be pinned by uncomfortable and unflattering memories of its own selfishness and abuses of power.

BORN IN THE U.S.A.: WAR, THE FLAG AND INVISIBLE VETERANS

One man who could speak profoundly and painfully about victimization at the hands of American power managers is Bobby Muller. Muller served in the United States Marine Corps during the Vietnam War, leading an infantry platoon as a combat lieutenant. Muller's service as a Marine ended in April of 1969 when he was shot in the spinal cord, leaving him paralyzed from the chest down. Upon returning home, armed with a record of combat and a college degree, he quickly committed to serving his country in ways much more meaningful and helpful than leading troops in a war that should have never been fought. He founded Vietnam Veterans for America which is currently under the moniker Veterans for America. This organization unites veterans of various wars to address veteran and service family-member needs, along with larger concerns about the devastating impact of war. Muller also founded the International Campaign to Ban Landmines, which won the Nobel Peace Prize in 1997. He is a dedicated peace activist and veterans advocate who, after losing the use of half his body in Vietnam during a war launched for specious reasons, made a conceited effort to summon all his energy and strength to oppose the policies that put young men like him in danger, and to fight for their protection and assistance when they return home in desperate need of medical or psychiatric care.

He is seen in Phil Donahue and Ellen Spiro's documentary *Body of War*, which profiles the life of Tomas Young — a veteran of the Iraq war who also became paralyzed in combat, and has dedicated a significant part of his life to working with Iraq Veterans Against the War. Muller speaks to Young about politics, and life without the ability to walk. He discusses how he got shortchanged as a veteran, never receiving the quality of treatment and services he needed. Then he asks Young how long he was in the hospital and Young answers "just a few months." Noticeably shocked, Muller takes a long pause before telling him he was in the hospital a year, and that Young "got screwed." Muller then takes a moment to encourage Young's activism, somberly explaining, "At a certain point, I decided that if I don't fight this system, I am going to die."

It is a powerful scene of documentary cinema — two men whose scars, along with their radically democratic and progressive narratives, offer catastrophic contradictions to the feel-good mythos of America — sitting side by side, both in wheelchairs, discussing how they are no longer in physical combat but are battling for visibility in a country uninterested in their important stories and monumental concerns. Muller and Young share a laugh over how during any anti-war demonstration the organizers want the "gimps up front," to understandably enhance the effect of their political point. They are both happy to help make an argument against unjust war by giving onlookers an intimate view of its consequences. However, they also wonder who would be there to look when the demonstration is over. This is what makes Muller's work and Donahue and Spiro's film so powerfully important — they show the calamities of the war, "the price in blood," so that America is forced to morally reckon with its foreign policy. As Donahue put it in an interview before the opening of his film, "Show the pain. Don't sanitize the war." In other words, do not allow the victims of war — whether it be a Vietnamese child running from napalm, an Iraqi family blown apart by U.S. attack, or Tomas Young — to remain invisible so that the empathy-deficient power brokers of American society can be massaged into a state of moral immunity.

On August 20, 1981, Bruce Springsteen and the E Street Band performed a benefit concert in Los Angeles for Bobby Muller's Vietnam Veterans for America. The concert began with a speech from Muller in which he discussed the importance of veteran advocacy, the never-ending need for vigilant citizenship (in order to prevent future Vietnam-like wars), and the unifying capability of rock 'n' roll. Springsteen and company followed his speech with a passionate and emotional performance, spanning well over three hours and including well-chosen cover songs, such as "Who'll Stop the Rain," "This Land is Your Land," and "Ballad of the Easy Rider," alongside classic Springsteen songs like "Badlands" and "Born to Run." It has long been considered one of Springsteen's greatest concerts, but more important than the musical quality and intensity of the night was its purpose. Muller would later confess that VVA was on the verge of bankruptcy, and would not have lasted much longer if it were not for Springsteen's charitable efforts.

One year later Springsteen wrote what would become one of his most famous songs, "Born in the U.S.A." He recorded it for *Nebraska* in a sparse, bluesy, acoustic arrangement that evoked feelings of dread, despair and disappointment. Springsteen thought it felt more like a "band song," and recorded it again in 1984 with the backing of E Street power. The first person he played it for was the man who inspired it, Bobby Muller. By both Springsteen and Muller's account, the Vietnam veteran-turned-activist broke down into tears when the song faded into quiet. The intensity, raw emotion and fury of rage that defines the thunderous drumbeat, vibrating synth riff and impassioned vocals were mistaken by some as leaning into triumph. But Muller knew it was nothing but pure anger — anger at being lied to, left behind and perpetually unseen. The song begins:

> Born down in a dead man's town
> The first kick I took was when I hit the ground
> You end up like a dog that's been beat too much
> Till you spend half your life just covering up
>
> Born in the U.S.A.
> I was born in the U.S.A.
> I was born in the U.S.A.
> Born in the U.S.A.

The protagonist describes the almost inevitable cowardice, which always leads to isolation, that can result from persecution. The image of a frightened dog with shaggy hair, slinking around the corners of the house, with its head hung down, cowering at the mere hint of confrontation, is a powerfully provocative way to begin a song about being born in America, and it indicates that although this song may be inspired by Muller, it is not directly about him — he is a fighter — this suffering protagonist has sunken into submission. The transition from "Till you spend half your life just covering up" into "Born in the U.S.A.," does not contain any words, and the musical lift separating verse and chorus is minimal. The lack of separation between

the reality of the character's birth and predicament, along with the persistence of the drum and snarled vocal, indicates that American citizenship is
no comfort. It only intensifies the torment of the character. The promised
rewards, prizes and protections granted to Americans by right of birth have
been denied to this man, even after he served the country overseas, as he
explains in the second verse. After returning from Vietnam, he finds himself in a land that seems foreign. The services intended to assist American
veterans and struggling citizens are either non-existent or ineffective. The
comforts that those around him try to bestow are superficial. His feelings
of invisibility and his inability to find opportunities for renewal culminate
in the third verse.

> Come back home to the refinery
> Hiring man says "Son if it was up to me"
> Went down to see my V.A. man
> He said "Son, don't you understand"

The men who are placed in positions of supposed assistance are unable to
even speak in complete sentences when responding to the humble requests
of the down-and-out vet. "Son if it was up to me" . . . "Son, don't you
understand" . . . The condescending designation of this character as "son",
as if he were a lost child or if he were asking for something unreasonable,
adds insult to injury. He cannot find a job and the Department of Veterans
Affairs is unable to point him in any hopeful direction. The V.A. man simply
throws up his hands and asks, "don't you understand" . . . Presumably this
sentence can be finished with a distressed sentiment about budget cuts,
service shortages or too many veterans with unaddressed needs. The same
problems of moral priority manifested in low V.A. budgets that collided with
the Vietnam veteran's hopes, run head on into the Iraq veterans returning
home from another unpopular, unjustified war. The overwhelming majority
of veterans deserving of psychiatric care do not receive it. V.A. health care
continues to be cut, which inevitably causes a weakening of services.[10] Walter
Reed Army Medical Center was nearly shut down after it was revealed that
rats were running through the hallways and soldiers were living in filth and
squalor with medical needs unattended.[11] Gender integration of the military
has been met with unthinkable horrors that receive cruelly nonchalant
reactions. Twenty-three percent of female users of V.A. health care reported
experiencing sexual assault in the military, and 11 percent of female National
Guards veterans have been raped while on active duty. It is unsurprising, but
morally indefensible, that services for reporting the crime in the barracks
and receiving psychiatric recovery at home are painfully absent. The report
detailing the severity of women's suffering in the military was written by

the V.A. in 2001 but suppressed by the Bush administration which deemed female veteran trauma as inconsequential and irrelevant. It finally saw the light of day in 2005 after a small number of congressional representatives released it to the press.[12]

Veterans are the grimmest reminder of America's moral failures. They are walking-and-talking contradictions to the scripts that politicians, media elites and delusional Americans write for themselves about the compassionate nature of American power. In order to avoid the damaging interrogation that would ensue after engaging veteran needs, America wipes them off the face of the Earth, keeping them hidden from plain sight — invisible. Paradoxically, the military itself, as an institution, is considered sacred to the American script because it symbolizes its imperial might. Soldiers are therefore given the prop treatment during presidential addresses, and sloganeering about "troop support" is a full-time business. This only adds to the essentiality of keeping veteran tales of dissent and disappointment under the cover of a child-crafted red, white and blue quilt on which American myths of self-stroking narratives are liberally written. Those that sleep under the quilt, and live on the neglected periphery of American life, have gained a deep understanding of despair-inducing truth that cultural and media brokers of the mainline narrative prefer not to discuss. In "Born in the U.S.A.," the listener's neutrality, apathy or acceptance in the face of such suffering is challenged — most especially in the final verse — after it is learned that the protagonist's brother died in Vietnam.

> Down in the shadow of the penitentiary
> Out by the gas fires of the refinery
> I'm ten years burning down the road
> Nowhere to run, ain't got nowhere to go

The implication is that he has spent time in prison and a brief period working at the old refinery where he previously applied and was rejected. Both periods of his life receive vague mentioning, as if they are equally insignificant and unfulfilling. They only help to provide some landmarks during the "ten years" he has spent "burning down the road." "Burning" conjures images of racing with intensity and passion. However, the character's passion and intensity are not channeled into sources of usefulness and meaning. We learn that despite his "burning down the road," he has nothing to do, nowhere to go and no place to call home, which means that he will eventually burn out. This terminal diagnosis of the character's hopes and dreams is followed by another chorus — another empty declaration of being "Born in the U.S.A."

The obvious difference between this dispossessed Vietnam veteran and Amadou Diallo is one of citizenship. Far from being "born in the U.S.A.,"

Diallo came from West Africa with the hope of obtaining what the vet seemingly already possessed — a strongly defined American identity that would serve as an admission ticket into the much vaunted arena of "life, liberty, and pursuit of happiness." He would soon learn, with the most brutal and vicious instruction, that he was not included in that identity scheme, and that his hopes for inclusion were denied. The Vietnam veteran was given the same lesson, only not with violence but with a slow, systematic smashing of hopes in which part of positive identification and optimistic projection into the future is chipped away each day, until the realization is made that one has "nowhere to go." He has tried all the standard avenues, only to find them obstructed by unforeseen road blocks that he has been told all of his life do not exist for an American willing to "work hard." The cross section of tragedy formed by the murder of Diallo and the societal denial of the Vietnam veteran's human value forms in the night side of America, where those relegated to roles of invisibility roam the streets, barred from the corridors of power.

Diallo and the vet do not share a common ancestry, but their geographic setting is the same. This is a point that Springsteen emphasizes throughout their respective songs; even the titles — "American Skin (41 Shots)," "Born in the U.S.A." — evince this shared identity. Many arbitrators of opinion in the media, along with various other public figures, promulgate the dogma that any evocation of the flag and American imagery must be positive and beaming with praise. Noam Chomsky has fun at the expense of those that make an idol of America when he discusses an article he wrote in the late 1960s comparing Japanese counterinsurgency documents from the imperial era of the 1940s to U.S. military counterinsurgency manuals used in Vietnam. Chomsky claims it was not a very popular article, but it garnered some interesting reaction in the U.S. press, which interpreted it as a "compelling justification" for Japanese atrocities.[13] According to the "manufacturers of consent," if anything is comparable to American activity and policy it is automatically virtuous. Springsteen removes the clothes of this dogma while unnerving and unsettling its preachers by evoking the flag and typical American imagery during disturbing portraits of the invisible victims of American power and marketplace politics. The importance of setting in storytelling is significant but that importance is surpassed in value by the human dignity Springsteen assigns to those who have been stripped of it in American life. Springsteen's geographic specificity gives listeners a reminder that tragedies exist in their own neighborhoods, while his uninterrupted call for recognition of common humanity forces them to develop their own empathy.

The identity, reputation and persona of the storyteller is especially noteworthy in this case because Springsteen is an American performer who has been lauded within the mainstream and bestowed by many as representing a true-blue American image built upon the iconography of Americana. An essential part of that iconography — to the singer, but more so to his audience — is his heterosexual bravado and strength. Springsteen's American manhood imagery culminated in the mid-1980s on the *Born in the U.S.A.* tour when he dressed similar to Rambo — a bandana tied around his head, tight blue jeans, biker boots — and appeared to be "pumped up" — to use the parlance of that decade. Following that tour, the wardrobe continued to change, but the way women and men in the audience viewed Springsteen remained the same. He was an American man whose place was alongside old cowboy movie characters and tough guys in commercials for trucks and cigarettes. Given Springsteen's alpha male status in American music, it is difficult to think of a more challenging songwriter to sing in the voice of an openly gay man dying of AIDS.

THE POWER OF A KISS: AIDS, DEATH AND HOMOPHOBIA

In 1992 film director Jonathan Demme approached Springsteen about allowing one of his songs to be used in the movie, *Philadelphia*, which starred Tom Hanks as Andrew Beckett, a corporate lawyer who is fired from his law firm after colleagues discover he is a homosexual living with AIDS and sabotage his work. Denzel Washington plays Joe Miller, who despite being an admitted homophobe, takes Beckett's case after he witnesses a shocking scene of discrimination against him in the Philadelphia library. Beckett is researching past cases of workplace biases against people living with AIDS. At one point a librarian approaches and speaks loud enough for other patrons to hear, "Here is the book you requested about living with AIDS." Mortified people stare at him in shock and then quickly move as far away as possible, leaving Beckett humiliated and isolated. The librarian then suggests that he continue his work in a private room. The dualistic nature of oppression is clear in this scene. Those in the library react first by staring at Beckett, while devaluing and belittling him, but paying more attention to him than they would someone they deemed of equal human value. Following that, they render him invisible by removing themselves from his presence. The librarian emphasizes his lack of visibility by asking him to physically move into an isolated area where it will be literally impossible to see him. To capture this invisibility in song is a seemingly more difficult task than to do so in film, considering the lack of visual tools at the songwriter's disposal. However, Springsteen accomplishes this feat with "Streets of Philadelphia" by embracing a minimalist style, often avoided by those attempting to tell a story with profound implications in any format or genre. Over a neutral hip-hop beat, an ominous and dread synthesizer riff plays, which reminds the listener of mourning and by doing so calls for the listener to mourn for a dying man that is not only different from the listener in supposedly crucial areas but has also been castigated by the American mainstream. Springsteen does not emphasize the political and social elements of the AIDS patient's suffering, although they are implicit, but instead speaks of the core of his humanity by emphasizing his similarities and commonalities with nearly anyone else — heterosexual and homosexual. His vocals are sadly whispered, unlike the angry Vietnam vet in "Born in the U.S.A." who shouts in a demand to be heard, or the prophetic observer describing a detailed truth in "American Skin (41 Shots)," the protagonist of "Streets of Philadelphia" speaks in the voice of a last breath.

> I was bruised and battered and I couldn't tell what I felt
> I was unrecognizable to myself
> Saw my reflection in a window I didn't know my own face
> Oh brother are you gonna leave me wasting away
> On the streets of Philadelphia

If one were able to separate the song from the movie in which it is featured, he or she would still get the impression that this character is suffering and struggling with both a physical ailment of the worst severity, and emotional emptiness. The role of the "brother" that this man addresses is unclear. He may be a lover or a friend who can provide the emotional comfort and opportunity for existential meaning to the suffering soul who is in a world where the good continues to vanish, both in physical and psychic terms. He may also be a personification of the social institutions that he believed would be there to assist him in his time of great need. AIDS in the gay community is still largely unaddressed in the political dialogue of America. In most cases, the epidemic in Africa is the focal point for charitable organization and social rallying. While that effort is valiant and necessary, it should not entirely eliminate any discussion of how AIDS has absolutely devastated a segment of the American population.

Social services for gay men with AIDS have not reached the quality and quantity they should have by now partly because of America's refusal to recognize the problem for nearly a decade. President Ronald Reagan hardly even broached the topic during his tenure in the White House, and subsequent Presidents have not done much better. The United States is a highly religious country, and therefore when supposed "spiritual leaders," such as Billy Graham, go on the record saying that AIDS is "God's punishment for homosexuality,"[14] far too many people take them seriously and believe that the best way to help the gay community is to demonize their lifestyle. In 2005, many religious figures blamed Hurricane Katrina on the high concentration of gay people living in New Orleans. Prior to that, bigoted lunatics like the late Jerry Falwell and Pat Robertson pointed their crooked fingers at gays for causing 9/11.

The most shocking and shameful aspect of America's mistreatment of gay people is that 32 states lack any workplace protection for homosexuals, meaning that an employer can fire a gay worker for reasons based entirely on sexual-orientation bigotry, and the employee will have no legal recourse. Jim Crow-style stories of harassment, cruelty and discriminatory firing practices have been reported in such backwater areas of the country as the Chicago suburbs, Philadelphia and New York. Surveys indicate that 40 percent of gay people have experienced workplace harassment or discrimination but without legal recourse they have no choice but to suffer daily indignities while either waiting to be fired or deciding when to quit.[15] This is precisely the form of socially germinated and institutionally supported bigotry that Harvey Milk, the assassinated member of the San Francisco Board of Supervisors and the first openly gay person to be elected to public office in America, battled against in his courageous campaign for freedom, equality and democracy. Attempts to fire all teachers in the Bay Area that were suspected of homosexuality ignited Milk's movement, which he would connect to a plethora of other gay rights issues, as well as civil rights for African-Americans, women, students and the disabled.

The status quo of American sociology and politics, which is still under assault from gay activists following Milk's courageous example, is what makes Springsteen's portrayal of not only a gay man but a gay man dying from AIDS so compelling. In the second verse of the song, the listener is confronted with an even more disturbing presentation of this man's shattered life. Unlike the first verse, the focal point is not his deteriorating physical condition, but his increased isolation from the things he loves and the people he trusts, and his inner torment.

> I walked the avenue till my legs felt like stone
> I heard the voices of friends vanished and gone
> At night I could hear the blood in my veins
> Just as black and whispering as the rain
> On the streets of Philadelphia

He is forcibly separated from his friends, who have either also died of AIDS or have abandoned him by condemning his lifestyle without sympathy for his suffering, and feels the corrupted and dirty blood flowing through his body, unable to serve its basic purpose or have any lasting positive effect.

Like the rain, it mixes with the unclean, trash-littered and publicly soiled pavement, but contrarily, will not evaporate the next morning. He lives with this virus, and the filthy bodily conditions it creates are permanent. His solitary confinement, imposed on him by America's institutions and populace, exacerbates these problems and causes him to question his own humanity. However, there still remains one fading source of hope that the protagonist calls out for in moments of pain and doubt while never losing sight of his inevitable and forthcoming physical and mental destruction.

> Ain't no angel gonna greet me
> It's just you and I my friend
> And my clothes don't fit me no more
> I walked a thousand miles
> Just to slip this skin

Perhaps the most haunting line of the song is that first line in the bridge — "Ain't no angel gonna greet me." It captures the character's perpetual hopelessness through a recognition that there will be no saving grace, whether it be supernatural, medical or communal. The overwhelming loneliness that results from physical immiseration and social invisibility motivates him to desperately call out for his last friend — presumably a male lover — yet again. His first request was made in doubt — "brother are you gonna leave me wasting away?" — while this is a more hopeful attempt at affection. The man is there, but he is unsure as to how much comfort his presence really offers. A creeping sadness has set in which does not prevent the character from reaching out to his lover but prevents him from taking a high level of solace in the potential intimacy. This is most likely because he knows that the intimacy will not lead to anything else, and it will stand alone as the single source of human connectivity and communal action available in his life. In the face of political indifference and social castigation, this well runs only so deep. His having "walked a thousand miles" is sufficient proof of his inability to find political sympathy or social acceptance. Each mile represents a crucial part of the labor he has invested into finding a loving community and "slipping this skin" cloaked with invisibility, seemingly transforming into a person whose humanity is reaffirmed and is thereby able to live his last days with hope and joy rather than depression and emptiness. It is clear that this transformative moment of communal welcoming does not occur, and listeners are left to contend with a dark and dreadful account of his life's conclusion.

> The night has fallen, I'm lyin' awake
> I can feel myself fading away

> So receive me brother with your faithless kiss
> Or will we leave each other alone like this
> On the streets of Philadelphia

In the dying moment of this man's life he requests a kiss. He needs to feel the touch of another's lips and bask in the power that it brings. It may be one absent of faith — it is universally understood that this man is dying and nothing has the capacity to save him — but it offers essential spiritual solace that brings a few seconds of peace and dignity to an otherwise tortuously painful and heartbreaking death. The need for a personal connection, which solidifies one's humanity, is at the heart of hospice care, which offers dying patients a close companion in their final moments of stress, need and terror. It limits their "fading away" to physical existence, and stops it from mutating into continual invisibility from the world of the living. It encourages them to remember that even though their physical existence is slowly vanishing, the value of their lives and presence is not forgotten.

The meaning and value of a kiss — perhaps the ultimate sign of personal intimacy — is expressed beautifully and emotively in Gore Vidal's description of the physical decline and eventual death of his 53-year "partner" (Vidal disapprovingly calls this the politically correct term). Vidal begins by recollecting a surprising request after Howard was given troubling news about the growth of his lung cancer and his need for risky surgery.

> A doctor friend in Rome, although officially retired, still worked at a private Roman clinic. We checked in. An MRI revealed a small dark bubble on the lobe of the brain that controls locomotion. He had also become incontinent. Several times I had to lift his deadweight off the floor until, finally, I ruptured a spinal disk. Donella, our doctor friend, arranged for a distinguished surgeon at Rome's Villa Margherita to operate. But when the professor had studied the MRIs of Howard's brain he said, "We must not wait." Unfortunately a long holiday weekend was coming up and such weekends are sacred in Italy. The operation was scheduled for the next week. As I left Howard's room, he said, "Kiss me." I did. On the lips, something we'd not done for fifty years.[16]

Howard's need for a human act of emotional intimacy expressed physically from someone he loved deeply comes from the fear and sadness all people must feel when they are confronted with their own mortality, vulnerability and weakness. The key difference between Howard's story and the one that belongs to the character in "Streets of Philadelphia" is that Howard was surrounded by people he loved and was confident he would receive the best possible medical care, along with the most empathetic and adequate social response free of moral classifications of inferiority. The man dying from AIDS in "Streets of Philadelphia" is not only confronted with mortality, vulnerability and weakness, but accusations of diminished human value and insufficient self-worth.

The response that Springsteen takes to the physical deterioration and social devaluation of the AIDS patient is a dramatic, prophetic and stirring call for empathy, mutual identification and community. This comes through the emotively descriptive lyrics of the song, but even more so in the music. Following each verse, Springsteen sings an extended "li, li, li, li, li, li, li" chorus that grows stronger with each repetition. It begins as a whisper in the middle of a storm — one dying man desperately struggling to be heard in a society and culture that ignores his pain, except when they can exploit it to make a narrow political or religious point — but after the second verse it grows a little louder and more noticeable. By the song's conclusion, it has grown in power and begins to resemble a small choir of voices singing this simple but terribly beautiful chant of a monosyllable repeated deliberately in a startling combination of sadness and urgency. The symbolic gesture of this simple act of musicality possesses a palpable power and clear message. Springsteen is calling upon those informed of this man's story to mourn with him, and provide him with the humanity-affirming community that will cause any doubts about his value and self-worth to immediately cease. We are all to fearlessly wrestle with the tragic circumstances and conditions of this man's life, and through that wrestling develop an understanding of his struggle and empathy for it while also taking into account how his suffering is worsened by the powerful institutions of a democratic society that ideally should function for the people's needs by the people's demand. Democracy is about choices, and in this case the choice is clear. Will citizens, after being made aware of another's unbearable pain, extend their love to him in an attempt to alleviate his psychic wounds that intensify the severity of his physical disease, and then respond publicly by demanding that others like him receive the social services and institutional hospitality they deserve? Or will they turn their heads? The chant that concludes "Streets of Philadelphia" attacks the listener's moral sensibility with the desire that it will be stimulated into collective action on behalf of suffering people.

LIVING AMONG GHOSTS: POVERTY, OPPRESSION AND AMERICAN MYTH-MAKING

A similar alarm to the sleeping moral conscience of America is sounded during the title track of Springsteen's 1995 release, *The Ghost of Tom Joad*. This traditional folk song gives listeners a raw and open-wound description of homelessness in the world's wealthiest nation. It begins with a harsh portrayal that angrily and cynically references President George H.W. Bush's promise about America ushering in a "new world order."

> Men walkin' 'long the railroad tracks
> Goin' someplace there's no goin' back
> Highway patrol choppers comin' up over the ridge
> Hot soup on a campfire under the bridge
> Shelter line stretchin' round the corner
> Welcome to the new world order
> Families sleepin' in their cars in the southwest
> No home no job no peace no rest
>
> The highway is alive tonight
> But nobody's kiddin' nobody about where it goes
> I'm sittin' down here in the campfire light
> Searchin' for the ghost of Tom Joad

The details, routines and daily activities of the homeless are placed within their proper hopeless, placeless and aimless misery. Social services are inaccessible and political concern is so minute it cannot be measured, save for an insincere declaration of vague reform, which places American power on a firm pedestal resting on the broken backs of oppressed citizenries here and abroad, from a cold marketplace manager President. The grim picture of America's night side does not grow any sunnier or more hopeful in the second verse, which describes a homeless preacher smoking butts of cigarettes and praying for Christian judgment day in which the alpha will become the omega. His hopes are relegated to metaphysical reward handed out to loyal earthly servants of a heavenly monarchy indifferent to class, income or portfolio. The chorus slightly changes but the alteration is not substantive, merely semantic. "The highway is alive tonight / But where it's headed, everybody knows." The iconic symbol of hope rooted in the American tradition of exploration and progression and which Springsteen cited consistently on early records has transformed into another structural manifestation of division, inequality and inaccessible opportunity. The highway may lead to transference from one location to another but not to transcendence from the inescapable and hellacious conditions that define their lives and dictate their social misery. The highway allows for visitation of different places but will not grant meaningful visibility to differently situated people with proximity to structural power. Therefore, without geographic deliverance into hopeful settings, these Americans are subjected to the locational margins — kept out of sight of tourists, politicians and wealthy consumers who prefer not to be disturbed by undeniable examples of race and class inequality. What follows is the sociological and political application of the old phrase, "out of sight, out of mind." As long as the homeless and desperately poor are invisible to the eye they are also invisible to the pen used to sign local, state and federal budgets.

In the final verse of "The Ghost of Tom Joad," the homeless find a thin source of hope, which may not be tangible, but is obtainable. However, it will only be obtained if there is direct cooperation and calibration from the portion of the populace able to bring its voting power, organizational capacity and political means of expression to bear on the powerful managers of society. The resolution to this conflict of political will and pervasive apathy, which results in the undue medical, social and psychological suffering of countless men, women and children, is obviously undetermined, as it hinges on the collective response of Middle America. But the goals of attentive and empathetic citizens are as finely marked in loud coloring as the responsibilities of freedom that accompany them. Springsteen ingeniously identifies both.

> Now Tom said "Mom, wherever there's a cop beatin' a guy
> Wherever a hungry newborn baby cries
> Where there's a fight 'gainst the blood and hatred in the air
> Look for me Mom I'll be there
> Wherever there's somebody fightin' for a place to stand
> Or decent job or a helpin' hand
> Wherever somebody's strugglin' to be free
> Look in their eyes Mom you'll see me."

When one lives in a country of political privilege where marketplace values of greed, selfish individualism and consumerism undermine democratic-humanistic values of love, service and equality, one must consciously choose a side — the marketplace or democracy — the oppressor or the oppressed. This dilemma lies at the heart of nearly every other major decision one makes in a free society. Who are your friends — so to speak — the ones who dictate marketplace policy or placate it with a favorable ideology, or those who are victimized by it? How deep is your love for those people who are struggling, and how much courage are you willing to conjure in the commitment to serving them?

Springsteen personifies this challenge in a resurrection of Steinbeck's character from *The Grapes of Wrath*, Tom Joad. The literary allusion to Steinbeck is important and revealing for all the obvious reasons. Steinbeck made a career of writing about the needy and embattled segments of American society pushed to the margins and made to live in financial desperation, psychic torment and public obscurity. Many critics believe that *The Grapes of Wrath* represents the peak of Steinbeck's writing; it introduces readers to characters living in the depression, fighting for labor rights, and clinging to thin hopes of shelter found in New Deal resettlement camps. Springsteen's invocation of Steinbeck reminds listeners that his prophetic platform rests upon a foundation built by literary, musical and artistic giants who came before him. It also provides an example to emulate. Tom Joad dedicated his life to not only assisting his struggling family but also fighting as a foot soldier in the war for organized labor, equality and opportunity for lives of decency and dignity. After killing a man during violent police disruption of an orchard-worker strike, he is forced to leave his mother behind. But before going on the run, he promises her that no matter where she goes or he ends up, he will be a tireless and relentless advocate for the oppressed. That is how she will be able to see him, in spite of his physical absence.

The deliberate citation of Tom Joad as a social hero and exemplary example functions as an invocation of past democratic traditions in creative production, and a challenge to listeners. Springsteen is clearly offering Tom Joad as a personification of a larger struggle that requires collective action. Obviously no ghosts are arriving under bridges where veterans live in squalor; in hospital rooms where citizens are denied care; or in school rooms where children do not have textbooks and are forced to learn in an environment that contains more metal detectors than computers. One could imagine the ghost of Katrina haunts these dark settings of the destitute, considering that the hurricane bearing her name, like no other event in modern American history, represents the deep class and racial divide that continues to widen in the superpower. Or one could say that the victims themselves are ghosts — invisible from institutions and media forums that matter — while the few that speak for them are treated with the same credibility and respect given to those obsessed with the paranormal.

However, in reality, there are no ghosts offering aid and comfort to the oppressed. Therefore, Springsteen is attempting an exorcism of collective political will and organization that seeks to mobilize and energize the apathetic American masses into summoning its financial, political and social power into "being there," when authorities of law or governance exploit the vulnerable or ignore the needs of the powerless. The invisible can only become visible once they are ushered into the public eye's trajectory by those that are already in it. This is the calling Springsteen offers to the listener. All attentive citizens must simultaneously work to bring awareness to those not paying attention, and provide comfort and hope to the victims of marketplace values and politics.

Throughout the entire *The Ghost of Tom Joad* album Springsteen places the otherwise invisible on a mantle of public display. In "Youngstown" — a song about the Ohio steel town that has been ravaged by economic changes of globalization and corporate greed told through the eyes of a mill worker — the protagonist indicts his boss with charges of profit-obsession and cold self-interest that borders on sociopathy: "Once I made you rich enough / Rich enough to forget my name." He is invisible in unemployment — forgotten, his needs unattended to even after years of dedicated and onerous labor — and invisible as the public interest and common good is neglected. This condition ranges from moral failures of foreign policy to the devastating economic consequences of worker mistreatment. The rest of the album tours through unseen and uncounted America, making stops in border towns where patrol guards feel conflicted over preventing young, goodhearted and impoverished women from pursuing their dreams in the States ("The Line"), and poor southwestern cities where young boys sell their bodies to feed themselves ("Balboa Park") and older men produce methamphetamine for a livable income ("Sinaloa Cowboys").

These stories are kept out of view in American life because they contradict the cozy Horatio Alger tales of "rugged individualism" that take place in a "land of opportunity" where supposedly anyone can succeed without significant obstruction if he or she is willing to work hard. It is far easier for those who reside in halls of power to transform suffering people into objects of invisibility than to deal with the moral consequences of their plight. This also comforts the millions of Americans who prefer to live in consumer cocoons, pursuing the perfect caffeinated beverage or pixilated digital screen while living in self-imposed ignorance to the struggling masses who spend their energy and time pursuing shelter, medicine and social acceptance.

The dichotomies of struggle without reward and hyper-visibility versus invisibility create an entire set of inevitable personal consequences that come with destructive social costs.

WHY NOT KILL YOURSELF? — ANESTHESIA AND MEANING IN INVISIBLE COMMUNITIES

If one looks at any group of people who have been systematically, institutionally and sociologically traumatized through a denial of equal human value and existence, one will find predictable results — alcoholism, drug use and a variety of self-destructive behavioral patterns. The pain that results from victimization at the hands of powerful external forces will often give way to self-medication and internalization of the oppressor's values, which result in self-hatred and self-disrespect. Examples of this virus, injected directly into the veins by institutions of power, and the symptoms that follow abound.

It may be useful to begin with two groups of people whose supposed lack of humanity was assumed and explicitly expressed by nearly every part of the American polity for most of American history: Native Americans and African-Americans. Whether one begins with the physical genocide, which was followed by cultural genocide in the form of brutally abusive residence schools and the current marginalization of indigenous Americans or the enslavement and subsequent terrorism of Jim Crow levied against blacks, one is likely to find varying forms of psychic trauma and self-medication that persists among both peoples. This behavior is the result of painful questions of self-worth that Springsteen brilliantly identifies in "American Skin (41 Shots)."

Wrestling with such a devastating confusion over identification and social value is often done with the assistance of a bottle or syringe, and usually coincides with the breakdown of family and peaceable neighborhood communities. Rates of alcoholism and drug abuse are far higher in Native and African-American groups than in the general population. Much scholarship and debate has been dedicated to solving this problem by beginning with attempting to determine why it exists in the first place. However, very few observers have even attempted to link self-medication to the root of the disease — devaluing, degrading and demeaning on a large and never-balancing scale. The trauma induced throughout this process stunts emotional maturity and growth, which causes many people to comfort themselves through mindless hedonism and self-destructive medication. Many brave and brilliant individuals are able to recondition their minds, and escape their stultifying scenarios. But those that cannot often fall prey to street therapy. The personal devastation wrought by drug culture permeates communities and begins to eat away their core, making even those abstaining from harmful substances victims.

Bruce Springsteen directs us through this haze of smoke, tears and blood with a deep understanding of how human suffering is either directly attributable to public failures or worsened by them. However, the real brilliance and challenge of Springsteen's music that throws light on the suffering invisibles of American society, especially "Streets of Philadelphia," is that it goes beyond public policy discussion to answer Albert Camus's psychological throw down that the most important question for a human being to answer is "Why not kill yourself?"

Suffering people, who are victims of oppression and are unable to find tangible hope in high quantity, certainly have to answer that life and death question more often and more seriously than anyone else. Springsteen demonstrates that even though institutionalized inequality, lack of representation in the political system, and faltering social services desperately need to be addressed, as they are a primary part of the problem, people still have to be provided with meaning and fulfillment, which will ultimately give them a reason to live with hope. In the absence of this meaning, people will sink deeply into depression until they are unreachable or answer Camus's question with a tragic answer. Several of Springsteen's characters, ranging from a grieving widow of a dead soldier ("Gypsy Biker") to a soldier himself ("Devil's Arcade"), either consider suicide or descend into a drug-induced, emotionally constructed cell, which confines them to misery and isolation, after they undergo trauma and find it unacknowledged by crucial communities and important institutions.

In another song about a veteran, a man who describes burying his friend killed in the Vietnam War summarizes the feeling that results after suffering through something that automatically isolates one from those that have not experienced it, and having that isolation mutate into something far worse when the dominant culture dictates that the suffering is invisible and unworthy of discussion, consideration or reconciliation. From "Brothers under the Bridge," released in 1998:

> Come Veterans' Day I sat in the stands in my dress blues
> I held your mother's hand
> When they passed with the red, white and blue
> One minute you're right there . . . and something slips . . .

This character's mental and emotional presence in this world changes from moment to moment. Holding the hand of his deceased friend's mother during a parade is an act of kindness, which illustrates his awareness and participation in intimately building qualitative relationships with beloved family and friends. But it is quixotic. Eventually, he slips away and is no longer part of the loving, lucid and waking world.

The goal of progressives should be to prevent any human being from slipping in and out of emotional consciousness by keeping them engaged and active in a community that reinforces their humanity and never allows them to feel invisible, despite the best efforts of dominant society. This community should also battle the hegemonic culture that places them within the night side of invisibility through institutional indifference, social discrimination and economic stagnation. The religious right, and superpatriots who worship country and receive any criticism of it as blasphemy have seen their ranks swell in recent years as the economic situation worsened and political opportunities for participation became more distant during the Dark Age of the Bush presidency because they provided people with false comfort through a shallow community that is deceptively soothing.

Activists with a progressive orientation can combat the despair of discarded people by waging a three-pronged assault against the forces that subjugate them to useless roles. First, as Springsteen has demonstrated, they must be brought into visibility through a commitment to truth-telling. Their stories must be told, highlighted and set against any phony, self-aggrandizing mythic narrative that American systems of power sell to an apathetic public. Awareness of their existence is crucial to enlisting others in the effort to overcome their oppression and to exerting pressure upon political representatives, economic elites, and cultural figures of influence. The second process that must be initiated is one already alluded to — namely solidifying their value as human beings by working with psychologists, social workers, faith counselors and other concerned and competent people to connect them to a beneficial community.

The granting of visibility and community will alleviate the individual calamities of suffering, trauma and torment. Alcoholism, drug usage and family abandonment, which stem from an overall hopelessness, would eventually decline. However, this is all dependent upon an eradication of social ills that persist in poor, black, indigenous and suffering communities. Activists must go beyond "superstructure" when dealing with suffering people, but cannot neglect it.

Sustained concentration and action must be given to altering the status quo in order to complement humanistic values of love, service and dignity by undermining marketplace values of greed, narcissism and selfishness. Institutionalized inequality and normalized political corruption must be ended with democratic energy, rhetorical shrewdness, political know-how and compassionate outreach.

Springsteen offers a useful launching pad for this campaign, but other political and artistic predicates can and should be applied. Humanizing the structural implementation of politics and economy throughout America requires a deep and profound grappling with the personal consequences of casting those not useful to the current implementation into invisibility. Political campaigns were humanized by the Obama victory, but this process must go beyond election cycles and penetrate into the deepest corridors of American society. It demands a thorough examination of the social consequences that come with marketplace subversion of democracy. In many cases, the political and personal are interlocked. The conditions responsible for their creation and conjoining cannot be toppled without a fearless confrontation with the social suffering wrought in their wake, and an understanding of how that suffering originates and is systematically recycled.

Once again, Springsteen provides a predicate for this confrontation in a prophetic and empathetic voice which cries out for its listener to make a lasting commitment to simply "being there."

Chapter 5

Down in Jungleland

The Politics of Urban Decay

We remain — in where blacks can live, what they subsist on, the quality of their lives, what future they can expect — still largely divided
into two Americas, racially drawn, estranged from each other. Even
among African-Americans who have managed to escape the under-
tows of the past enter the comfortable preserves of the middle-class,
there can be heard, for the very reason that they presumably made it
into the American promise, the most bitter angers of alienation. Most
critically, in our inner cities, there steadily expands a kind of Third
World country within the United States, a population of inner exiles
empty of any sense of possibilities or any connection to the rest of the
national community — millions of those whom James Baldwin once
described as "the most dangerous creation of any society . . . that man
who has nothing to lose." The enormous combustible potential of such
a situation is obvious, and it is fearful to ponder what might ensue if
the distraction and anesthesia of drugs were ever actually removed
from these masses of the unhoping.

— Marshall Frady, Foreword to *Jesse: The Life and*
Pilgrimage of Jesse Jackson, 1996

Throughout the first three decades of Bruce Springsteen's career
American cities disintegrated into high-tension, high-crime and
high-drug areas of social division, political liability and economic
depression that engendered paranoia in mostly middle-class and largely
white America. The declining state of American inner-cities inspired a
bastion of cultural and entertainment production which diversely ranged
in quality and style. Mickey Spillane made a fortune writing books about

Mike Hammer, a hard-nosed, ruthless and misogynistic private investigator battling the mean streets of New York City. Even though Spillane's most-popular Hammer novels were written in the 1940s, '50s, and '60s, they remained popular in later decades — so much so that television dramas featuring the Hammer character found not one, but two airings in the '80s and '90s. Hammer's influence was widespread and visible in Clint Eastwood's *Dirty Harry* films, and Charles Bronson's *Death Wish* series of movies about a victim of crime turned vigilante. All of these stories glorified tough and emboldened loners who were contemptuous of civil liberties and who chose to operate outside of the legal system to assure the survival of justice — almost universally relying on violence to do so. Bronson's character was the most controversial, due to the fact that he was not a police officer nor was he investigating one particular criminal or organized crime faction. He was merely patrolling the streets at night with a gun, waiting to be attacked so he would have provocation to kill. Many critics condemned the series for glamorizing violence and encouraging aggressive vigilantism. But audiences, increasingly paranoid and angry about rising crime rates and gang violence, cheered while getting a vicarious thrill from Bronson's street judge, jury and executioner. John Carpenter's *Escape from New York*, starring Kurt Russell, depicted a futuristic New York City where criminals ruled the streets with violence and intimidation. Anarchy characterized the Big Apple's daily activities in a world where every man had to fight for himself in a blood match in which the most savage and least humane participant always had the advantage. The film's sequel, *Escape from L.A.*, time-warped viewers into a Hollywood transformed into a giant prison without any guards or order. Visual portrayals of city life became bleaker and more and more colored with danger, while popular music provided a complementary soundtrack.

Some singers took a sympathetic view of city woes — outstanding examples being Buddy Guy with "Cities Need Help," Marvin Gaye's "Inner City Blues," and Lou Reed's late '80s concept album *New York*. However, no music captured angst in inner-cities better than hip-hop, which entered the musical arena in the 1970s and rose to incredible heights in the 1990s. Rap artists spoke directly, in explicit terms, about life in the expanding ghettos and slums surrounding majestic skylines throughout America. They affixed a spotlight on to the portions of America long kept in the dark — although many of them could not do this without revealing faults of their own. "Gangsta" rappers were accused, with good reason, of glorifying and glamor-izing the destructive vices of many men in inner-cities — booze, bling and bitches. Substance abuse, mistreatment of women and criminal disrespect of authority justified many of the worst and most idiotic stereotypes white America held against black people. Record companies and music television networks promoted these forms of hip-hop while they ignored or dismissed edifying and enlightening hip-hop artists, which gave way to a much amplified public debate about the pervasive influence of hip-hop.[1]

Politically, the demonization of inner-cities, along with their inhabitants, continued to court favor with much of the media and voting public. Ronald Reagan infamously lambasted fictional "welfare queens," who according to him drove around impoverished streets in Cadillac cars, wearing fur coats, while their children starved. This cartoon opened the door for "Welfare to Work" reform passed during the Clinton administration which effectively ended social assistance programs by turning them into ushering services for low-wage, no-benefit jobs which do not have much opportunity for upward mobility. It also had the power to make careers. The myth of Rudy Giuliani's single-handed slap-down of crime in New York City has become an incontestable part of American politics. Inconvenient statistics that prove crime of all kinds was declining prior to Giuliani's mayoral election are universally muted. The Giuliani case is indicative of the entire hysteria surrounding inner-cities, which relies on exaggerations, hyperbole, scare tactics and a refusal to discuss substantive issues.[2] Despite the endangerment of inner-cities, and the hopelessness that persists there today, the urban picture is not as grim as some would have it. Urban decay is a real phenomenon created by deindustrialization but crime rates in America are not much higher than the rest of the developed world — save for two categories: use and sale of illegal drugs, and gun-related violence. Also, in the 1990s crime across the country went down while, paradoxically, fear of crime increased. This is because coverage of crime has become much more pervasive as media outlets have grown in size and stature, and "tough on crime" politicians have ratcheted up their rhetoric.[3] Predictably, social hysteria over crime and drugs defeats rationality in American life — as it did with communism and continues to do with terrorism — and more realistic depictions of cities, along with practical solutions for urban problems, are thrown into the dustbin in favor of deranged ranting and borderline-racist paranoia.

Many intelligent, critical and creative responses have been made to this politically expedient narrative by activists, politicians, artists and journalists. One of the most challenging and meaningful creative challenges has come from Bruce Springsteen — a singer who always identified with cities, spending much time in New York City, and making Asbury Park, itself a victim of urban decay, a second home. Both of those cities, one — a mid-sized shore town with a once vibrant culture and the other, the capital of the world — receive a lot of play in his early records with songs like "4th of July, Asbury Park," "It's Hard to Be a Saint in the City," "Does This Bus Stop at 82nd Street?" and the beautiful "New York City Serenade." These songs, along with several others, portray cities as geographic sources of hope and opportunities for self-improvement. By driving into the city one is connected to bountiful resources that allow the individual to obtain culture, romance and joy-induced meaning. Once when introducing "New York City Serenade," Springsteen said, "This is what New York should be like." That succinct summary of a ten-minute song reveals the underwhelming and disappointing nature of urban life when matched against the dreams that fuel transit to its host cities. Every year, countless Americans move to cities — most likely New York City or Los Angeles — hoping to "hit it big." They are seeking fame and fortune in film, music, business or fashion and make serious sacrifices while in pursuit of their dreams.

A recent New York Times article chronicled the lives of several young people who moved to the Big Apple and became so strapped for cash because of exorbitant rent fees that they skipped meals and lost any semblance of a social life. However, they all shared one thing in common — a steadfast faith that one day they would achieve success beyond most people's expectations and be able to laugh about their previous lives of desperation.[4] Springsteen tapped into that energy and belief when he penned those early tunes, which have exciting or emotive melodies set against romantic stories of young people seeking redemption. Although these tales of individual exploration possess an American character, and make good fodder for film and television plot lines, there is also a flip side to American cities that is less exciting and triumphant but more real, honest and indicative of collective American failures in economic justice, social equality and political representation.

The flip side is not accurately represented by the cartoon narrative presented in Death Wish and other depictions of anarchic war zones permeating throughout American life. These sensationalized portrayals of inner-cities often encourage some of America's worst social practices: white flight, bigotry, suburban purchasing of firearms, and distrust of neighbors. The underside of America's cities is complex, conflicting and contradictory. It reveals how even after exciting personnel change in the White House, which has the power to emotionally uplift and empower the mostly African-American residents of inner-cities, real policy changes are needed to eradicate poverty, hopelessness and the deadly social viruses that infect those depressed epicenters of crime, unemployment and drug rings. It includes people making bad choices, which should be condemned. But, in many cases those people also deserve sympathy that comes from considering their bad and occasionally cruel choices as deriving from hideous social and political contexts. Economically, cities simultaneously showcase America's vast wealth and destabilizing poverty. A child's familiarity with riches and luxury or bankruptcy and violence depends solely on which part of the city she is born and raised in. Urban juxtapositions of wealth and poverty, and personal irresponsibility and societal immorality, exist from the northwest tip of Seattle all the way down to Miami, and deserve deep probing which will offer indispensable lessons for American public policy, economic structuring and social interaction.

ACROSS THE RIVER: TOXIC ENVIRONMENTS, SICK BODIES, AFFLICTED ECONOMIES AND SAXOPHONE SOLOS

In 1975, with the release of *Born to Run*, Springsteen began to take a less optimistic look at American cities, even though that seminal album is imbued with romanticism on such songs as "Thunder Road" and the title track. Springsteen, when describing the album, has discussed two creative agendas that guided him throughout the writing and recording processes. First, he wanted to be responsible for "the greatest rock 'n' roll record of all time." That kind of arrogance and self-significance would be mocked if he had not succeeded — *Born to Run* almost always ranks in the top five on any list judging the greatest popular music albums ever released. More importantly, from an intellectual and musical standpoint, he also wanted to create a loosely conceptual album that provided vignettes from the lives of different people in the same location — presumably New Jersey and New York City — during one day. The album begins with a screen door slamming on a front porch as a young man pulls into a driveway attempting to persuade Mary into getting into his car in a search for redemption with the promise of love ("Thunder Road"), and ends with a girl shutting out a bedroom light oblivious to the "death waltz" taking place on the streets below her apartment window ("Jungleland").

If *Born to Run* is to be understood as a morning-to-night musical documentary, then "Meeting Across the River," being the second-to-last song on the album, must be set in the late evening hours, just after sundown, and moments before the night either ends or begins — depending on a person's lifestyle, vices and responsibilities. For the characters in this song it is definitely beginning, along with, according to their hopes, the rest of their lives. It begins with a trumpet blowing jazzy notes of blues-inflected sentimentality that would provide the perfect soundtrack for any noir tale of a perpetually down-on-his-luck outcast desperately gripping at one last, big score. Piano notes are set against the wailing trumpet to evoke action and fill in the gaps. If the trumpet sounds like observation, the piano rings of movement. As a piano riff takes control, opening up room for the singer, with the trumpet still moaning in the background the listener begins to learn about the nature and purpose of this movement, but only in mysterious generalities that loyally serve its master: a haunting and vaguely threatening melody.

Hey, Eddie, can you lend me a few bucks
And tonight can you get us a ride
Gotta make it through the tunnel
Got a meeting with a man on the other side

Hey Eddie, this guy, he's the real thing
So if you want to come along
You gotta promise you won't say anything
'Cause this guy don't dance
And the word's been passed this is our last chance

We gotta stay cool tonight, Eddie
'Cause man, we got ourselves out on that line
And if we blow this one
They ain't gonna be looking for just me this time

The protagonist of this song sings in a voice of urgency — prone to fluctuation and self-confidence — that is deep and occasionally slyly whispering. He is an unnamed loser, petty thief or wannabe gangster with a fledgling career in crime. It is clear that he is not in good shape. He needs money, transportation and a trustworthy partner. Although Eddie can provide all three of these necessities, he is gun-shy, in need of coaxing, and not to be given a role in shadowy negotiation. However, in case the duties of friendship are not enough to inspire assistance to the protagonist's problems, he is reminded that the stakes of this con, score or "heist" (the song was originally called "The Heist") affect his life and livelihood with the cryptic warning, "if we blow this one / They ain't gonna be looking for just me this time." One gets the feeling that Eddie has heard this pitch a hundred times before, and that he has responded with weak and ultimately destructible resistance on every occasion.

It is also clear that these two men live on the margins of society, either due to personal failure, difficult social circumstances or most likely a combination of both. It would take the imagination of a fine novelist to think of a scenario in which two doctors or wealthy legitimate businessmen would have this conversation at a late hour. These two men — whether because of a situation of their own making or social forces beyond their control — find themselves in a moment of personal crisis devoid of viable options alternative to the nefarious activity they are plotting. Upon observing a story of this kind, many Americans would ask obvious questions such as "Why not get a job?" This line of inquiry about personal responsibility and smart decision-making is understandable and may be entirely relevant, as biographical information on Eddie and his hustling friend is not provided. They may have been committed to crime from an early age, eschewing opportunities to make it straight and believing they could live lives of easy, care-free glamor as depicted in the first half of the film *Goodfellas*. One does not easily assume that these guys are not culpable in their own marginalized social statuses. Beyond that, it is difficult to precisely nail down their respective biographies without taking narrative license. "Meeting Across the River" possesses such a haunting melody and such an imagination-energizing story that it has inspired some of America's best fiction writers to fill in the blanks for themselves with directly referential, but creatively reaching, short stories. These musically guided literary experiments have been collected in a book edited by Jessica Kaye and Richard J. Brewer called *Meeting Across the River*.

Most authors, from Eric Garcia to Pam Houston, cast these characters in deadbeat roles of struggle and petty criminality. Garcia gives perhaps the most literal reading of the song in his story, "Meeting Across the River," which features Jimmy as the protagonist. He is the clichéd born loser who passes time either working for peanuts at a Jersey waterworks or serving out a sentence at the penitentiary. Jimmy's brother, Eddie, wants little to do with him and is unwilling to lend him a car or money when he gets the bright idea to rob parked trains while the conductors polish one off in a nearby watering hole. After being flatly rejected from his brother, he ends up stealing the car, with the intention of giving it back, and meeting his partner — a sleazy character he met in prison — outside the train yard. After finding a crate of money, he alerts his partner, who reacts by clubbing him over the head and stealing all the loot for himself, leaving Jimmy alone and on his back when the police arrive. He winds up back in the joint, and seemingly at the beginning of another unsatisfying, impregnable cycle of low-end jobs and criminal schemes gone awry.

C.J. Box's interpretation of the underrated Springsteen song, also contained in *Meeting Across the River* under the title "Pirates of Yellowstone," dramatically differs from Garcia's literal reading, but holds the same racing-to-a–dead-end quality for its characters. Box casts Vladdy and Eddie, two immigrants from the Czech Republic, as main characters who live in Wyoming. Unable to find suitable employment due to language and educational barriers, they keep their eyes open for a lucrative con, and soon discover they live near a rogue scientist who steals bio samples from Yellowstone Park. They plan to steal the samples from the thief and offer them back to him for a few thousand dollars. Meeting any reader's expectations, the story ends tragically with Eddie being shot in the head by the not-so-naïve mark and Vladdy narrowly escaping, but not without a possible homicide charge hanging over his head after he kills Eddie's murderer in a vengeance-driven rage.

The rest of the stories, impressively collected by Kaye and Brewer, widely vary in scope, setting and circumstances. But, they all seem to capture a restless embodiment of sordid city life (even those like Box's that do not take place in an urban center) that defines the powerful drama in the original "Meeting Across the River."[5]

The importance in recognizing the inspirational effect of Springsteen's *Born to Run* album on American fiction, and the significance of analyzing the nature of that influence is not merely literary or musical, but political. If politics can be understood as the public debate, deliberation and decision-making processes that produce societal governance, and good governance can be measured by how efficiently, adequately and democratically it responds to citizen needs, then any political observer interested in urban policy must begin with the lives of urban people. Springsteen, in "Meeting Across the River," gives listeners a small but precisely positioned window into the desperation that characterizes the lives of many embattled inhabitants of American cities. The talented authors who follow in his footsteps attempt to broaden that window — some with greater success than others.

Not forgetting that *Born to Run* is a conceptual album, one moves next to the epical song immediately following "Meeting Across the River" — "Jungleland." Since 1975 Springsteen has rarely played the former without following it with the latter. Both in the studio and on the stage, "Meeting Across the River" serves as a lyrical and musical prelude to the ten-minute "Jungleland." With its jazz-saturated, quiet melody and soft vocals, "Meeting Across the River" is a musical representation of a stirring of the pot or a ticking of a time bomb. Its successor is a catastrophic explosion, annihilating everything in its path. From city dreams to urban failures, and from unachieved redemption to unmitigated disaster, no topic is left unaddressed in Springsteen's emotively engineered epic. The song begins with the orchestral sounds of a violin which contains beauty normally not heard on a rock 'n' roll record, signaling that Springsteen's narrative, as well as his characters, have moved from planning to action — from mapping to moving. The piano accepts the baton from the violin and is played with pulsating frenzy, again placing emphasis on activity and movement. The story that unfolds is fit for rock 'n' roll opera, with mountainous highs and ocean-floor lows, relying on wildly romantic descriptions and exciting musical breaks. It begins with the singer softly establishing setting and character development over quick and melodic piano which is eventually assaulted by a wall-of-sound fury that Springsteen and band unload on the listener after he shouts, "Down in Jungleland!" as if he were a military captain ordering "Fire!" While the song's very title evokes a sense of social Darwinism and isolated, cutthroat struggle, its lyrics, along with dramatic musical shifts, produce an unforgettable tragedy of hope, fear and sadness in urban America.

Well the Rangers had a homecoming
In Harlem late last night
And the Magic Rat drove his sleek machine over the Jersey state line
Barefoot girl sittin' on a hood of a Dodge
Drinkin' warm beer in the soft, summer rain
The Rat pulls into town, rolls up his pants
Together they take a stab at romance and disappear down Flamingo Lane

Well, the Maximum Lawmen run down Flamingo
Chasin' the Rat and the barefoot girl
And the kids 'round here look just like shadows
Always quiet, holdin' hands
From the churches to the jails, all is silent in the world
As we take our stand
Down in Jungleland

A romanticized pair of desperate lovers attempt to evade law enforcement after an unnamed act of crime in a battle that seemingly paints the criminal with a sympathetic brush and the cops as heels. Their surroundings are implicitly dangerous, while socially, institutionally and empathetically unavailable. Muted children and silent institutions, which according to their own standards house the sacred and profane, either watch or turn away in indifference to the human suffering outside of their walls. This unhealthy social and political reality prompts the desperate and downtrodden to stake their own claim and single-handedly fight their own war in a lonely and animalistic conflict for turf, money and status. With this imagery and musical narrative, Springsteen brilliantly and ironically turns the self-congratulatory American myth of "rugged individualism" on its head by depicting it not as an exercise of triumphant strength but as a futile act of desperation.

The second verse extends the description of struggle beyond Magic Rat and his lover to the masses tightly huddled on the margins of the city. He emphatically sings of kids who "flash guitars just like switch blades," a "ballet being fought out in the alley" and an "opera out on the turnpike" while the saxophone, dueling guitars, thunderous drums and rapid-fire piano work as a well-oiled machine to force along this urban tragedy with power and purpose. Just before the second verse comes to a crescendo, the singer indicts "local cops, Cherry Tops" who "rip this holy night." Once again casting the cops as villains, Springsteen underlines the distrust and resentment directed towards police in inner-cities where law enforcement is viewed as a brutality-prone, exploitative and power-hungry harasser.

After a quick bridge, which has Springsteen singing in an Elvis-like baritone about "Lonely-hearted lovers" who "struggle in dark corners" before vanishing without a trace and "backstreet girls dancing to the records that the D.J. plays," the music widens to create space for Clarence Clemons's transcendent saxophone. It is the sound of someone coming out of something — perhaps the successful evasion of police during a deadly chase or another person finding existential redemption through love or positive attainment of identity. Musically, it provides a climax for Springsteen's philosophical romanticism, which resides in romanticized cities. The Springsteen-penned and Clemons-performed sax solo may be rock's greatest. But, perhaps more importantly, it is the sound of Springsteen's career and vision taking a sharp turn from romance to realism — from Thunder Road to the darkness on the edge of town. When Clemons brings his beautiful and emotionally reeling performance to a conclusion, the singer ends this tragedy with a glimpse into catastrophic circumstances and the social apathy that keeps their blood pumping.

> Beneath the city two hearts beat
> Soul engines running through a night so tender in a bedroom locked
> In whispers of soft refusal and then surrender in the tunnels uptown
> The Rat's own dream guns him down as shots echo down them hallways
>   in the night
> No one watches when the ambulance pulls away
> Or as the girl shuts out the bedroom light
>
> Outside the street's on fire in a real death waltz
> Between what's flesh and what's fantasy and the poets down here
> Don't write nothing at all, they just stand back and let it all be
> And in the quick of the night they reach for their moment
> And try to make an honest stand but they wind up wounded, not even
>   dead
> Tonight in Jungleland

As the hero dies, presumably by the hand of another but by the command of his own dream, "the girl" (his barefoot lover now separated from him?) shuts out the bedroom light in cold indifference to her former lover's brutal death. Even more pernicious, the poets, who can be understood as those supposed to bring a crucial and critical perspective to bear on issues of suffering, stand in silence, similar to the muted children, at the sight of an every-man-for-himself war zone, too cynical and disengaged to voice dissent and too withdrawn to inspire. For those that do attempt to snatch victory and happiness from the jaws of Jungleland only a wounded status remains. They cannot even count on a martyr or warrior's burial to get them through an inhumane surrounding.

This is the culmination of Springsteen's creative transformation from romance to realism. The city does not offer any of these characters a hopeful future, and the tragedy of "Jungleland" does not bode well for Eddie and his hustling friend making plans for profit and a quick getaway in "Meeting Across the River." The writing is on the walls; those who try to defeat the predatory city streets will not succeed, and may not even survive.

Any realistic look into cities must thoroughly take into account the grim realities that result from economic decline, institutional failure and political indifference. Throughout the past 30 years in America inequality has grown, wages have stagnated and poverty has intensified. The inner-city has been victimized by these developments more painfully and fatally than any other geographic contingency, while the response from white Middle Americans has been to relocate with as much distance between them and the city as possible, leading to long commutes and suburban isolation. The collective reaction of most elites has been to ignore inner-city suffering, save for exploiting the occasional drive-by shooting or drug bust to impersonate Wyatt Earp with "tough on crime" speechmaking.

Largely, American democracy has not addressed the laboratory of social ills afflicting the entire country but which is most pervasively damaging the inner-city. It has not ushered the United States into the twentieth-century First World (never mind the twenty-first) by establishing a fair, efficient and universal health-care system which does not ration treatment and services according to wealth. Instead it continues to implement an insurance industry-dictated, profit utility-managed system which is expensive, unfair and unethical. The wickedness of this system, in which people die or suffer because of bottom-line decision-making, harms the lives, finances and morale of the poor, working class and middle class. However, the impoverished inhabitants of inner-cities suffer the most lasting wounds and deepest scars because they are the most likely to be employed in low-end jobs or not employed at all, and are therefore kept out of employer insurance coverage packages. Social programs aimed at alleviating this trauma — Medicaid and SCHIP — are either underfunded or overly controlled by the corporate sector, whose agenda not only contradicts the purpose of such programs but also subverts it. The results of this undemocratically designed and poorly implemented system, along with the weakening social programs intended to fill its ever-widening gaps of coverage, can be tragic.

In 2007, 12-year-old Deamonte Driver complained to his mother of a toothache. His mother was a low-wage worker and his father, like all too many in cultures defined by poverty, was not in the picture. Deamonte's mom, Alyce, desperately searched for a dentist that would accept Medicaid and provide the $80 tooth extraction that her son needed, but she was unable to find even one dentist who would perform the simple procedure. Deamonte continued to tell his mother he was in pain, and Alyce did what any good mother in their predicament would do — she rushed him to an emergency room where she hoped someone would do something for her boy. The tooth was not removed and Deamonte was sent home with medicine for headaches and a dental abscess. However, he would soon return to the hospital when his condition took a horrible turn for the worse, and it was discovered that because the abscessed tooth was never removed, the bacteria had spread to his brain. Two emergency operations were performed in a last-ditch effort to save the young boy's life. But it was all too late. At the age of 12, Deamonte died. He lost his life, before it really began, because the American health-care system, with its market agenda, determined that he was not worth the cost of an $80 tooth extraction.[6] Unfortunately, and to the suffering of children and parents across the country, stories like Deamonte's are not rare exceptions in the world's richest nation. They are all too common.

The World Health Organization ranks the American system 37th in the world, due to lack of access. The WHO also reports that among the developed world, the U.S. ranks first in infant mortality and is among the lousiest-performing nations in life expectancy.[7] This poisonous health-care status quo that harms the collective American polity but tortures the inner-city makes the lives of its confined residents, needless to say, traumatic. They not only must rectify having the most obstructed and obstacle-filled path to affordable health care but also have to live in the toxic waste-dumped, urban-sprawl squalor which results from city, state and federal officials treating the communities of poor and politically frail minorities as oversized trash cans and gigantic ash trays. Poverty-defined and dilapidated city outposts with strong black or Hispanic demographics have traditionally been exploited as dumping headquarters for waste typically produced by, or because of, profit-producing city activity enjoyed by people who live safely and comfortably outside of the socially miserable inner-cities. Far too often the environmental agenda ignores the poor people of the United States and many other countries who are most infected by wasteful and pollutant policies.

Toxic waste, pollution and health-care inaccessibility culminates in a severe threat to the right of poor Americans to live healthy lives, making nearly everything else secondary. The personal solution to this predicament — to escape current conditions by becoming upwardly mobile — is impeded to a near point of unavailability. American deindustrialization and job outsourcing has left under-educated inhabitants of inner cities, especially black men, with a lack of tenable financial options. This produces a pervasive "nowhere to go, nothing to do" virus of inconsistency and instability in poor communities that formerly relied on industry for an economic base.

Closed factories have become a common eyesore along any American highway, and the exportation of blue-collar manufacturing jobs has hit families hard. Even prior to the financial crisis, *Business Week* analyzed the American job market and dubbed it the "health care economy," because health care was the single field of employment with an expanding field of available jobs.[8]

Systematic deindustrialization, which is the product of globalized trade agreements that benefit multinational corporations able to exploit fatally poor people of the Third World while stripping salaried jobs from First World workers has caused many American cities to crumble in its wake. One illustrative example of this unfortunate economic development is the Ohio steel city, Youngstown. Since the decline of the steel industry in the 1970s, and later drops in revenue gained from auto plants, Youngstown has wallowed in economic malaise. The mid-sized city captures the battle for resuscitation and revival being waged throughout the Midwest Rust Belt, where rural communities have been maimed by the loss of family farming and smaller cities have suffered a tough blow from deindustrialization.

Springsteen identifies this ongoing struggle through the eyes of one worker in the city once famous for its steel production in his ballad "Youngstown." It was originally introduced to audiences on *The Ghost of Tom Joad* as a guitar-and-fiddle folk ballad which possessed an eerie musical quality and a quietly bereaved, half-whisper vocal delivery. Youngstown was the first stop for Springsteen on the tour conducted in support of his 1995 release. His next tour was backed by the E Street Band, and a completely remade "Youngstown" was featured prominently in each night's set. The song had been transformed into an angry, hard rock classic fueled by Springsteen's hellfire howling vocals, the late Danny Federici's cultural tip-off accordion riff, and a closing guitar solo by Nils Lofgren that makes the hairs on anyone's neck stand at attention. The bitterness, pain and resentment of the folk version are amplified into outrage with the E Street Band, and the worker's final plea, "When I die I don't want no part of heaven / I would not do heaven's work well / I pray the devil comes and takes me / To stand in the fiery furnaces of hell" is entirely believable after being assaulted by this worker's hellacious depiction of his town and life, which cannot possibly end with an ascension into a celestial paradise. The story begins happily and triumphantly with Youngstown heroically making the "cannon balls that helped the union win the war."

The listener is transported ahead into the late 1960s, just prior to the city's demise, in the second verse, when the son of a steelworker describes returning home from Vietnam and making a stable and secure living at the mill.

> Well my daddy worked the furnaces
> Kept 'em hotter than hell

I come home from 'Nam worked my way to scarfer
A job that'd suit the devil as well
Taconite, coke and limestone
Fed my children and made my pay
Them smokestacks reachin' like the arms of god
Into a beautiful sky of soot and clay

Here in Youngstown
Here in Youngstown
My sweet Jenny, I'm sinkin' down
Here darlin' in Youngstown

The comparison of smokestacks to the "arms of god" not only provides the song with powerful imagery but also gives one a sense of the unmatched importance of the steel industry to Youngstown life. It was a benevolent giver of jobs, livelihood, opportunity and identity. It helped individuals maintain decent lives for their families and established value and meaning for their larger community. Pride and purpose could be found in the assistance that Youngstown's labor gave to American foreign policy. That is, until the foreign policy became confusing and ignoble, and the American steel industry folded. The worker recalls his father, no doubt at this point an elderly man, expressing scarred bewilderment over how the world's evilest men could not destroy Youngstown, but wealthy American elites with their own agenda could.

Well my daddy come on the Ohio works
When he come home from world war two
Now the yard's just scrap and rubble
He said, "Them big boys did what Hitler couldn't do"
These mills they built the tanks and bombs
That won this country's wars
We sent our sons to Korea and Vietnam
Now we're wondering what they were dyin' for

The original version of the song is the lament of a defeated man who is at the end of his rope, and seems to be telling his story reluctantly, while the E Street rendition functions as a violent confrontation between worker and structural authority. Those in its path are blown over by an enraged victim of cruelly misplaced American economic priorities who is prepared to extract accountability from the corporate traitors, and their enablers in politics, who denied him his prideful livelihood and robbed his city of its identity, value and purpose. The three-guitar pileup riff, accented by a folksy accordion, sounds like the harsh hum of manufacturing and Springsteen's voice resembles a prophet screaming knee deep in a lake of fire. When condemnation of economic exploiters, political pirates and a system that encourages them is issued, one is forced, spine thoroughly chilled, to morally and existentially reflect on the often ignored victimization process playing out in far too many American homes and cities.

> From the Monongaleh valley
> To the Mesabi iron range
> To the coal mines of Appalacchia
> The story's always the same
> Seven-hundred tons of metal a day
> Now sir you tell me the world's changed
> Once I made you rich enough
> Rich enough to forget my name
>
> And Youngstown
> And Youngstown
> My sweet Jenny, I'm sinkin' down
> Here darlin' in Youngstown

Without the hope for any decency to emerge from the betrayal of corporate elites, and without the expectation of recognition from political elites, all that remains is that haunting prayer for his destroyed soul to find sanctuary in hellfire, which will bring the worker back to the heat of the mill, and allow him to hold on to his only remaining sources of independence and pride: hostility, rage and violent instinct.

Some Rust Belt cities, not willing to descend into hell, have attempted revitalization — Youngstown among them. However, many of them have been unable to find tenable alternatives to steel and have thus far had difficulty in getting ahead. Joliet, Illinois and Gary, Indiana have relied on vice distribution in the form of riverboat casinos to stay afloat. City leaders and rational residents have little reason to morally oppose gambling but most of them realize that while it may not destroy the moral fabric of city life, as some puritanical critics believe, it certainly does not uplift it. Therefore, they hope that the financial rewards will be greater than the social costs by manifesting themselves in increased jobs and entrepreneurship surrounding the casino. The economically beneficial effect of gambling on small-to-mid-sized, formerly manufacturing-driven cities has either been inconsistent or felt only at the margins.[9]

THE WRONG SIDE OF THAT LINE:
EDUCATIONAL INEQUALITY, JOBLESSNESS
AND CRIMINAL SOLUTIONS

Citizens not contemplating city planning but merely clawing for lives of stability and dignity are forced into considering college enrollment for future opportunities because the knowledge-based economy, which includes fields like health care and digital technology, requires at least an undergraduate degree from most applicants. The near absolute necessity of college presents a problem for sufferers of urban decay, one of the worst consequences of which has been the breakdown of public education. This American institution, which more than any other was designed to be a great equalizer to ensure the fertility of the "land of opportunity," has deteriorated into an inequality processing plant where poor children are prepared to be poor adults. Promising proposals for reforming the property-tax funding mechanism for public schools, which institutionalizes inequality, and interesting ideas for filtering out incompetent teachers while attracting inspiring ones, have been consistently ignored in American politics. The American marketplace has deemed the replication of excellence in public schools a non-priority, and has thereby denied school systems adequate funding. Its only discussion of reform is a mind-numbingly narrow debate about the effectiveness of the No Child Left Behind Act which simplifies education into the passing of rudimentary, high-stakes tests written by bureaucrats outside of students' communities without providing districts with sufficient funds to implement its mandated reforms. Although the Act has the potential to be marginally successful in the worst schools where children cannot read by the eighth grade and accountability is good in principle, it does not even begin to look at the two most debilitating factors in public education: structural disparities and communal despair.

These conditions create a disgraceful city public-school system that produces hopeless and detached young adults who have little chance of attending college. The *Wall Street Journal* reports that America has slipped to seventh in the world among nations that graduate the highest percentage of their citizens from college. The same paper pointed out that the current generation of American men is the first to graduate college at a lower rate than their fathers, which explains the even more disturbing revelation that this is also the first generation of men less financially secure than their fathers.[10] The most obvious reason for this drop in degree-earning males is the unbelievable and unjustifiable rise in college tuition. Since 1980, average tuition costs have more than doubled across America. Simultaneous with rising tuition has been a significant drop in aid. Pell Grants have been consistently cut while interest rates on loans have increased with the same frequency, making college financially unfeasible for many Americans.[11]

The calamitous combination of these circumstances — a deindustrialized and deunionized jobless economy, toxic environment, lack of affordable health care and miserable school systems that result in low prospects for higher education — overwhelms those living among urban decay with dread, despair and dejection. The lack of hope that afflicts inner-city communities not only leads to personal torment, but also a torrent of social trauma.

Ironically, the social trauma is inflicted upon these communities by its own members who take to crime as a means of addressing their individual desperation. They prey upon the poor and vulnerable people in their neighborhood — most often women and children — in an attempt, albeit a cruel and vicious one — to selfishly right the wrongs in their own lives. This inevitable series of events can be explained by what sociology has long called "strain theory."

Sociologist Emile Durkheim was the first to identify the strain being imposed upon some people who live under circumstances and conditions that may actually encourage them to commit crime. He classified the strain in two ways: structural and individual. Structural strain is the product of inadequate social structures that fail to address a person's basic needs. The pain and friction that results from this systemic reality is what typifies the individual strain people feel when they determine that merely achieving societal goals is more important than the means used to do it. Robert King Merton expounded on strain theory by adding that culturally assigned goals and aspirations are structural and are therefore heavily reliant upon more traditional structures, i.e. the acceptable means to fulfill the culturally assigned goals — obeying laws, following social convention, living responsibly. When there is no balance between these two structures, society cannot normatively function because there will inevitably be a large group of people who feel intense pressure to achieve material success but cannot do so with legitimate means, and will thereby resort to deviance.[12]

On 1982's *Nebraska*, Bruce Springsteen portrayed an American underworld and night side that was bleak, grim and potentially deadly to those that are either forced or choose to live within it. Most of the stories told in eerie folk balladeering on that album are set in cities — places beaming with life, vitality and activity but dead to those that, for whatever reason, cannot tap into its energy. One of *Nebraska*'s most powerful and classic moments is the song "Atlantic City," which not only offers emotive musical excitement and fulfillment but also epitomizes what Durkheim, Merton and many others had in mind when they brilliantly claimed that most crime can be explained with strain theory.

The song begins by referencing mafia violence in Philadelphia; specifically the killing of underboss Philip Testa (nicknamed the "Chicken Man"). It also captures the uncertainty of gambling's ability to resurrect and revitalize Atlantic City. Its original incarnation is a sparse and haunting ballad which features a soft strumming of a guitar at a somewhat brisk pace. Springsteen deeply sings in the voice of a defeated observer, while another vocal track, by the same singer but shouting and howling off-time, plays in the background to effectively express the character's inner turmoil and desperation. Its music video emphasizes the defeated observer status of the character by being composed only of black-and-white images of Atlantic City, which cannot be characterized as anything but bleak and depressing.

> Well they blew up the chicken man in Philly last night now they blew up
>   his house too
> Down on the boardwalk they're gettin' ready for a fight gonna see what
>   them racket boys can do
>
> Now there's trouble busin' in from outta state and the D.A. can't get no
>   relief
> Gonna be a rumble out on the promenade and the gamblin'
>   commission's hangin' on by the skin of its teeth
>
> Well now everything dies baby that's a fact
> But maybe everything that dies someday comes back
> Put your makeup on fix your hair up pretty
> And meet me tonight in Atlantic City

The chorus, with its hauntingly fatalistic prayer, "Everything dies baby that's a fact / But maybe everything that dies someday comes back," speaks not only to the uncertainty of this character and Atlantic City residents about the fate of their city but also to the lack of certainty throughout America regarding its future. From Youngstown to New Jersey, what lies ahead may not only be unexpected, but terrifying and disheartening.

Exactly like "Youngstown," "Atlantic City" was dramatically rearranged with the E Street Band. Instead of beginning with an acoustic guitar, Max Weinberg pounds the drum to create a deeply ominous audio representation of the "rumble out on the promenade," just before a dark and sparse electric guitar starts sending out lost signals that are unable to find frequency underneath the violent and bitter rumble. Immediately following the first chorus, Steven Van Zandt plays a simultaneously chaotic and soulful mandolin which, with its hearkening back to traditional folk instrumentation and sound, serves the same purpose as Federici's accordion on "Youngstown"; to evoke the marginalization of the neglected individual that folk music so often expresses. Before the second verse begins, the music slows down again and resembles the song's opening, as if to imply that the hope and energy gained from heading to Atlantic City is temporal and fleeting.

> Well I got a job and tried to put my money away
> But I got debts that no honest man can pay
> So I drew what I had from the Central Trust
> And I bought us two tickets on that Coast City bus

With just a few words, shouted by the singer in a mad howl that epitomizes existential angst and social devaluation, it becomes clear that this character is without financial comfort and personal place. After another chorus, the music rises to a transcendent level as the protagonist expresses his loftiest and fondest dreams to a woman who may or may not be even listening. Regardless of her level of communicative reciprocation, she is essential to this man's idyllic, perhaps fantastical, painting of the future. The final verse of "Meeting Across the River" features the protagonist vowing to get his girlfriend Cherry back, despite her anger about him pawning her radio without permission. In "Jungleland," Magic Rat's dangerous pursuit of happiness is meaningless without his companion — the barefoot girl — and in "Youngstown" the embittered steel worker delivers his lament to Jenny — a woman whose exact relationship with the worker is indefinable. These desperate pleas made by painfully lonely men are directed towards the single source of companionship, compassion and communion in sight: A woman who feels scorned or unappreciated. Unable to find stability and humanity on the street, embattled men seek it out with romantic companionship, even when the love has grown, by their own admission, cold.

> Now our luck may have died and our love may be cold, but with you
>   forever I'll stay
> We're goin' out where the sand's turnin' to gold so put on your stockin's
>   baby 'cause the night's getting cold
> And everything dies baby that's a fact
> But maybe everything that dies someday comes back

After the words, "everything that dies someday comes back," the music comes to a crashing halt. Hope has died, and it has a long shot of coming back, only if this character is willing to pay an unenviable price. The singer orders the song to begin again with a count of four and after one mandolin riff, the music becomes sparse — slow with a noticeably softer drumbeat and winding guitar with gaps filled by a faint mandolin. The protagonist's life has taken a wrong turn down a potentially even darker road and this moment of silence signifies the careful consideration of options, and reflection on guaranteed risks versus potential rewards.

Now I been lookin' for a job but it's hard to find
Down here it's just winners and losers and don't get caught on the wrong
    side of that line
Well I'm tired of comin' out on the losin' end
So honey last night I met this guy and I'm gonna do a little favor for him
Well I guess everything dies baby that's a fact
But maybe everything that dies someday comes back
Put your makeup on and fix your hair up pretty
And meet me tonight in Atlantic City

In three lines this protagonist encapsulates the heart of strain theory. Legitimate avenues of success are obstructed by immovable objects, while the stakes riding on overcoming this societal obstacle course are ultimate. Eventually, this dislocation becomes unbearable — hence the fatigue over "comin' out on the losin' end." He has struggled far too long with social norms and convention and has gotten to the point of being willing to achieve security and stability by any means necessary. He has agreed to "do a little favor" for "this guy" he barely knows. No further details are provided, but this character is obviously preparing for something unsavory. It may be deemed small, but most people can predict how the story ends. One favor leads to another, and pretty soon he has reached a point of no return. He is a criminal, and the cemetery or penitentiary is his most likely destination.

Those removed from the situation can rightfully label his choice to enter a life of crime as unfortunate and harmful. But to him, incapable of accessing mainstream institutions of opportunity and success; surrounded by a fledgling economy dependent upon the distribution of vice; living among a violent mafia war; and ignored by public policy, it is entirely rational and seemingly beneficial. The song ends with the singer, repeating several times over, in a voice increasingly angry and erratic, "Meet me tonight in Atlantic City," while Van Zandt, Nils Lofgren and Pattia Scialfa echo his refrain. With each repetition the singer's plea becomes more violent, desperate and urgent. He has placed everything he has on the table, and is waiting for the cards to come up. It is his final bet and his last hope — his attempt to break out of this hopeless cycle of misfortune and dislocation, and be relieved from an intolerable strain.

While there is an undeniable element of rationality involved in the decision-making process of many (potential) criminals similar to the man in "Atlantic City," others react to being submerged in a toxic pool with no lifeguard on duty, while their humanity and value are systematically denied, with a despair that mutates into derangement. One example of such a dreadful human condition is contained in the Springsteen song "Johnny 99," which also appears on *Nebraska*. The fast-paced folk tune is accentuated by a quickly strummed guitar and singer who belts out the story in the third person with urgency. Later E Street Band versions lend themselves more to dancing than heartbreak, which offers a distinctive down-playing of the story — as if it is not anything out of the ordinary. These are the stories Americans read in the newspapers and hear about on the television nearly every day. Life always goes on, and the prevailing attitude is to be unaffected by such triviality.

Singing and playing this song with whimsicality contradicts its central narrative, which adds a fascinating aspect to its appeal. It begins with a common description of deindustrialization — a closing of an auto plant, which leaves Ralph unemployed and, without any other sellable skills, suddenly unwanted. Like so many who suffer from self-doubt and questions of self-worth, he turns to self-medication. After "mixin' Tanqueray and wine" too heavily, he purchases a firearm and eventually winds up in the "part of town where when you hit a red light you don't stop."

He can be seen maniacally waving his gun around, threatening to kill himself, just before an "off duty cop" sneaks up on him, detains him, and hauls him into the station. Listeners are then taken to his sentencing hearing and find out that he is sentenced for "98 and a year," hence the nickname "Johnny 99." With that, the judge grants Ralph one final opportunity to speak for himself. "Johnny 99" obliges and with little words, offers a stirring reflection on the personal pain that thrives on social misery.

> Now judge I had debts no honest man could pay
> The bank was holdin' my mortgage and they was takin' my house away
> Now I ain't sayin' that makes me an innocent man
> But it was more 'n all this that put that gun in my hand
>
> Well your honor I do believe I'd be better off dead
> And if you can take a man's life for the thoughts that's in his head
> Then won't you sit back in that chair and think it over judge one more
>   time
> And let 'em shave off my hair and put me on that execution line

Ralph's bitter lament adequately summarizes the pernicious influence of poverty but he goes beyond issues of survival to questions of uniquely human concerns that many people never have the misfortune of trying to answer. He may have had "debts no honest man could pay" — the exact same phrase appears in "Atlantic City" and the selection of the word "honest" reveals the breaking point for would-be criminals when they decide the ends of personal profit justify the means of illegality — and was on the verge of homelessness, but he admits it was "more 'n all this that put that gun in my hand." The intensity of his depression that motivated him to behave so chaotically and dangerously cannot only come from economic malaise, even though it was an essential component of his condition. He must have felt isolated, invisible and hopeless — unable to apply his human value of actualization to anything useful, and incapable of identifying the meaning of his own independent existence. Similar to the distraught protagonist of "Youngstown," his only comfort is an upcoming grisly death which will liberate him from conscious suffering and allow him to hold tightly onto his anger, resentment and bitterness in his final moments.

After losing his job, and on the verge of foreclosure, Ralph obviously feared becoming part of the permanent lower class and combating the symptoms of such an incurable condition — devastating poverty, existential emptiness and societal neglect. Millions of Americans, whose basic needs are unmet, emotional needs unfulfilled, and institutional needs unattended, make up this beleaguered segment of the populace. They are most intensely concentrated in cities, and are therefore prime examples of the corrosive effect of urban decay. The permanent under-class is a group of people who, barring sweeping institutional and cultural reforms, will continue to live in poverty and unemployment, and be forced to contend with instability and hopelessness on a daily basis. As long as the United States is governed as a marketplace and not a nation, these social ills will continue to spread in pandemic fashion, without diagnosis from policy makers. The increased failure of public schools, obstruction to health care, and breakdown of infrastructure in inner-cities demonstrates the growth capacity of urban decay-engineered social woes.

The structural and institutional problems of impoverished inner-city life are abundantly clear. What also must be considered, and not in some narrowly conservative cultural critique but within the context of urban decay, is the breakdown of a small but priceless institution of support, hope and dignity — the family.

STRIPPING THE EARTH TO ITS BONES: FAMILY BREAKDOWN, "THE WAR ON PARENTS" AND STREET GANGS

While regressive forces on the right blather on about "family values" by defining them as genital supervision and religious indoctrination, they, along with the collective American polity, largely ignore how raising children as responsible parents becomes more strenuous, materially devastating and emotionally difficult with each passing year. Examining this modern, yet Dickensian, tragedy requires advocacy of progressive politics for poor and working-class parents. However, the examination must begin with a truthful and accurately measured account of the deck that is stacked against modern parents, as opposed to one-sided moralistic ridicule of "welfare queens" and absentee fathers launched from safe, stable and sterilized cocoons of wealth and privilege.

Cornel West and Sylvia Ann Hewlett eloquently and effectively summarize the struggles of parenting in their 1998 book *The War against Parents*. In an attempt to conceptually lay out the unbearable burdens of becoming a parent, West and Hewlett contextualize that decision and commitment in broad terms after describing the large financial costs of child rearing to the age of 18, which they estimated to be an average of $145,000, without including college tuition.

> Large numbers of well-meaning moms and dads may still elect to invest large quantities of money and time in child-raising, but for the first time in history their loving energies are not reinforced by enlightened self-interest. This is a tall order in a society that venerates the market. We are asking parents to ignore the logic of their pocketbooks and buck the dominant values of our age. Contemporary moms and dads are trapped between the escalating requirements of their children, who need more resources for longer periods of time than ever before, and the signals of a culture that is increasingly scornful of effort expended on others. Parents often feel as though they are expected to read from two or three scripts that diverge completely in terms of how they lead their lives. Should they take on a second job to pay for college, or should they stay home in the evening to do a little bonding and turn off the TV? It is easy for a bewildered parent to become paralyzed as he or she is besieged by a host of contradictory demands.[13]

West and Hewlett describe parenting as a loving and self-sacrificing task that is undermined by defective schools, polluted environments and hedonistic culture, along with crime, drugs and conservative economic policies. They also deal with how fathers are excluded from well-meaning social programs and henceforth discouraged from taking an active role in their family's lives, even though they may not be able to find suitable employment with decent wages, livable benefits and opportunities for promotion. Placing parents at a disadvantage has been a consequence of unfettered market deregulation and impotent political representation of poor and working people.

West and Hewlett demonstrate that progressives should not be bashful when speaking about family and parenting. They should demand that American "family values" go beyond media censorship and gay bashing, and extend to equal access to health care for sick children, affordable housing for parents, schools that mothers and fathers can trust, and an economy that gives opportunities to those already raising children. While the left pathetically tinkers, and the right continues to undermine parental efforts while hypocritically vowing to protect families, countless unprotected children slip into a malaise of pain, heartbreak and self-destructive behavior. Their parents may be unable to fill the voids in their lives because they are hooked on narcotics or too tired after working long hours. Their fathers are most likely uninvolved in their lives, leaving a dangerous void of male guidance and nurture. They look around and see a school system that is not equipped to prepare them for the modern world and a social structure that fails to address their suffering. They become trapped in a swarm of despair, dread and disappointment and soon find themselves reaching out to the nearest role models that ironically enough are glorified and glamorized on the electronic screens that always seem to be flashing — drug dealers, gangsters and pimps.

The breakdown of the American family living among urban decay is a common phenomenon that is contradictorily often discussed but rarely investigated for root causes. In 2005, Bruce Springsteen released his third collection of sparsely arranged, mainly acoustic folk ballads, *Devils & Dust*. One of its most moving and emotive story-songs is called "Black Cowboys" and it chronicles the lives of a young mother and son living in the Bronx. With deliberate strumming of the acoustic guitar, soft background piano and whisper vocals, Springsteen tells a haunting and heartbreaking tale of losing love and family. Female background vocals that simply cry "ooooh" in a sweeping style underscore the young boy's search for home and peace. The song begins by describing the transformative love between a parent and child as a lifejacket in a tumultuous and stormy sea.

> Rainey Williams' playground was the Mott Haven streets
> Where he ran past melted candles and flower wreaths,
> Names and photos of young black faces,
> Whose death and blood consecrated these places.
> Rainey's mother said, "Rainey stay at my side, for you are my blessing
>   you are my pride. It's your love here that keeps my soul alive.
> I want you to come home from school and stay inside."

The second verse provides some texture to the Rainey character. He is fascinated with the long forgotten "black cowboys" who are barely discussed in history classrooms and even less frequently portrayed in Hollywood productions. Lynette, Rainey's mother, collected books and photos of black cowboys so that her beloved boy would have something to look forward to on his walk home from school. But, what really made him happy and brought him everlasting joy was simply the sight of her.

> Summer come and the days grew long.
> Rainey always had his mother's smile to depend on.
> Along a street of stray bullets he made his way,
> To the warmth of her arms at the end of each day.

In a world of instability and danger, a mother's love can provide a physical, emotional and spiritual sanctuary for a child, just as his love keeps his mother's "soul alive," despite degrading and demeaning conditions. When that love disappears, depression, torment and trauma ensue with painful and permanent consequences. The listener learns that Lynette has somehow, for reasons unexplained, lost her way, and has found companionship of the worst kind. Perhaps, she needed to have her femininity affirmed or sought refuge from economic troubles. She might have viewed this new man as a means of protection against the gang wars and "stray bullets" that define the Mott Haven streets. In any event, her decision to stay with him, and consume his deadly product, has devastated her son and robbed him, along with her, of the most valuable and precious thing in their lives.

> Come the fall the rain flooded these homes, here in Ezekiel's valley of dry
>   bones,
> It fell hard and dark to the ground. It fell without a sound.
> Lynette took up with a man whose business was the boulevard,
> Whose smile was fixed in a face that was never off guard.
> In the pipes 'neath the kitchen sink his secrets he kept.
> In the day, behind drawn curtains, in Lynette's bedroom he slept.

> Then she got lost in the days. The smile Rainey depended on dusted
>   away,
> The arms that held him were no more his home.
> He lay at night his head pressed to her chest listening to the ghost in her
>   bones.

Rainey's longing for the ghost inside his mother, the spirit that once gave him everything he needed in a cruel world, is a heart-piercing evocation of the lovelessness that many urban children must bear throughout their lives. It is a state of being that neither I nor anyone who has not undergone it can pretend to understand. It makes innocence impossible, the expression of outwardly love muted, and must reduce human life to an animalistic instinct of survival, devoid of the spiritually sustaining elements of love, hope and abiding companionship. Urban decay not only renders its youthful inhabitants as economic liabilities and social outcasts; it also makes them deeply disconnected from life-giving forces that human beings everywhere rely on for dignity, energy and mobility. If children grow up under these hellacious conditions, it should not be shocking that they may be the first to falter when they are parents themselves, creating a perpetual cycle of loss, sadness and hardened hearts. Just as predictable is the overwhelming desire that many young people feel to escape their conditions or worse yet to find solace in mind-altering substances or organizations that resemble families but are akin to domestic terrorist groups. Rainey escapes the old-fashioned way, which is preferable to the alternatives, but tragic given that one senses a better way was possible if only the love between him and his mother could have survived urban decay and the pernicious influence of a drug-dealer boyfriend.

> In the kitchen Rainey slipped his hand between the pipes.
> From a brown bag pulled five hundred dollar bills and stuck it in his coat side
> Stood in the dark at his mother's bed, brushed her hair and kissed her eyes.
>
> In the twilight Rainey walked to the station along streets of stone.
> Through Pennsylvania and Ohio his train drifted on.
> Through the small towns of Indiana the big train crept,
> As he lay his head back on the seat and slept.
> He awoke and the towns gave way to muddy fields of green, corn and cotton
> And an endless nothin' in between.
> Over the rutted hills of Oklahoma the red sun slipped and was gone.
> The moon rose and stripped the earth to its bone.

The uncertainty of Rainey's future is depressing upon reflection. His transformation from an innocent boy, fascinated with black cowboys and bathed in the welcoming glow of his mother's smile, to a young man riding though the countryside with stolen drug money and no one by his side is catastrophic. He has become one of those photographed cowboys he adored but his frontier freedom is unwanted and unhealthy. It is not a glorious search for self-improvement and adventurous discovery. It is the consequence of not having a home.

As dispiriting as this story is, it still possesses a thin vestige of hope. Rainey could amount to something and find happiness on the open road. It seems unlikely but it is an undeniable possibility, whereas for many inner-city youth who suffer from the same tortured hopes and tattered relationships as Rainey, achievement and sustaining happiness are largely unattainable.

Rainey's unannounced exodus from the Bronx and his mother's home must also be viewed as an act of incredible courage. Most people lack the necessary strength to leave everything they know in search of a better future without a reliable plan to get it. His problems are sadly common — living without a dependable family unit and without economic opportunity — but his solution — to board a train for across the country without looking back — is rare and indicative of a belief in himself that was given to him by his mother and managed to survive her decline into a drug-induced haze. Rainey's willingness to buck his human urge for tribal belonging is not shared by most of his peers surviving urban decay who, rather than attempt to build reserves of self-reliance, enter hierarchical tribes of mutual support and dependence called street gangs. These destructive units serve two purposes for the enlistee. First, they provide opportunities for financial profit in a destabilized and disorganized local economy that is characterized by poverty. Second, they fulfill the universal need for family support and community belonging. Due to these two basic needs that growth of gangs thrives on, they are certainly not new or unique to modern urban areas or black and Latino peoples.

The much glamorized and glorified Italian-American mafia originated in urban areas in the late nineteenth and early twentieth century because of severe anti-Italian bigotry that flourished throughout America. Italian immigrants were unable to find good jobs, were the victims of vandalism in their own neighborhoods, and were often harassed by police when they would file complaints. Constant humiliation, degradation and intimidation motivated a group of Italian men to form the "Black Hand" which, in addition to operating as a neighborhood protection unit, extorted local businesses and kidnapped community leaders for a costly ransom. This thuggish gang eventually evolved into the Italian mafia and conducted the organized crime for which it is famous.[14] The Irish mafia's development is strikingly similar.

Organized units of criminality and deviance are almost without exception formulated by marginalized groups of despised people who, without foreseeable mainstream opportunities for success, begin relying upon themselves by victimizing others. They become families that are equally — if not more — important than biological relations. This emotional and occupational tug of war provided the fascinating conflict for Tony Soprano on perhaps the greatest television drama in the medium's history, *The Sopranos*. His central struggle was the attempt to balance dualistic loyalties that did not always complement each other. This was captured most brilliantly in an episode that depicts him taking his daughter, Meadow, on a road trip across New England to visit prospective colleges. During the trip he sees a "rat" who went into witness protection after betraying several mafia colleagues in a court of law. Tony decides that this opportunity for revenge and mob code enforcement is too great to pass up, and therefore begins plotting a vengeful homicide while chauffeuring his daughter around various campuses and protecting her image of him as a loving father. In the end he succeeds on both accounts, but not without being forced to confess to Meadow that he "makes a lot of his money from illegal gambling and other things like that."

Jesse Guajardo, a leader of the Latin Kings in Chicago, "fought back tears," according to the *Chicago Tribune*, when his act of balancing membership in two diametrically opposed families failed. He had been a member of the gang since he was eight years old and was overwhelmed with emotion when betraying his "second family" in order to avoid a lengthy prison sentence that would separate him from his daughter.[15]

The conclusion to Guajardo's tenure in the Latin Kings is unlikely to be shared by many future members. The life expectancy of a street gangster is not very long, and those that do survive more often than not live most of their remaining years behind bars. Considering the potentially fatal risks associated with gang membership, one has to stand in awe of the devotion and commitment its leaders, enforcers and foot soldiers make to their newly formed families. As they suspend all ethical judgment, moral sense and rational long-term planning, they are fed, financed and protected by the other members in the gang. These vital services are precisely the same ones most likely missing from their domestic lives. The fulfillment of basic physical and emotional needs is central to the gang's appeal, and pivotal to its motivation of fierce loyalty.

Street gangs can be conceptually analyzed from a distance by discussing the psychological and financial value they provide to their members. However, it must be remembered that their methods of business and tactics of enforcement are akin to domestic terrorism. They prey upon the weak and victimize the vulnerable, while thriving on the misery of others. Taking into account the complex political, economic and social factors that fertilize the poisonous plant of gang growth should not inhibit moral condemnation. By the same token, that worthy condemnation should not preclude empathy and understanding, as even gang members are not monsters. They remain human beings.

One of the finest achievements in television history was the HBO series that ran from 2002 to 2008 called *The Wire*. Its deep exploration of political, sociological and legal issues in inner-city Baltimore was shockingly comprehensive and artistically satisfying. Creator David Simon identified one of the themes of the series as institutional failure, which is evident in the constant disorganization of the Baltimore Police Department, inefficiency of the Baltimore school system, corruption of city politics, and lack of loyalty and honesty in street gangs. Regardless of which institution a character allows to regulate his or her life, he or she will deal with disappointment and dejection.

One such character, Michael Lee, who is introduced to the viewing audience as a pre-teen and makes his last appearance as a 14-year-old, has a mother who is hooked on crack and a father who goes through cycles of absence or abuse. Michael has been barely educated by a school system without sufficient supplies, competent teachers or committed administrative staff. He is surrounded by a jobless economy and maintains a daily struggle to feed and clothe his little brother. During one episode a local gang leader — a man of considerable wealth and power — approaches Michael, hands him some cash, tells him that he can be "one of us," and if he wants more money to come to see him about work. Michael accepts the gangster's offer and soon begins selling drugs, robbing stores and committing murder. Within that context and under those conditions, it is easy to understand gang enrollment and any honest and fair observer would have to admit that he would probably make the same choice if he were in Michael's shoes.

The Wire excelled at depicting individuals, even those who make horribly unethical choices, with a degree of holistic understanding and sympathy because it presented a detailed context for those choices. Simon has said that the series "is a deliberate argument that unencumbered capitalism is not a substitute for social policy; that on its own, without a social compact, raw capitalism is destined to serve the few at the expense of the many."[16]

Perhaps there is no better visual artistic companion than *The Wire* to Bruce Springsteen's folk albums, *Nebraska* and *The Ghost of Tom Joad*. Those dark and depressing albums successively survey the scenes of America's broken cities, dilapidated economies and useless institutions by examining the toll they take on the lives of individuals. "Atlantic City" and "Youngstown" depict urban decay, deindustrialization, and the systemic betrayal of the American working class with musical power and potency, while the former provocatively shows how these factors present a compelling influence for crime. "State Trooper" portrays the anxiety and paranoia of isolated urban misfits who drive the highway at night desperately seeking a human connection, and "Balboa Park" tells the horrifying story of a teenage boy who prostitutes himself underneath a bridge in San Diego to old, rich men. Many of the boys whom he has met performing the same dehumanizing work have "poison in the blood," which is no doubt a reference to AIDS. One night, Spider (the boy in the song), hears the border patrol moving towards the bridge and begins running down the highway. He gets hit by a car, and the driver does not even bother to stop. He continues down the freeway as if he just hit a piece of road kill, which ironically is what Spider has been rendered throughout his life. Spider takes shelter in an underpass, holds his stomach, tastes his own blood, and helplessly lies among the filth, possibly awaiting his death as he "listened to the cars rushin' by so fast." This is a side of American cities that most people know exists — which is why more and more of them are suffering long commutes to live in white, peaceful suburban areas — but rarely discuss and never confront.

Also on *The Ghost of Tom Joad* is a barely melodic folk song that provides insight into the supply side of the drug trade while presentations of street gangs and inner-city despair capture the demand angle. "Sinaloa Cowboys" chronicles the lives of two Mexican brothers, Miguel and Louis, who jumped the border into California and began working in orchard fields for pennies a day. Unable to make financial progress, they accepted an offer to "work in a deserted chicken ranch" cooking up methamphetamine, despite its illegality and physical dangers, during which hydriodic acid could "burn right through your skin." This choice is made because, listeners are told, "You could spend a year in the orchards / Or make half as much in one ten hour shift." Their decision to accelerate their monetary earnings and material progress by participating in a dangerous and criminal enterprise does not come without consequences. By the end of the song, a major turning point has occurred in the lives of these characters.

> It was early one winter evening as Miguel stood watch outside
> When the shack exploded, lighting up the valley night
> Miguel carried Louis' body over his shoulder down a swale
> To the creekside and there in the tall grass, Louis Rosales died
> Miguel lifted Louis' body into his truck and then he drove
> To where the morning sunlight fell on a eucalyptus grove
> There in the dirt he dug up ten-thousand dollars, all that they'd saved
> Kissed his brother's lips and placed him in his grave

Louis was another casualty of drugs and, it is fair to say, drug policy in the United States. Inner-cities and urban decay cannot be fairly discussed without taking an in-depth look at the American "war on drugs," which has a long, sordid and unimpressive history. *The Wire* examined many issues afflicting the inner-city, but none more than illegal substances — individual abuse, criminal prosecution and economic exploitation. But, as far as cultural output goes, that HBO series, along with some of Springsteen's songs, possesses an exploratory quality that is rare in American politics and art. Political discussion of drugs is exclusively punitive, as any mention of decriminalization is a third rail, while most television and film portrayals of the drug war depict enforcement agents as the good guys and dealers as the bad, without placing the conflict in a social, economic or historical context.

UNDERCOVER OF THE NIGHT: DRUG WARS, UNSTATED AGENDAS AND BLACK AND BLUE CONFLICT

If one peers into American history with both eyes open, it becomes clear that criminalization of substances has more to do with class than chemistry. America's first experiment in this area was the prohibition of alcohol which, like the current war on drugs, failed miserably. Puritanical support from religious groups made legislation banning consumption of alcohol possible. However, its aim was to exert social control on immigrant groups who took to drinking and socializing in bars after work, which explains why police raids most commonly took place in working-class beer establishments in city areas while upper-class wine and liquor drinkers living well past the city limit sign enjoyed their beverages in comfort and leisure.

Marijuana was criminalized almost immediately after the prohibitive laws against alcohol were repealed and bureaucrats once devoted to the mindless task of prosecuting alcohol consumers needed something to do. Many reasons were provided for the smokable substance's criminalization. However, acting Drug "Czar" Harry Anslinger explained it pretty directly in the 1930s: "Most marijuana smokers are Negroes and Hispanics. It causes white women to seek sexual relations with Negroes."[17]

Lawmakers are almost always drunk and high on racism and xenophobia when they draw up plans to criminalize certain substances and penalize a very specific portion of its users. Not coincidentally, all efforts supposedly designed to eliminate drug use miss their goals by a very wide margin. Drug use has not significantly declined in 30 years. Yet, in the United States, the current policy of interdiction and criminalization remains largely unchallenged, despite that its failure can be observed by anyone with the slightest amount of literacy.[18] If the stated agenda of a policy has not been accomplished in decades, and there is little discussion of reform, that policy must be succeeding at accomplishing an unstated agenda. If one views the drug war from that angle, its purpose and achievements become clear, along with the motivation for refusing to examine policies that may actually have an impact on drug addiction, namely ones that speak to the despair and poverty of its users — greater access to jobs and heavier emphasis on rehabilitation coupled with a drastic reform agenda to revitalize decaying inner-cities which would help keep the family unit intact and strengthen struggling schools.

Instead, current drug policy is intended to exert social control on Middle America by inculcating irrational fear about minorities, crime and drugs while it discards an unwanted and unusable portion of the population that does not complement marketplace needs. The criminal justice system gives this policy muscle and, unsurprisingly, it is flexed most excruciatingly when its hand has a tight grip on poor, black people who mostly derive from urban areas. The Justice Policy Institute reports that although white and black people use drugs at similar rates, blacks are more likely to be arrested on drug charges, more likely to be tried and convicted, and ten times more likely to go to prison than whites. Human Rights Watch has studied the same disparities of justice and found similar results.[19]

Criminalization of drugs, and deliberate legal targeting of black people, largely explain why the United States has the largest prison population in the world, both in terms of sheer numbers (over 2.3 million) and percentage of general population (over 1 percent of adults). Of course, blacks represent the majority of U.S. prisoners and most of them are incarcerated for non-violent drug crimes.[20] This enables the flourishing of the prison-industrial complex in the United States, which is both big business for corporate elites and job stimulus for white, working-class, rural America. In addition to providing financially desperate people opportunities for employment, the construction and opening of a prison also helps the local economy by establishing a need for new motels, restaurants, and various other businesses. Congressional representatives welcome the prison-industrial complex, which has been almost entirely privatized, into their districts because it comes with pork spending which often translates into votes.[21]

All of this adds up to mean that the United States' power structure currently has a political agenda, executed through a policy deceptively called a "war on drugs" and an economic program of prison expansion and industry stimulation, which thrives on urban decay and the social misery associated with it. This tragic turn of events was prophetically predicted by sociologist and writer Sydney Wilhelm in his 1970 book *Who Needs the Negro?*

To succinctly summarize Wilhelm's thesis, it essentially describes how, after World War II, returning white veterans drove black men out of manufacturing jobs. Eventually, when foundry work became unappealing to white workers and the primary source of employment for working-class African-Americans, deindustrialization began to take hold of cities and leave black men without work. Service employment is the last remaining option but, as indicated by Devah Prager's studies of hiring patterns in New York City and Milwaukee (referenced in Chapter 4), employers tend to prefer a white face to represent their businesses and therefore discriminate according to pigmentation. The combination of these circumstances and developments makes the poor, uneducated black man useless to powerful economic and political institutions in America and therefore their placement in prisons is, in their eyes, at best a societal relief and at worst a minor social problem not worthy of attention.[22]

Certainly, individuals making stupid choices fill American prisons, and personal responsibility should be emphasized in any message directed towards any group of people — rich, poor, black or white. However, the "drug war" is a national policy which receives state and federal funding to be enforced by police and prosecutors and essentially removes a "bothersome" bulk of the population from mainstream economic and power structures. Policies like this, along with those instrumented in education, make personal irresponsibility more hazardous to the health and prospects in poor, black neighborhoods than in white, middle-class neighborhoods, along with ensuring that personal responsibility is more beneficial to inhabitants of white neighborhoods than those that are multicolored.

The drug war provides a social and political foundation for Bruce Springsteen's comment on the harmful and potentially deadly consequences of viewing people of color through a "veil of criminality." The application of a prejudiced lens to the observation of black people is tacitly supported by active public policy — at the heart of which is criminal justice and law enforcement. Therefore, it should hardly be surprising that within urban decay, the relationship between police officers and poor, black people is characterized by distrust, adversity and hostility.

The paranoia and mutual fear that permeates throughout the inner-city in both black and blue worlds is a direct product of public policies that have allowed poor urban areas to decline into near Third World conditions while simultaneously focusing on putting as many of its inhabitants in prison as possible, even for non-violent offenses. Add to that a multi-century legacy of social strife between white and black people and one is left with a mostly white police force that is encouraged to view black people with suspicion, and black and brown communities that automatically put a guard up against any interaction with the police out of fear of brutality or harassment.

All of these political failures to bring democracy to poor people, and social failures to create peaceful relations between differing groups culminate in tragedies like the Amadou Diallo shooting which provided the inspiration for Springsteen's "American Skin (41 Shots)." When police and a West African immigrant met in that vestibule which will be forever marked with an innocent man's blood, the space between them was filled with failures of American democracy, politics and social will which have shattering impact upon the lives of many uncounted and unacknowledged struggling citizens who, if not physically suffering, are facing spiritual death on high-crime, low-financed, crumbling American streets.

The tension between police officers and ordinary citizens exacerbates the instability in inner-cities, and the cynicism directed towards American institutions that reverberates across those communities. Although the Diallo tragedy, and far too many like it, provides hideous examples of the strain felt when black and blue people interact, there are more subtle and pervasive consequences of mutual distrust and dislike.

Dateline NBC conducted an interesting social experiment not too long ago by wiring a young black man with a hidden camera and microphone before sending him into several police stations on Long Island, New York, to request a civil complaint form. The young man, who asked for the form politely, was consistently questioned with suspicion and threatened with detainment for not cooperating. If this is at all indicative of the treatment black people can expect when dealing with law enforcement, and it most likely is, there should not be any cause for questioning why cops are seen as an enemy that is responsible for more harm than good. On certain occasions, understandable anger over police policies and tactics mutates into ugly sentimentality, which intensifies an already blazing conflict. Witness controversies over rap lyrics that advocate violence against police to get an idea of this unhealthy ingredient mixed into the toxic soup. Far worse than rap lyrical content is the effect that drug criminalization has had on police officers, effectively making them victims as well. Forced to deal with victimless crimes, which are the product of an illegal enterprise that will never shut down, police are distracted from real police work, namely investigating much more important capital crimes, such as rape and homicide. The drug war has also alienated the policeman from his communal beat, making even the well-intentioned officer an object of suspicion from neighborhood residents. Law enforcement can be a heroic, courageous and noble vocational calling to serve the community. Drug policy in the United States has sacrificed that service for cheap statistics and big prison money.

One of the reasons that "American Skin (41 Shots)" is such an important song is that it takes an important issue, typically confined to a ghetto of "black politics" and dismissed by mainline discussion as a "black issue," and holds it right in the collective face of white America. It is hardly a secret that Springsteen's audience is composed mainly of white people, and despite "American Skin (41 Shots)" being awarded by the NAACP and praised by Diallo's mother, it was performed most often and most intensely to white people who are most likely reticent to confront such a messy issue and then wrestle with the disturbing questions it presents.

The television drama *NYPD Blue* served the same function for 12 seasons on ABC. While it consistently gave viewers suspenseful stories that revolved around street-savvy detectives tracking down ruthless criminals, it also contained deep insight into important issues of urban decay — modern race relations (especially between police and the poor), family separation, poverty and the multifaceted influence of drugs and policies aimed to eradicate them.

NYPD Blue's best vehicle for driving important points, or at least inquiries, into the living room of white America was its main character — the recovering alcoholic Detective Andy Sipowicz brilliantly portrayed by

Dennis Franz. From the outset of the program he is paradoxically the most troubled and sympathetic character. Despite his penchant for boozing, and his array of prejudices against minorities, gays and poor people, he is likable because of his willingness to learn from mistakes and new experiences. He is open to change and is therefore perpetually struggling to become a better cop and, more importantly, a better man. It is almost as if Stephen Bocho and David Milch (the creators of the series) were making a concerted effort to present a mirror image of a bigoted white man to the viewing audience to demonstrate that transformation and progress is possible.

Kenneth Meeks, author of *Driving While Black* (an in-depth review of racial profiling policies), analyzes a redemptive and transformative moment for Andy Sipowicz in an essay collection edited by Glenn Yeffeth called *What Would Sipowicz Do? Race, Rights and Redemption in NYPD Blue*. It is the first among many that offer redemption for Sipowicz and allow him to grow into a more loving, open-minded and accepting person:

> A little African American girl named Hannah helped Sipowicz move even further toward changing his racially prejudiced views. Hannah was the daughter of a black community activist named Kwasi. Sipowicz and Kwasi had previously had a racial altercation involving the "N-word." After a series of complicated events that led to Kwasi's murder, Sipowicz tried to make a peace offering to the little girl, who had just learned her father was dead. It was a fragile moment in Sipowicz's character development. I believe he honestly tried to look beyond the race of this little girl and see her humanity, not her skin color. But the tables turned. The girl's mother rejected his offering because of his fight with Kwasi. Though Sipowicz tried to make amends for his prejudices, racial prejudice still kept Hannah's mother from accepting Sipowicz's attempt at making things right. This scene demonstrated just how stupid racial prejudices are, and how they interfere with human compassion.[23]

The tendency of *NYPD Blue* to depict complex issues of urban decay and inner-city turmoil through human drama runs parallel with the preferred tactic of empathy employed by Springsteen. It expresses a belief that political progress and social salvation are reliant upon individual willingness to expand communal action to include fair and open relationships with different, and even demonized, people. This will foster personal growth, but also encourage the empowerment of democratic energies.

TURNING SAND TO GOLD: EMPATHY, UNDERSTANDING AND ACTIVISM

When Springsteen demonstrates belief in subversive empathy, politics are typically removed from the narrative or accessible only through implication. On *The Ghost of Tom Joad* track "The Line" he weaves a story, once again set to barely melodic folk music, of Carl, an ex-military man who, while grieving for his recently deceased wife, takes a job with the California Border Patrol preventing embattled Mexicans from forging a passage way to Southern California cities that, to them, possess salvific possibilities. The patrolman resists a dualistic dichotomy, which places him on the side of the righteous and his darker-pigmented objects of enforcement on the other, because his partner, Bobby Ramirez, is a Mexican immigrant and listeners are told that his ethnicity makes the job "different for him." Bobby, with a certain kind of casual wisdom, informs the protagonist that these desperate border jumpers "risk death in the deserts and mountains," "pay all they got to the smugglers," and do it all over again if they get caught. Such irrational behavior has nothing to do with the intellect or deliberate planning. It is the product of the most basic of urges, which Bobby clearly identifies when he somberly states, "hunger is a powerful thing."

It cannot be determined through the brief but powerfully nuanced character development in "The Line" how deeply Carl reflects upon the nature of his work, and the behavioral motivations of his would-be-immigrant objects of patrol. He assures listeners "I was good at doin' what I was told," and that he categorizes "drug runners" and "young women with little children by their sides" vaguely under the following rubric: people we would try to "keep from crossin' the line." Although Carl's precise feelings regarding illegal immigrants cannot be identified, it is clear that whatever they were before going to work one night — complacency towards policy, mild empathy — they dramatically changed when Carl meets a beautiful young woman who instantly captures his heart and imagination.

> Well the first time that I saw her
> She was in the holdin' pen
> Our eyes met and she looked away
> Then she looked back again
> Her hair was black as coal
> Her eyes reminded me of what I'd lost
> She had a young child cryin' in her arms
> And I asked, "Senora, is there anything I can do"

By either blind luck or invisible fate, Carl is reacquainted with this mysterious woman a few hours after their jailhouse introduction. A brief but transformative moment transpires and in the process pushes Carl to commit to neglecting his occupational duties and military-engendered code as easily as tossing out an old hat.

> There's a bar in Tijuana
> Where me and Bobby drink alongside
> The same people we'd sent back the day before
> We met there she said her name was Louisa
> She was from Sonora and had just come north
> We danced and I held her in my arms
> And I knew what I would do
> She said she had some family in Madera County
> If she, her child and her younger brother could just get through

One night, presumably not too long after their romantic dance in the bar, Carl provides Louisa with the crucial assistance she needs to reach Southern California which, although suffering from debilitating poverty and social strife of its own, provides visions of celestial paradise to those without a hope in their own country. They share a kiss in the second before Carl offers her help that is the equivalent of a lifeboat to a drowning child. This assistance requires Carl to make a fateful stand against his Mexican partner, who does not offer one solitary word of protest.

> We were just about on the highway
> When Bobby's jeep come up in the dust on my right
> I pulled over and let my engine run
> And stepped out into his lights
> I felt myself movin'
> Felt my gun restin' 'neath my hand
> We stood there starin' at each other
> As off through the arroyo she ran

Six months after this night of daring disregard for his occupational mission and surprising moral growth, Carl quits, takes "what work he can find," and dedicates himself to tracking down the woman who "reminded him of what he lost." Still captivated by Louisa's beauty and transfixed by her spirit, he "searched the local bars and migrant towns," looking for her with "the black hair falling down." A simple connection with her, made in a state of loneliness and purposelessness, revitalized his spiritual sense of existence and thereby changed his vision for future living. He would no longer be happy merely following orders to smash the hopes of families attempting to cross a border into land that once belonged to their ancestors. He would be motivated and mobilized by the memory of a brief but transformative moment of love. As Springsteen stated in a spoken introduction to the song during The Ghost of Tom Joad Tour, "California was Mexico until 1848. Mexican writer Carlos Fuentes says that the border is more like a scar than a borderline. This is about a young guy trying to figure out where that line really is."

Through Carl's deep and profound wrestling with such a vital and universally applicable question it is not only his voice that changes in tonality and visionary amplification. The inner-city landscape bleakly painted on Springsteen's 1995 folk record begins to etch out a silver lining. The album begins with the title track, which presents listeners with a merciless portrayal of poverty, and continues with the story of an ex-convict struggling to make "straight time" for lack of work and self-worth. The story of a bank robbery gone awry comes on its heels, which leads into "Youngstown" and "Sinaloa Cowboys." The sparse musical arrangements, which lack any semblance of rock 'n' roll and are completely devoid of the excitement of "Jungleland" and "Atlantic City," demand full attention be paid to every syllable of the singer's story — no detail is to be ignored because the details are vital to understanding human drama and socio-economic circumstance. Narrow moral judgment is dependent upon muddy details and black-and-white main ideas, and this brand of judgment, which is almost always characterized by prejudice and self-righteousness, has no role to play in serious deliberation of urban decay and its corrosive influence on individuals and families.

Through the darkness of deindustrialization in Youngstown and the invisible death of a man who with his brother turns from migrant worker to methamphetamine cooker in an effort to stock enough money to pursue a decent life, a tiny, but guiding sliver of light emerges when Carl opens his eyes, mind and heart to the suffering of others and in a small but meaningful way responds with emotional comfort and physical assistance.

His quest to "figure out where that line really is" — the line that divides Mexico from the United States and the line that stands between people with the same needs but different skin shades or social backgrounds — gives him hope for personal redemption; Louisa hope for quality living; and listeners a weathered hope for city revitalization and national reform.

The flimsiness of socially drawn dividing lines, no doubt constructed of sand and not steel, is revealed throughout Springsteen's story-songs of personal probing into the commonalities of the human heart and spirit made under the harshest conditions. Sipowicz's attitude-altering moment with a grieving black child demonstrates the same capacity for change. These stories contain undeniable propensities for resonance that apply to anyone who has evolved into a stronger, more holistic and liberated person due to the pronounced presence of another human being. Acceptance of minorities throughout American history — whether it be blacks, women or gays — has relied upon personal familiarity from the majority. Exploring the emotional and ethical geography of borderlines made of fences, which prevent transit that is essential for understanding, and poisonous rivers that ooze into the water supply, which cause moral constipation and spiritual malnutrition, is long overdue in the world's "last remaining superpower." Especially considering that this very nation has allowed poverty to expand, inequality to rise, and the lives of millions to be rendered meaningless while they live in unconscionable Third World conditions. The most promising sign indicating that this process may be beginning is Barack Obama's ascent to the White House. This dramatic and powerful change provides inspiration to those struggling in inner-cities, and assures them that they have the potential of upward mobility and realization of an improved quality of life. It also demonstrates that white America has progressed to a point of accepting a black man in the ultimate role of leadership.

Despite reasons for hope and seismic signs of progress, intellectual and emotional deliberation on one's internalization of social division cannot solve the problems of inner-city inhabitants. Public policy changes that restore equality to schools, economic opportunities to impoverished neighborhoods, and social assistance to struggling peoples are essential. Without the institutional support that many Americans take for granted, urban decay's victims will have difficulty escaping the mind-numbing and nightmare-inducing despair that inspires self-destructive substance addiction and communally devastating gang activity. This must be remembered constantly as right-wing exploitation artists and well-minded but out-of-touch moderates attempt to use Obama's victory as a bludgeon against policy change intended to eradicate poverty by claiming, as former Secretary of Education Bill Bennett did so eloquently on election night 2008, that this puts an end to "excuses of 'there is so much built in this and that.'"[24] However, individual growth that allows cultivation of compassion, love, service and empathy against the values venerated by the hegemonic market — greed, impregnable self-interest, all-encompassing apathy — can positively impact the lives of suffering people and engender a swelling dissatisfaction with the status quo of city meltdown and the spreading, but perhaps deliberate, malfunction of American social, political and economic institutions.

Without an underground exploration of culturally emboldened borders, the nation will continue to split into two groups traveling down separate roads that only meet at rare, but tragic intersections previously mapped by Diallo and Katrina. One group will continue to expand without hope and without sense of belonging and self-respect, while another will grow more frightful, paranoid and prejudiced in an unblissful state of ignorance.

In between will arise a stronger, more ominous and threatening mutation of "Murder Incorporated" — the term that Springsteen used to denote the machinery, mechanizations and managers of the "compounded violence of life in America" in a song of the same name. The lyrics tell a vague story of one man's attempt to remain secure in the inner-city. He purchases a firearm, and lives in an apartment that "feels like it's just a place to hide." The music possesses overwhelming power — thunderous drums, screaming guitars, top-of-the-lungs shouting vocals — and captures the violent chaos of city life for its less fortunate inhabitants. It contains a bloody ending that the cops report as "just another homicide," as if it has no importance or shock value, but which the singer chalks up to frustration from "livin' with Murder Incorporated."

The song surveys a nightmare waiting to awaken into a tragedy enveloping the entire country. But, when Springsteen describes its meaning, it is clear that the song is not futuristic but sadly and regrettably present-tense: "Gated communities, the loss of freedom, and the mistrust of your own neighbor are the price we pay for writing off generations of young people to poverty, drug dependency, and severely limited hopes and dreams."[25]

Murder Incorporated is a beastly enterprise that has been collectively created by nearly all segments of American society. The urban exploitation by the market and the failure of American politics to rectify the situation are the most obvious culprits. But the majority of citizens who have allowed it to continue without raising protest or complaint are also culpable. Their indifference makes catastrophic conditions and immunity for those that helped create them possible. This is a destination that all Americans have arrived at together. Similarly, the only way to reverse course is to also move together.

Springsteen revamped "Atlantic City" for this tour with the Sessions Band in 2006. The tour contained songs from his folk revival album, *We Shall Overcome: A Tribute to Pete Seeger*, which featured culturally diverse songs that offered solace to the afflicted and oppressed that were often covered by the left-wing troubadour who is honored in the album's title. The tour was about the fun style of musicality that can be created by talented people who are attuned to music history and play portable instruments. It served the higher purpose of invoking the past tools of society's marginalized people who, lacking outlets for production and solidarity in the scornful mainstream, created their own culture with cheap technology but priceless values and vision. Irish immigrants in Appalachia who helped invent country music and Africans in the slave fields who invented American gospel music used music to offer hope, life and sustaining purpose during severely troubled times. Springsteen's invocation of this process was a musically pleasing, politically powerful, and historically timely venture (right in the middle of the Iraq War, and just after Hurricane Katrina).

The Sessions version of "Atlantic City," which often opened shows near the end of the tour, is driven by a banjo, fiddle and ringing organ. However, its most dramatic deviation from its original incarnation is the call and response of "Meet me tonight" between Springsteen and a mini-choir of backup singers that culminates in a "li, li, li, li, li" sing-along. The desperate plea for meeting in a struggling city transforms from a vain pronouncement offered by a character who will most likely fall harder than ever before, into a vision of solidarity, solidified by hope and standing on communal shoulders. Sands won't "turn into gold," but beneficial developments of new possibilities, which rest upon reinforcement of humanistic ideas of love, trust and mutual support, may emerge from the dusty and debased city streets. These developments may open the door for the policy change that is needed to revive America's cities. Nothing short of a full-scale Marshall Plan which addresses joblessness, health care, education, housing and infrastructure will do. Although that seems like a tall order, especially during hard economic times, past American achievements prove it is possible. If the U.S. could defeat Nazi Germany, put a man on the moon, and dominate nearly every major industry at one point or another, surely it can muster the determination, intelligence and finances to rescue its own cities and citizens.

Each time Springsteen presents a chance at redemption it is either preceded or followed by a dose of fatalism (remember "Down here it's just winners and losers and don't get caught on the wrong side of that line") which rightfully warns "Easier said than done."

It is essential to examine what forces are preventing that saying and doing in disparate communities across the country while remembering throughout the entire process that the hopes of disintegrated families, crime-ridden residencies with barred windows, and tragically cynical children rest on the results.

Bearing Springsteen's rightful fatalism in mind, and never forgetting the height of the deck that is stacked against struggling city communities, those concerned with suffering people, and the future of a struggling nation, must forge ahead by maintaining faith in the promise that "everything that dies someday comes back."

Chapter 6

Ain't Nobody Drawin'
Wine from This Blood

The Politics of Religion
and Humanism

S uffering people, whether they are struggling in a politically neglected
and socially castigated neighborhood; deteriorating from a wasting
disease that brings social stigmas; or simply the victim of self-created
conditions, desperately search for meaning which will help them understand
their suffering and possibly alleviate it. Bruce Springsteen's music has com-
plexly and carefully dealt with the search for meaning in the modern world,
and has offered an uncommon directive.

The most typical method used for finding meaning by Americans is the
one handed down by religious leaders. Faith-based approaches to answering life's ultimately unanswerable questions are accepted by more people in
America than in any other developed nation. However, the spirituality and
religiosity that has prevailed throughout the richest nation of the world is
too often shallow, self-absorbed and hollow in its application of spiritual
directives to serve others and reshape the world according to justice. The
altar is too often replaced by an ATM, and the cross is too often concealed
for the comfort of conformists.

America is in great need of a political, moral and, yes, spiritual counter-
balance to the dominant presence of the anti-intellectual, intolerant and
regressive religious right. Since the 1980s, forces of Christian conservatism have not only gained stature and rank in American politics but have
presided over a shifting of political values — from science to superstition,
from constitutional mandates to biblical decrees, and from intelligence and
democratic expansion to hateful exclusivity and silliness. Richard Dawkins,

Sam Harris and Christopher Hitchens have scored big publishing hits with their anti-religious texts, which is indicative of the demand for opposition to theocratic movement. Although many of the new atheism movement's points are brilliantly argued and deserving of consideration in social and legislative circles, it would be unwise and unhealthy to entirely dismiss the capacity for humanitarian and democratic change to emerge from religion. To be sure, religious forces are responsible for a great deal of bigotry, hostility and stupidity. But they also, in their highest moments, give spiritual subscribers a means of adopting a pledge of cultural resistance to the dominant order of individually minded materialism. Spiritual forms of living have been historically reliable for encouraging people to be dedicated to justice and devoted to democracy engineered by love and charitable hope. They have often preached and practiced this in isolation, as the culture turned more money obsessed and the political process became more oligarchic. A Christian left in America, accompanied by practitioners of other faiths acting in unity, could empower currently complacent citizens into action on the collective's behalf and reintroduce a nation in which the prosperity gospel has been destroyed by financial meltdown to the social gospel.

The point that Dawkins and Hitchens argue most convincingly in their polemics is the need for religious influence to be removed from the political system of the United States, which is supposed to be constitutionally protected from the dictates of the church. John F. Kennedy wrestled with this during his presidential campaign, which represents a unique moment in history. In an attempt to quell anti-Catholic hatred that poisoned the atmosphere of his time, he gave an address to the Houston Ministerial Association in 1960 that contains words which, if any serious contemporary candidate used, would land him in a scandal threatening to his future career:

> I would not . . . look with favor upon those who would work to subvert Article VI of the Constitution by requiring a religious test, even by indirection. For if they disagree with that safeguard, they should be openly working to repeal it . . . Whatever issue may come before me as President . . . I will make my decision in accordance with these views, in accordance with what my conscience tells me to be in the national interest, and without regard to outside religious pressure or dictates.[1]

The religious test that Kennedy refers to has been applied in several presidential elections since the contest he won, by a radicalized and emboldened constituency which is assisted by a media that bizarrely does its bidding.

Much of that constituency can be found in the great numbers of bright-eyed people shuffling into the stale doors of megachurches because their lives have suddenly become devoid of meaning and direction as civic traditions are weakened, political institutions become less accessible, and financial stability is threatened. Progressive advocates of equality must not only be prepared to offer them a form of politics that addresses their suffering and anxiety but also present a prophetic spirituality that sustains them through ongoing struggles and enlivens their dormant sense of community and compassion. Bruce Springsteen's music has often demonstrated how the love, justice and charity ethic not only provides edification to practicing individuals but also serves as a vital, humanizing check and balance of a political system dominated by unaccountable elites.

On personal matters of faith, he has taken a more conflicted approach, showing how one can acknowledge the sacred and the mysterious but still find happiness without solely leaning on the promises and platforms of organized religion. Ultimately, a similar national and communal approach may heal many of America's ills by revealing the needlessness of much of the conflict that inhibits political and personal progress in America while showing exactly where polarization and strife are desperately called for. Once people begin to make personal progress — finding fulfillment in their own lives and happiness in their own communities — beneficial public policy solutions to national problems will be granted a window of opportunity for entrance. At that point they are also more likely to embrace religious traditions that resist the dominant order, and instead of creating division, encourage ecumenical love, solidarity and unity in service to a common good.

DROP THE NEEDLE AND PRAY: SPRINGSTEEN'S SECULAR SPIRITUALITY AND HUMANISTIC HAPPINESS

Bruce Springsteen makes no secret that he was raised Catholic, and often relies on the language of Roman Catholicism to artistically communicate his spiritual and political vision. Its poetic metaphors and rich symbolism provide great opportunity for expressing personal points about human issues on a fertile and commonly explored spiritual geography. However, this does not make him a Christian singer. He professed personal secularism as early as 1978 and as recently as 2005. But this has not stopped many fans, critics and Christian media members from attempting to claim Springsteen as their own. Priest and columnist Andrew Greeley wrote a long missive for the Catholic publication *America* in which he explained the virtues of Springsteen's supposed Catholic message, and *Christianity Today* has made a habit of reviewing his albums as testimonials of a devoted faith. Greeley correctly identifies commonalities between Springsteen and the communitarian spirit of Catholicism but reaches too far when attempting to co-opt the singer for the Catholic Church. *Christianity Today*'s appropriation requires both a stretch of the imagination and leap of faith to accept because a close listening to Springsteen's music reveals a grappling with issues of faith and dogmas of religiosity that often leads to an advocacy of spiritual, but also humanistic, modes of achieving happiness, peace, comfort and stability.

This process of self-discovery and spiritual suggestion has been emphasized by Springsteen through his use of theological language to describe humanistic activity and fulfillment. By cleverly and creatively flipping the script of conventional thought, Springsteen uses sacred terminology to express the importance and meaning in the secular. This shrewd application of language demonstrates that what people often search for in tabernacles and temples claiming contact with an outer world can be found in the terrestrial. Transmitting that message in the art form of music requires the creation of drama and theater, as music speaks first to the emotions and second to the intellect. Considering that religion is drama, and drama is religion, evoking Christian symbols and metaphors which come out of a tradition most familiar to Springsteen's primarily Western audience successfully wraps his subversive message in a narrative that speaks to a shared emotional core.

Examples of Springsteen songs that embody this approach to music and life abound. The finest among them may be the uplifting and committed rocker from *Magic* called "I'll Work for Your Love." Melodically there is something pure and innocent about the song. Its piano opening, set against a limited musical backdrop, reminds one of *Born to Run*'s romanticism as it serves as an invitation for the rest of the song, just as Springsteen said the tunes from his 1975 masterpiece all featured such "invitations." The beauty of the piano invitation is appropriate for the song's emotionally pure and lovingly unwavering lyrics which like most declarations of love walk the line between poetry and naïveté. The invitation ends with a crashing declarative drum which precedes Springsteen's jubilant, unbreakable vocal that accentuates the character's commitment to his much lusted-after and dreamed-of barmaid. It is the kind of melody that creates a mood. Joy, hope and surrender to the high that follows love's induced rush of dopamine attacks the listener, just as it surrounds the character who is teetering on ecstasy from simply being in his would-be lover's presence. He confesses the depth of his feelings, perhaps just internally in mental preparation for the real thing, but it is a confession nonetheless. It is a kind of secular prayer without a specific address, voiced to assist him in finding his emotions, willingness to commit and claim of identity.

> Pour me a drink Theresa
> In one of those glasses you dust off

> And I'll watch the bones in your back
> Like the Stations of the Cross

The tone and condition of the character's plea is made abundantly clear from the opening lines, sung in that certain, deliberate and focused tone by Springsteen. He views Theresa with the same reverence, adulation and faith that congregants are commanded to view God and, as she turns, he concentrates on sacred ground — her flesh — which, like the ground that Jesus is said to have walked on during his bloody trip to Calvary, symbolizes the sacrifice he is ready to make for her. He continues his plea, not in desperation or despair, but in total confidence. Perhaps not confidence that Theresa will reciprocate his interest and devotion, but confidence in the absoluteness of his commitment and purity of his love that even a denial cannot shake.

> 'Round your hair the sun lifts a halo
> At your lips a crown of thorns
> Whatever other deal's goin' down
> To this one I'm sworn

The acknowledgment of his deistic, angelic way of viewing her is dead on with the vision of a sun-drawn halo around her head. Just as clear is his sympathy for the suffering, pain and tribulation she has endured under unspoken conditions. The crown of thorns at her lips symbolizes her struggle with trauma deriving from an external source — to which the character has an antidote: His undying, unconditional, and uncompromising service.

> I'll work for your love, dear
> I'll work for your love
> What others may want for free
> I'll work for your love

Clearly vesting her love with salvific powers, he commits to a life of service, simply called "work." Much like the tradition of the Roman Church, reward does not come after mere proclamation of faith; the bargain requires "good works" made in the spirit of love, generosity and self-sacrifice. As Augustine explained in *A Treatise on Faith and Good Will*:

> Unintelligent persons, however, with regard to the apostle's statement: "We conclude that a man is justified by faith without the works of the law," [*Romans 3:28*] have thought him to mean that faith suffices to a man, even if he lead a bad life, and has no good works. Impossible is it that such a character should be deemed "a vessel of election" by the apostle, who, after

declaring that "in Christ Jesus neither circumcision availeth anything, nor
uncircumcision," *[Galatians 5:6]* adds at once, "but faith which worketh
by love." It is such faith which severs God's faithful from unclean demons,
— for even these "believe and tremble," *[James 2:19]* as the Apostle James
says; but they do not do well. Therefore they possess not the faith by which
the just man lives, — the faith which works by love in such wise, that God
recompenses it according to its works with eternal life. But inasmuch as
we have even our good works from God, from whom likewise comes our
faith and our love, therefore the self same great teacher of the Gentiles
[apostle Paul] has designated "eternal life" itself as His gracious "gift."
[Romans 6:23][2]

In this passage, as well as several others, Augustine implores the faithful
to bolster their faith which "worketh by love." Acting on knowledge not
had by any other human in his time nor after, he amazingly assures the
reader that this combination will guarantee him "eternal life." There is no
mention of earthly happiness — such a concept would be difficult to find
in the writing of Augustine, Aquinas or other theologians of the time. Most
of them promised a heavenly reward for terrestrial torment and preached
the masochistic hard line that suffering was to be received as a blessing, as
it makes one closer to God. However, there is a great beauty found in their
philosophy and one can easily see its influence on Springsteen, regardless of
his questionable level of devotion to Catholicism. Augustine, Aquinas and
most especially St. Francis of Assisi strongly emphasized that Catholics be
guided by love, selflessness and sacrifice in a commitment to community.
They viewed the world as fundamentally absurd, and therefore rejected the
pursuit of happiness, but insisted that meaning could be found through love
and service to others.

The character in "I'll Work for Your Love" is not only searching for meaning through service to Theresa but also counting on earthly happiness once
he receives her love. He does not expect it to come free, nor should he, but
he does expect it to come while he is breathing. The promise is emphasized
later in the song when he sings, "The pages of Revelation / Lie open in
your empty eyes of blue / I watch you slip that comb through your hair and
this I promise you," before declaring his intentions with another chorus.
Revelation is intended to be read as a prophetic template of the second coming of Christ, which will precede ascension into paradise. For this straggler
sitting on a worn-down bar stool staring at an object of human beauty, the
better world waits in her arms.

Each chorus is followed by a sweeping riff of a violin or harmonica which
captures the character's existential shift. Religion promises transcendence to
the devoted worshipper and claims to have a monopoly on it, but as anyone

who has been in love can relate, this man is elated and elevated by merely having Theresa in his visual periphery. Following the harmonica, a bridge leads into a final verse where the music falls down to make a clear path for the signer's still swaggeringly stable voice. His final appraisal of the situation and proposal takes shape:

Your tears, they fill the rosary
At your feet, my temple of bones
Here in this perdition we go on and on

Now our city of peace has crumbled
Our book of faith's been tossed
And I'm just out here searchin'
For my own piece of the cross

The late afternoon sun fills the room
With the mist of the garden before the fall
I watch your hands smooth the front of your blouse and seven drops of
    blood fall

Once again Theresa's pain is referenced, this time in the form of tears, and she is assured that she is not alone. They both share a state of perdition — spiritual ruin, devastation and destruction. Their "city of peace," presumably their communal sense of belonging and spiritual home, "has crumbled" and he informs her that he is there to find his own "piece of the cross" — that which gives him hope for a better future, purpose for the present and meaning for the past.

The last verse shows a maturity of vision which up until this point has been unexpressed. The barroom resembles the "garden before the fall" and he witnesses "seven drops of blood fall" from her fingertips. These ominous signs of imperfection and possible disappointment linger in the patron's perception of Theresa and a future life together. But he commits anyway. He suffers through it with an intelligent expectation of failure. He is content with humanistic love and relationships, even if they are flawed and destined for setbacks, error and periodic descent. To achieve happiness he does not require the perfection promised by the sellers of the supernatural. He needs only the redemptive love of the flesh, which offers emotional comfort, spiritual solidarity and peaceful sanctuary in a crumbling city. The supernatural articulation of this vow accentuates the mystery that dominates human love and emotion, which may very well be the property of the sacred. Theresa's admirer has embraced the mystery and has invested his labor, energy and hope in it, creating a perfect example of faith.

The last two lines of the chorus are repeated with power, possession and purpose: "What others may want for free, I'll work for your . . . / What others may want for free, I'll work for your . . ." until one last promise is made, the last "love" held before the song comes to a crashing halt when all one can hear is the triumphant final ring of an organ — the sound of spiritual energy and redemptive joy.

Throughout this underrated gem, the sanctification of the flesh reoccurs: "Pour me a drink Theresa / In one of those glasses you dust off," "I watch you slip that comb through your hair," "I watch your hands smooth the front of your blouse." These common, seemingly mundane activities are paramount to the character's faith in humanly earned and independently induced happiness. Simple acts of bodily movement and physical contact foreshadow delights of transcendental pleasure and unmatchable delight: Real acts of human satisfaction, connectivity and joy that have been thoroughly and uniformly despised and preached against by organized religion, perhaps because they act as unwanted and unbeatable competition.

Throughout his career Springsteen has drawn battle lines between sex and religion, where the pleasures of the flesh always emerge victorious. Most often the tactic used to mobilize forces in the listener's mind is similar to that of "I'll Work for Your Love." In "Leap of Faith," he joyously sings, "Your legs were heaven your breasts were the altar / Your body was the holy land," directly assigning her skin sacred value. One of Springsteen's best songs to go largely unnoticed is a treasure from *Devils & Dust*, titled "Maria's Bed." The story of a drifter's lifestyle is described by a man whose only comfort and solitary saving grace is the sexual companionship of a generous woman named Maria. He obsesses over her while he trucks down the road in ecstatic anticipation of when their hands will fasten, lips will touch, and bodies will blend into one. Although the song is rich on metaphor, the conflict between earthly sustenance and vague notions of heavenly reward is described more directly than in any other Springsteen song: "Holy man said 'hold on brother there's a light up ahead.' / Ain't nothin' like the light that shines on me in Maria's bed."

With that philosophically radical rejection of the preacher's proposal, the character actually places his loyalty in the world of the flesh, and is content "living in the light of Maria's bed." The song's gospel-flavored backup vocals, swinging fiddles and triumphantly hard driving guitar and drum-engine beat celebrates this man's joy and in doing so endorses his decision to focus his energy and devotion on physical love and human companionship. The meaning in his life is to be found through exclusively humanist activity, and throughout his onerous and unsatisfying work, and his otherwise lonely existence, that meaning is what ultimately saves him. Confidence and trust in that meaning is obtained after a brief flirtation with religiosity: "I was burned by the angels, sold wings of lead / Then I fell in the roses and sweet salvation of Maria's bed." This all occurs after the character has described a similar perdition to the patron in "I'll Work for Your Love," one where he was "out of luck" and "left for dead." "Maria's Bed" can be interpreted as the transformation that may occur for that patron should Theresa reciprocate his desires in "I'll Work for Your Love." Suffering men find solace in the loving generosity and hospitality of a good woman. While this may not be an original theme — it has provided fodder for centuries of literature and decades of film — it strikes a truthful and resonant note when juxtaposed with the selling points of religion. It also returns one to the question of how suffering people search for meaning.

As people's suffering increases, their search for meaning becomes more obstructed, difficult and seemingly futile. In America, as the financial situation has greatly worsened for working people, civic traditions have weakened, public institutions have wallowed in failure and unaccountability, and catastrophic events like the September 11 attacks, the carnage of the Iraq War and Hurricane Katrina have devastated people's faith in American democracy and each other, citizens have increasingly turned their faces upward, desperately hoping to find answers in the sky while missing the opportunities planted at ground level. They have not only counted on the easy answers of religion to put to rest their rightful confusion and anger over the disappointments of modern life but have also gravitated towards pseudo philosophy and pop psychology, which preaches mindless narcissism and attempts to provide excuses for the negligence of responsibility. Best sellers like *The Secret* inform readers that their thoughts control their universe and are thereby responsible for their station in life, as well as the lot of others. There is no need to worry about the poor or cast the slightest concern in the direction of public affairs because everyone is responsible for their own thoughts and are therefore responsible for their own bliss or misery, without exception.

While positive thinking is practical advice for anyone, and no one has ever benefited from drowning in pessimism and negativity, the secret of *The Secret* is incredibly shallow and, much like many religious edicts, allows people to alleviate themselves of the responsibility (thoughts can easily change, behavior cannot) for not only their own happiness but also the shared responsibility of shaping their society in a democracy where they are endowed with the freedom to either approve or disapprove of the actions taken by power.

Political questions are essential to the search for meaning from suffering people, as are ones of personal fulfillment. Once one is willing to work for personal fulfillment by not settling for easy prescriptions doled out by a pastor or simple-minded self-help author, one can begin to maturely address the public policy component of their suffering or the struggles of others. Springsteen's music written in the aftermath of 9/11, which deals with loss, grief and crushing pain, is applicable to this process in crucial ways. He acknowledges the importance of religion to suffering people, and even directly summons it on the album's closing track, "My City of Ruins." But up until that point Springsteen ties meaning and hope to secular points of human love and activity, thereby artistically showing what the black church has projected for centuries. Spirituality can be obtained through a variety of important non-religious sources but when it is to be found in the church it must be connected with some earthly struggle exigent to the supernatural narrative. The fight for freedom, respect and dignity in black communities was symbolically and morally connected with Moses leading escaped Israelite slaves to the Promised Land. Through fear, pain and diminished hopes and dreams this story, and others like it, gave them promise for a better future. On September 11, all Americans felt vulnerable and afraid, and were engulfed by sadness after witnessing people jump out of skyscrapers to escape an even more grisly death in a blazing inferno; planes full of people crash into buildings; and heartbreakingly delusional family members holding up pictures of their loved ones and pleading for those who may have seen them to immediately inform the proper authorities. Springsteen sorts through this deluge of heartache, anger and bitterness throughout *The Rising* — released less than a year after the attacks — by focusing on the timeless themes that were dramatized on that day: loss, grief, family and faith.

On nearly every song on *The Rising* Springsteen places himself in the position of a grieving and ailing person — someone whose life has been torn apart by an unspeakable tragedy. The character in "Empty Sky" looks up to see not only the emptiness where those colossal buildings once stood but also the void left by his deceased wife. "Into the Fire" pays tribute to the heroism of firefighters who sacrificed their lives to save others through the voice of a grieving widow, and "You're Missing" places the listener in the bewildered, depressed and angry condition of a father who is unsure how to answer his children's questions about their lost mother. These trauma narratives, set against a repetitive melody which utilizes piano and violin to almost funeral-parlor effect ("You're Missing"), delta blues-inflected wailing ("Into the Fire") or a hip-hop beat with sparse instrumentation similar to "Streets of Philadelphia" ("Empty Sky") remind listeners of the simple internal devastation wrought in the hearts and minds of people, which makes for thousands of individually psychic ground zeroes. Things begin to take a more complex and hopeful turn when Springsteen examines just how people move forward after being nearly destroyed by such a staggering attack on their happiness, stability and consciousness.

"Mary's Place" is the most familiar-sounding track on *The Rising*. If one did not know any better, one could easily believe that it was some lost out-take from the early 1970s, with its soulful *Asbury Park* sound completed by a choir of backup singers, rhythmic accentuation from a full horn section and black gospel-influenced vocal styling. The lyrics provide an interesting account of a grieving person's attempt to find peace and comfort by perusing a smorgasbord of religious doctrinal systems and narratives. Despite literally "pulling all the faith I can see" in an arbitrary and disloyal fashion, he cannot escape what continues to haunt him.

> I got seven pictures of Buddha
> The prophet's on my tongue
> Eleven angels of mercy
> Sighin' over that black hole in the sun
> My heart's dark but it's risin'
> I'm pullin' all the faith I can see
> From that black hole on the horizon
> I hear your voice calling me

The voice calling after him may not only be reminding him of the greatness, beauty and love that he has lost as she faded away into the dark but also how best to overcome his psychological torment and existential anguish. The "angels of mercy" and "the prophet," who both supposedly hover overhead, are not solely required for comfort and solace. The path upward may be obstructed but even so there is no need to despair. The obstacle to some metaphysical delight, along with its ominous characteristic, can be welcomed as long as one makes a righteous substitute.

> Let it rain, let it rain, let it rain
> Let it rain, let it rain, let it rain, let it rain
> Meet me at Mary's place, we're gonna have a party
> Meet me at Mary's place, we're gonna have a party
> Tell me how do we get this thing started
> Meet me at Mary's place

The rain, which falls from the home of the prophet and the angel, may otherwise appear troubling and defeating. However, for this bereaved wanderer it is not immobilizing — quite the opposite. He gets his joy, strength and spiritually sustaining energies started in the company of others — the friends and family he loves — and surrounded by the human-created sources of pleasure and liberation which have given him renewal for a lifetime. The picture is drawn clearly in the second verse.

Familiar faces around me
Laughter fills the air
Your loving grace surrounds me
Everybody's here
Furniture's out on the front porch
Music's up loud
I dream of you in my arms
I lose myself in the crowd

Let it rain, let it rain, let it rain
Let it rain, let it rain, let it rain, let it rain
Meet me at Mary's place, we're gonna have a party
Meet me at Mary's place, we're gonna have a party
Tell me how do you live broken-hearted
Meet me at Mary's place

Familiar faces, the sound of laughter and the permanently renewable resource of music gives this lost soul a temporary sanctuary. Back in the environment of friendship, solidarity and joy he is surrounded by his lost companion's "loving grace" but is unable to free himself from the unshakable dream of her presence in his arms. In an attempt to do so he loses himself in the crowd. The only attempts at living a spiritual life worth the time and energy are those that take the individual outside of himself and connect him with the world surrounding him, other human beings and an overpowering feeling of mutual humanity. The grieving widower finds this at Mary's place in the middle of a party, beaming with communal energy, joyful recreation and a collective temperament that eschews martyrdom, servility to suffering and angst. He answers the critical questions — "how do you live broken-hearted?," how do you endure through tragedy and trauma and continue to find reason to struggle and reason to fight? — with a simple declaration universally understood by those who in their lowest moments have found ascension only in the company and comfort of others: "meet me at Mary's place."

Even within this uplifting sanctuary, the problem of loss lingers like a cloud of smoke hanging over the air and it returns to focus after a wild musical break full of horn solos and ebullient choir repetition of that simple declaration. There is no melodic contradiction to the lyrical narrative in "Mary's Place." This is the kind of song one would expect to hear at a house party and it would provoke dancing, singing and erratic outbursts of energy. Then the song instantly breaks down, leaving only the tapping of a cymbal and a light horn riff to accompany the singer. In live versions Springsteen would sing in his best Smoky Robinson impression "I been missin' you," while Patti Scialfa, Steven Van Zandt and Nils Lofgren would croon the same phrase in the background. Eventually, the singer begins to whisper the third verse in a timid, embattled and much less joyful voice before breaking free and increasing the volume with the line "Seven days, seven candles." From that point on the voice grows more confident, jubilant and triumphant — as if he is forcing his way through the dark, finding his way over the mountain of regret and defeat, and gaining strength and speed with each step. What finally provides him with the energy, mobility and connectivity he has been longing for is as unusual as it is inspirational.

> I got a picture of you in my locket
> I keep it close to my heart
> A light shining in my breast
> Leading me through the dark
> Seven days, seven candles
> In my window light your way
> Your favorite record's on the turntable
> I drop the needle and pray (Turn it up)
> Band's countin' out midnight (Turn it up)
> Floor's rumblin' loud (Turn it up)
> Singer's callin' up daylight (Turn it up)
> And waitin' for that shout from the crowd (Turn it up)
> Waitin' for that shout from the crowd (Turn it up)
> Waitin' for that shout from the crowd (Turn it up)
> Waitin' for that shout from the crowd (Turn it up)
> Waitin' for that shout from the crowd (Turn it up)
> Waitin' for that shout from the crowd (Turn it up)
>
> Turn it up, turn it up, turn it up
> Turn it up, turn it up, turn it up, turn it up
>
> Meet me at Mary's place, we're gonna have a party
> Meet me at Mary's place, we're gonna have a party
> Tell me how do we get this thing started
> Meet me at Mary's place

After all of his evocations of the supernatural and theological — angels, prophets, Buddha — it is not until he reaches for the shelf and puts on his loved one's favorite record that he begins to feel hope and sense transference outside of himself and onto her level. With the dropping of the needle and the opening chords of her most beloved song — one they most likely danced, made love and sang to on many nights — he finally is influenced to pray. He may be directing his prayer to his perception of God, possibly to her, or it may not have a specific addressee. It may be the kind of prayer that philosopher Jacques Derrida held in high regard; one that is an absolute "secret act," but involves "common ritual" and "coded gestures." It is fundamentally "childish" because it is dependent upon a suspension of belief and certainty. Contrarily, it also requires enough skepticism for the prayerful to acknowledge that the "object of prayer is indeterminable."[3] Considering the prayer is expressed in a search for connection with the dead, it easily falls into Derrida's categorization of prayer. Belief has obviously been suspended and the object is by definition indeterminable because one can hardly be sure that the dead receive the message and one is doubtful of their ability to be responsive. The "common ritual" and "coded gesture" of the prayer is characterized by the call and response between the singer, backup singers and audience (when performed live) while the music intensifies, becomes louder and returns to its danceable beat. The response of "Turn it up" to a variety of descriptions and proclamations by the singer underscores the importance of music to the life and vitality of the grieving character, showcases its redemptive power and is reminiscent of the call-and-response prayers which are so often meditatively read throughout Catholic churches every Sunday. Repetition is essential to this prayer's strength because with each shout of "Turn it up" the music becomes stronger and the singer's voice begins to triumph with more power. The repeating of that simple command hastens the removal of one from oneself by directing all energy and concentration onto the external source of hope, love and joy in such a communally expressed way, both in a concert and in the song's narrative, that redemption and ascension above grief can be obtained. These are not entirely supernatural edicts that provide stability and hope to the bereaved widower. These are human-created, human-induced and humanly shared concepts: friendship, community, compassion and music. They come through because they are dependably present — even when those most loved and longed for are forever absent.

The excruciatingly painful absence of loved ones is addressed by organized religion through varying conceptual narratives of an afterlife. Eastern thought has the tendency of believing in reincarnation — a system of cosmic justice which punishes or rewards an individual's behavior with a fair placement in a next life. For instance, the soul of a mercenary may return in the bodily form of an abused dog while the soul of a self-sacrificing and charitable organizer may reside in a king or eventually reach nirvana — a state of earned bliss. Western religions — namely Christianity and Islam (Judaism places almost no focus on questions of life after death) — believe in an afterlife which contains two physical settings: Heaven and Hell. Rather than rewarding behavior, these monotheisms reward intellectual obedience, unwavering belief and servility to the divine ruler. Under Christianity, believers ascend to Heaven where they will live out eternity in a celestial paradise free of pain, sadness and disappointment. They will also reunite with deceased family and friends. Non-believers, charged with crimes of free thought and independently minded belief, will be punished with eternal torture, torment, beating and burning in the fiery pits of Hell. The same is true of Islam, only under their equally wicked version of the tale only Muslims will be rewarded with posthumous joy and everyone else, including Christians, will be permanently banished to the torturous and demonic dungeon.

Although this is not news to anyone remotely connected with Western culture and, oddly enough, many Christians do not subscribe to this narrowly totalitarian version of the afterlife, it does present an interesting context for another Bruce Springsteen song from *The Rising* — one in which the very name evokes visions of post-death living: "Paradise." Coming in the aftermath of 9/11, the song plants itself in the middle of a time period that hosted an interesting but contradictory discussion of afterlife ideas. The sickening tactic of suicide bombing, which resulted in the deaths of thousands of Americans, led many to become curious about this horrific and murderous martyrdom that characterized radical Islam. All of the hijackers were convinced that they were committing heroic acts for which they would be thanked by God with Heaven, everlasting joy and a high supply of prone virgins. This theological adulation of violence elicited widespread fear of Muslims and deflection of policy inquiries that put assumed U.S. moral immunity and superiority in question. Simultaneously occurring with rightful and understandable denunciations and repudiations of extreme Islamic ideas of afterlife was the celebration of the Christian concept. Sympathy for the viciously murdered victim's family members, along with a firm standing in the Christian tradition, prompted an outpouring of church services and media forums in which pastors and politicians assured everyone that following their unimaginably gruesome and unfair deaths the passengers of the hijacked airplanes, workers in the Twin Towers and Pentagon employees rose into Heaven where they were greeted by their previously deceased family members, a plethora of pleasures and a loving God. Billy Graham went so far as to say that "many" of the dead victims were "happier than they've ever been" and if they were "given the choice to come back, they wouldn't."[4] One cannot help but observe that Graham's promise is divisive, exclusionary and bigoted. The implication of his phrasing — "many of the victims . . ." — is clear. Those who died at the hands of terrorists on 9/11 who were not Christian, no matter how charitable, caring and compassionate, would be transported directly to Hell. Graham's promise, which was undoubtedly echoed by countless preachers during the weeks after 9/11, also bizarrely attempts to relieve Christians of the human duties to be hurt, angered and grief-stricken by the terrorist atrocity. If the victims are genuinely "happier than they've ever been," why not thank Bin Laden for improving the lives of thousands of people?

This question is morally idiotic and intellectually absurd on its face but entirely logical after hearing Graham's statement on the afterlife. The overall conflict over which visions of post-death living are good and which are evil also presents some monumentally difficult political realizations. First and foremost, as noble and necessary as the separation of church and state is, it may be impossible to uphold as long as there are aggressive theocrats with apocalyptic hopes in our presence. The belief that one must murder infidels for heavenly assumption, along with the less deadly belief, because of its passivity, that Jesus Christ will soon return to Earth to smite all non-believers while his meek worshippers are beamed into heaven, are by no measure apolitical. The Islamic hope for theocracy, with mullahs in Iran waiting for the second coming of their clerical leader, and promise of reward for terrorism has influenced global politics in an assortment of destructive ways, while Christian Armageddon preachers have a damaging influence over U.S. policy towards Israel. While these fatalistic "holy" men proctor for position in their respective country's politics, citizens should remember that it is best to proceed with extreme caution when dealing with people who look forward to the end of the world. These visions of the apocalypse, and in many cases the more benign idea of an afterlife, can often be at best distractive from more important earthly concerns to be addressed in the right now and at worst, as demonstrated by the egregious example of 9/11, deadly, destructive and disastrous.

In "Paradise," Springsteen brilliantly and emotively reveals how these visions come with a cost for the individual in moments of personal pain, but in such a way that can be projected on to societies and nations determining how to politically and socially progress without the hindrance of regressive religious edicts. He manages to accomplish this impressive feat not only with his psychologically and philosophically astute lyrics but also with an evocative melody which captures the devastating catastrophe of loss, along with the tragic suffering and despair that so often accompany it.

The song begins with a dull hum, which quietly fades into the background as the song progresses. It is the repeating sound of some machine left barely functional after a blast. A sparsely arranged and lightly played acoustic guitar provides fills over a sweepingly sad synthesizer riff. The melody remains so soft and distant that once the singer begins to paint a grisly scene, the listener is absolutely compelled to hang on every word of this haunting tale.

> Where the river runs to black
> I take the schoolbooks from your pack

> Plastics, wire and your kiss
> The breath of eternity on your lips
>
> In the crowded marketplace
> I drift from face to face
> I hold my breath and close my eyes
> I hold my breath and close my eyes
> And I wait for paradise
> And I wait for paradise

The music has a spooky element to it which underscores the basic creepiness of the suicide bomber. This terrorist, committed to his martyrdom and the deaths of innocent people, makes a final farewell to his child and enters a crowded marketplace. After taking a cold survey of his unknowing victims, he closes his eyes and eagerly awaits his reward. Because the song's narrative at this point — sung by an emotionally neutral Springsteen as if he himself is recounting the events with an otherworldly detachment — exists only within the head of the bomber, the scene ends as he "waits for paradise." The listener's imagination, along with memories of terrorist aftermath seen on the news, is given free will to explore the carnage of this heinous and hideous act of cruelty. "Paradise" also resists the tempting urge to moralize. Anyone with the basic human instinct for reciprocal ethics understands why the condemnation of suicide bombing should be without limit and they are given the perfect illustration in the next verse.

> The Virginia hills have gone to brown
> Another day, another sun goin' down
> I visit you in another dream
> I visit you in another dream
>
> I reach and feel your hair
> Your smell lingers in the air
> I brush your cheek with my fingertips
> I taste the void upon your lips
> And I wait for paradise
> And I wait for paradise

The song suddenly transports the listeners overseas to the widow of a man presumably killed in the Pentagon. The days begin to fall into one long depressing moment for her as her pain engulfs her emotional and waking life. Her only comfort comes in a fleeting and always disappointing dream where she sees her lost lover and attempts to make physical contact but in the end is left only with a dead and empty "void" upon his lips. The psychic depression and existential devastation inflicted upon this woman by terrorism is held in direct contrast to the first verse, which presents the story from the angle of victimizer rather than victim. The only thing they share in common is a hope for and vision of an afterlife where they will find an all-curing sedative for their earthly pain. They both "wait for paradise," neglecting the opportunities for life, vitality and mobility that may exist in their immediate grasp. She chooses to live only in dreams of sleep and death, while he accepts membership in a despicable cult of homicide. As different as their decisions may be, and while one character may be sympathetic and another contemptible, they do share a wish for and belief in life after death. The first verse examined the final moments of one who is willing to not only kill others but kill himself in the process to get to paradise. The song continues by taking a surprising turn where the grieving widow wrestles with thoughts of her own suicide. She never entertains the idea of killing others and thereby expanding her misery, but the promise of instant ascension into an afterlife where she will be reunited with the one she lost is tempting.

> I search for you on the other side
> Where the river runs clean and wide
> Up to my heart the waters rise
> Up to my heart the waters rise
>
> I sink 'neath the river cool and clear
> Drifting down I disappear
> I see you on the other side
> I search for the peace in your eyes
> But they're as empty as paradise
> They're as empty as paradise
>
> I break above the waves
> I feel the sun upon my face

The music continues to float along with an atmospheric lingering, noticeable in the background but somehow remaining out of reach, symbolically relating the notion of an afterlife. When the widow, in a moment of trauma and desperation, attempts to reach it through intentional drowning, the music remains distant. She searches for the lost, looks for the peace in his eyes that she has been told arrives with death but finds only emptiness and concludes that this notion of paradise must too be empty, meaningless and sterile. It does not provide the comfort, hope and joy for which she was hoping nor does it give the essential meaningfulness that a happy life depends upon. The music remains cold, inaccessible and without lift until that declaration of life is made. She breaks above the waves and for the first time can feel something real and dependable — the heat coming from the sun. The natural world provides her with vital connection to her surroundings and finally reaffirms her existence in the present. She is no longer hopelessly kissing at a void or wishing for death. She has chosen life, and after the listener is informed of that choice, the overpowering notes of an electric guitar overwhelm the light percussion, synthesizer and acoustic guitar that barely kept the song afloat. Soon after a chorus of backup singers provide a fill and as the widow, by her own independent volition, is finally connected with life, the listener is given musical elevation.

Springsteen creatively captures the important message that individuals and nations must stop relying on vague promises of happiness and peace in an afterlife and must begin doing the hard work of making it exist in the present tense — regardless of their religious beliefs. Human concerns in the human world require everyone's undivided attention and unbreakable concentration — while the spirit world will be responsible for its own work. This means that individuals must awaken, break above the waves of sorrow and seek out their own earthly meanings. Public affairs must be guided by the best tools of humanity — reason, logic and free inquiry — while being strengthened upon a bedrock of solidarity, compassion and emotional maturity.

Men and women must labor, fight and struggle to cultivate their own virtue and ensure equally virtuous communities. If they choose to incorporate religious comforts into humanist-derived sources of meaning, joy and pleasure they may but the sole reliance on theological promises and doctrinal systems leads to personal darkness, unnecessarily divisive social treatment of the other, and a politics unable to move forward into the light of progression, fairness and reasoned change. Clearly, as Springsteen has depicted while using the unimaginable pain of the bereaved following 9/11 as a muse, a better way is possible.

SPRINGSTEEN SAYS: BRUCE SPRINGSTEEN THE CONFUCIAN

Listeners who equate Springsteen's theological language with devout Catholicism are clearly shortsighted. However, even though Springsteen takes a humanistic approach to issues of love, happiness and meaning it would also be inaccurate to claim that the rock singer's vision is entirely secular. He endows sacredness within humanity, as long as it is acting in accordance with some greater community guided by moral conviction and spiritual maturity. Through narrative form he constantly depicts men and women struggling and striving past many obstacles and through many setbacks to reach an ultimate, but earthly, setting which is not so much a destination but a spiritual, moral and existential condition. The music of Bruce Springsteen consistently affirms the holy dignity of humanity and makes it clear that the expression and cultivation of that dignity is not dependent upon absolute possession of the individual, independent of others, as some part of the divine, as preached by megachurch Christianity. It is reliant upon a ceremonial dedication of enlistment and improvement of a community. It also acknowledges the sacred mysteries that emerge in moments of love and loss and that remain incomprehensible to even the finest minds.

In these respects, and several others, Springsteen finds a most surprising and unpredictable ally and companion. Not Jesus or Socrates — not even a thinker of Western origin. Bruce Springsteen's depiction of man's purpose, ability to cultivate virtue and achieve happiness, and role in a larger society finds most parity with the Chinese philosopher and sage Confucius.

Confucius rarely spoke of divinity as something independent of humanity and on the few citable occasions that he did it was in request or acknowledgment as a source of virtue, claiming it derived from Heaven. However, even under those assumptions, the role of Heaven was unclear and unelaborated under Confucius's teaching. He was not particularly interested in the possibilities of supernatural speculation, aside from this vague notion of virtue. Similarly, in one of the few songs of Springsteen's that overtly and directly calls upon God the prayer is not for world peace, personal happiness or societal stability. Instead, it is merely a request to be assisted in the struggle to attain virtue. "My City of Ruins," one of Springsteen's best from *The Rising*, is a gospel song driven by an organ and a choir of backup vocalists who repeat "With these hands," as Springsteen shouts, "We pray for your love, Lord . . . We pray for the strength, Lord." His request shows an acknowledgment of the supernatural but it also demonstrates an understanding that the responsibility and burden of solving human problems rests squarely on human shoulders. As beautiful as "My City of Ruins" is, with its heartbreaking and mournful description of a city and people lost in physical destruction and emotional devastation, and its joyless prayer for heavenly assistance in matters of love, faith and strength, it emerges as an exception among Springsteen's corpus, which has the tendency to employ doubt when considering how much help Heaven can offer — not an outright denial of its existence but doubt of its ability to play a relevant role in human affairs. The humility of "My City of Ruins" not only exemplifies a mature spirituality — one which does not attempt to understand the sacred as if it could possibly be understood — but also a responsible vision of virtue. A prayer for assistance can be sent but humanity must do the heavy lifting.

Similarly, Confucius never denied a spiritual existence but cautioned his followers not to rely on it when attempting to achieve personal happiness and serve a moral order. He commanded, "Devote yourself to man's duties . . . respect spiritual beings but keep a distance,"[5] and when asked directly about the supernatural he took a dismissive tone: "Until you are able to serve men, how can you serve spiritual beings? Until you know about life, how can you know about death?"[6]

This is in opposition to the monotheistic worldview, which implores followers to know life by knowing God and serve men by serving His kingdom. Springsteen, on the other hand, nearly echoes Confucius on "The Long Goodbye," a song from *Human Touch* which maps his journey from dread to joy, and bewilderment to understanding.

> Same old faces it's the same old town
> What once was laughs is draggin' me now
> Wailin' on rain hangin' on for love
> Words of forgiveness from some God above
> Ain't no words of mercy comin' from on high
> Oh no just a long goodbye
> Yeah yeah just one long goodbye

The singer's joy and fulfillment comes after he decides to stop waiting for it to arrive in the form of God's blessing and actively seeks it out for himself. As Confucius instructed his followers to devote themselves entirely to following a moral order, without concerning themselves with the metaphysical, Springsteen also describes a politically and socially moral vision and endorses the idea that happiness is to be found on Earth, and one does not have to beg for heavenly mercy to earn it nor wait patiently for a post-death reward. This is put very simply in "Happy."

> Some need gold and some need diamond rings
> Or a drug to take away the pain that living brings
> A promise of a better world to come
> When whatever here is done
> I don't need that sky of blue
> All I know's since I found you, I'm happy when I'm in your arms

One must tread cautiously when making this comparison because Springsteen has clearly shown a consistent interest in the psychological while Confucius, keeping closer to the Eastern tradition, did not emphasize "inner" life or psychological disturbances. However, compelling similarities can be found between the ancient teacher and the contemporary rocker. Their shared insistence on committing oneself to a moral order based upon humanistic ceremonial rites is perhaps the most important example. Confucius saw dignity, even sacredness, in the ceremonial aspects of living — when a person acts with love, loyalty and other virtues in accordance to the communal tradition without conflict and without motivation for self-gain. As Herbert Fingarette explains in his pamphlet, *Confucius: The Secular as Sacred*:

> The image of Holy Rite as a metaphor of human existence brings foremost to our attention the dimension of the holy in man's existence ... Rite brings out forcefully not only the harmony and beauty of social forms, the inherent and ultimate dignity of human intercourse; it brings out also the moral perfection implicit in achieving one's ends by dealing with others as being of equal dignity ... Furthermore, to act by ceremony is to be completely open to the other; for ceremony is public, shared, transparent; to act otherwise is to be secret, obscure, and devious, or merely tyrannically coercive.[7]

Reading this passage, one is immediately struck by how Confucius saw holiness in human existence. Springsteen's "I'll Work for Your Love" and several other songs make that same discovery by using, just as Confucius did, "Holy Rite" as a metaphor to explain human affairs and emotion. More important than this similarity, however, is their common moral vision and their demand that it be expressed publicly — Confucius as a teacher and Springsteen as a performer. One also learns that Confucius, much like Springsteen, extolled the ultimate importance of community. Fingarette continues: "Human life in its entirety finally appears as one vast, spontaneous and holy Rite: the community of man. This, for Confucius, was indeed the 'ultimate concern; it was, he said, again and again, the only thing that mattered, more than the individual's life itself."

Over the course of his career Springsteen has not provided a more beautiful, stirring and emotional tribute to communal love and individual sacrifice than the song he wrote for the firefighters who sacrificed their lives on 9/11 by climbing the stairs of a crumbling inferno in desperate hope to save others' lives. It is difficult to think of an action more loyal to the holiness of the human community, more enshrined in love, and more affirming of an equal dignity among men. "Into the Fire," with the classic Springsteen formula of blues verses and gospel choruses, juxtaposes suffering and healing. The suffering is obvious — loss of life, devastation, shattered families. The healing comes in the recognition of a profound example of moral truth and beauty which, if we tirelessly labor and persist, we may begin to understand and replicate.

The sky was falling and streaked with blood
I heard you calling me then you disappeared into the dust
Up the stairs, into the fire
Up the stairs, into the fire
I need your kiss, but love and duty called you someplace higher
Somewhere up the stairs into the fire

May your strength give us strength
May your faith give us faith
May your hope give us hope
May your love give us love

Springsteen chooses an example that Confucius would cherish. The emphasis on "love and duty" can be found in the *Analects of Confucius* — as they express the communal and ceremonial aspects of living which contain moral perfection and spiritual maturity. In order to reach this condition, one must constantly battle, labor and travel through obstacle and obstruction. Confucius relied heavily on the metaphor of traveling a road to describe man's quest for moral and spiritual development. Any fan of Springsteen can immediately name an abundance of songs which use rivers, roads or highways as metaphors for human growth. "American Skin (41 Shots)," "Racing in the Street" and "Streets of Philadelphia" are three examples already analyzed in this text — many more remain unmentioned.

Throughout this journey, Confucius instructs his followers that they must naturally choose to follow "The Way," which includes personal dignity and social harmony based on mutual respect rather than it being forced or coerced. Fingarette identifies the "central moral issue for Confucius" as "the factual questions of whether a man is properly taught the Way and whether he has the desire to learn diligently."[8] In this respect, another similarity to Springsteen's approach to morality, meaning, the sacred and the secular emerges. In the song "Real World," Springsteen outlines a rebirth in which the singer feels emboldened and enlivened to a world of possibilities, as long as he remains curious, open and ready.

I wanna find some answers I wanna ask for some help
I'm tired of running scared
Baby let's get our bags packed
We'll take it here to hell and heaven and back
And if love is hopeless hopeless at best
Come on put on your party dress it's ours tonight
And we're goin' with the tumblin' dice

Ain't no church bells ringing
Ain't no flags unfurled
It's just me and you and the hope we're bringing into the real world

Once again Springsteen takes no comfort in mystical and religious symbols and instead places his fate in human hands. But his willingness to mold the fate by seeking intellectual, emotional and spiritual help from those around him demonstrates a Confucian appreciation for cultivating a life following the Way. "Real World" also captures Confucius's idea of public, "outer" spirituality which is bound together by shared humanity and not embodied exclusively in gods or other non-human beings.

The virtues that Confucius stressed are all best expressed and cultivated in social settings and conditions — as they are all dependent upon other human beings to thrive. Mutuality in human relations, loyalty, love and trust are the most commonly instructed virtues throughout the *Analects*. These are the virtues that possess the power to create community and embed cultural unity — despite religious, racial and class differences. This is precisely why and how Confucius was able to call for political-social unity in ceremonial form. Fingarette surveys the Confucian community:

> It is essential to see that Confucius was concerned not merely with communal order but with human dignity, with a culture that was founded in a sense of the beautiful, the noble and the sacred as distinctive dimensions of human existence. Cultural unity was to be the consummation of humanity, not an order imposed upon sheep in human form.[9]

This deeply profound vision goes beyond mere sloganeering about "diversity" and "multiculturalism" and reveals a community in which diverse members can find common cause to organize monolithically, despite varying differences. Springsteen also captures this insight in the cross-cultural anthem from *The Rising* called "Worlds Apart." Musically, it is homage to multiculturalism — featuring a Pakistani choir, searing rock guitar solos and a hip-hop drumbeat. It is one of Springsteen's most interesting and eclectic musical creations, while lyrically it repeats some familiar themes — the power of love, community and an unflinching clutching on to the truth and beauty to be found in life, or in Confucian terms — the beautiful, noble and sacred.

Where the distant oceans sing and rise to the plain
In this dry and troubled country your beauty remains
Down from the mountain road where the highway rolls to dark
'Neath Allah's blessed rain we remain worlds apart

Sometimes the truth just ain't enough
Or is it too much in times like this
Let's throw the truth away we'll find it in this kiss
In your skin upon my skin in the beating of our hearts
May the living let us in before the dead tear us apart

We'll let blood build a bridge over mountains draped in stars
I'll meet you on the ridge between these worlds apart
We've got this moment now to live then it's all just dust and dark
Let's let love give what it gives
Let's let love give what it gives

The more one examines the philosophy of Confucius in comparison with Springsteen's music, the more one becomes surprised, enlightened and entranced by their endless commonality. They both expound the virtues and importance of a community guided by love, loyalty and companionship. They both believe that nearly every man is a work in progress to be crafted, chiseled and sculpted into moral maturity and spiritual significance. They also profess that these communal values should guide society into a peaceful, compassionate and dignified place that is loyal to the inherent holiness of human existence. Both the sage and singer are leery of heavenly decrees and theological speculation — choosing instead to invest in human responsibility and accountability — but respectful of its potential existence. Amazingly, even their preferred method of instruction is the same. Confucius spoke often in narrative form because of its symbolic power to relate what is important and meaningful to human life. Springsteen has made a career out of captivating people's hearts and imaginations with storytelling songs which make them think more of their own challenges and progressions than the singer's career.

While these similarities are fascinating on intellectual, cross-cultural and philosophical grounds, they also contain a provocative political truth. Namely, that the individual's responsibility is to live a morally ordered life that positively contributes to the creation of a fair, just and generous community. Through this process humanity can find unity, virtue and happiness. Springsteen and Confucius share a political, philosophical and even religious vision which, in the words of Fingarette, "reveal[s] humanity, sacred and marvelous, as residing in community, community as rooted in the inherited forms of life."[10] These forms of life are traditional and should be preserved but communities must also modernize as culture, technology and lifestyles change in order to preserve unity and virtue. Our most important traditions, rites and ceremonies, which provide sacredness, are rooted in our common humanity. As Springsteen so brilliantly and emotively captured in the early 1990s rocker "Human Touch," we are responsible for our own joys and accountable for our own dread. We also must seek comfort, consolation and community in each other, as those are the only places in which they can truly be found:

Girl, ain't no kindness in the face of strangers
Ain't gonna find no miracles here
Well you can wait on your blesses my darlin'
But I got a deal for you right here

I ain't lookin' for prayers or pity
I ain't comin' 'round searchin' for a crutch
I just want someone to talk to
And a little of that Human Touch
Just a little of that Human Touch

Ain't no mercy on the streets of this town
Ain't no bread from heavenly skies
Ain't nobody drawin' wine from this blood
It's just you and me tonight

Tell me, in a world without pity
Do you think what I'm askin's too much
I just want something to hold on to
And a little of that Human Touch

We inherit responsibilities of "human touch" (community creation, acts of kindness, distributing love) and for too long have surrendered them to power brokers in the halls of government or religion. Certainly there are fine servants of humanity to be found in both settings but often those in both arenas of power serve only to divide and weaken the American community. Confucius and Springsteen not only remind us of our humanistic passions and duties but also that unity should not be programmed into us like machines. The elites of American empire wish to subvert our faculties to an unthinking and all-encompassing jingoism which allows for no independence or critical thought, while the elites of religion too often demand we sacrifice our individuality and shared destiny to harsh dogmas that are inapplicable to modern life. And all the while they do this with severe attacks upon the vital principles of its unofficial but most practiced religion. The social gospel of Jesus Christ is an important documentation and demand for self-sacrifice to values of radical love, ecumenical service and persevering empathy. St. Francis of Assisi and Dorothy Day exemplified the social gospel with their dedicated identification with the poor and tireless devotion to assistance for the suffering.

The best elements of Christianity provide a usable example for spiritual maturity and national growth, along with the foundation of America — even with its hideous and bloody stains of slavery, slaughter of the native population, and subjugation of women. The United States was not founded during a power-hungry grab for territory but as a living and breathing physical embodiment of revolutionary ideas. Freedom, equality and political participation bound all citizens together in a shared vision — even those, like African-Americans, who for far too long were brutally excluded from the arrangement.

These are the values and principles that give people's lives meaning, and as they have slipped away, suffering citizens have sought them out in unqualified replacements — power worship and dogma deference. Confucius was a visionary who mapped all of this ahead of his time, albeit using Eastern examples of social strife and Eastern traditions for the solution. As American power has increasingly betrayed America's foundational values, Springsteen has taken a prophetic, principled and powerful position of protest and in the process has demanded that a communal solution — based upon love, mutual respect and democracy — be applied to communal problems, all the while desperately and passionately pleading, "Say 'amen' somebody!"

BENEDICTION: JESUS AS A SECULAR SYMBOL OF SUFFERING

Even though Bruce Springsteen may most often treat religious narratives and lifestyles with skepticism, doubt and uneasiness, he certainly maintains a respect and reverence for the idea of the sacred and the role it can potentially play in an individual's quest for meaning — as long as that role does not become dogmatic. Those who are secular find meaning through love, family, friends, the arts and satisfying work. Religious people derive meaning from the same generous sources but, depending on their level of devotion, apply a certain dosage of religion to those activities and the rest that fill their passing days. As long as religious passion is not allowed to influence public policy or be co-opted as a bludgeon to belittle the differing viewpoints, lifestyles and dreams of people of other, or indeed no, faith, it should be celebrated when it enables people to preserve a sense of meaning and a commitment to service and goodness. Springsteen has battled with the Christian tradition and made a compellingly convincing case of its shortcomings but neither he nor many others can doubt that at its best — Martin Luther King Jr., Dorothy Day,

Roy Bourgeois — it provides an example of compassionate, communitarian principles in action that are guided by viewing the world through people's suffering. This makes the important question for thinking and feeling people one of how to respond to that suffering, and hopefully alleviate it. Christians often fail to exemplify this approach and therefore cannot claim monopoly. Their successful examples are inspirational just as examples of their failure are dreadful, and equally inspirational and courageous examples can be found in other traditions — religious and secular.

Springsteen makes this point most eloquently, poetically and movingly on *Devils & Dust* by examining the life of Jesus Christ. Through the song "Jesus Was an Only Son," — a soulful gospel tune sustained by an organ and Springsteen's soft, mournful vocal — he provides a portrait of suffering and gives listeners a predicate for understanding pain, misery and despair, and for applying that understanding to community creation. What makes the song so captivating is that it removes the divine from Jesus and insists upon viewing him as a real human being who underwent unjustifiable physical pain and emotional torture. Springsteen explained his songwriting process during live introductions simply as deciding to "write a song about Jesus just as someone's son." By using the mother-son relationship as a window into Jesus's life, Springsteen forces listeners to confront the trauma and tragedy that must have overwhelmed the pair when they recognized and attempted to deal with the finality of their inevitable separation. During live versions — performed majestically on a piano — Springsteen speculates if Jesus — the man — wondered about what he would miss as he marched down his fatal path. Did he think of the children he would never have? The love he would never feel? Or did he simply focus on his pain-stricken mother and consider his last goodbye?

These questions induce a meditation on death, catastrophe and the irreparable hearts that crack in its wake.

> Now there's a loss that can never be replaced,
> A destination that can never be reached,
> A light you'll never find in another's face,
> A sea whose distance cannot be breached

By posing these questions through a presentation of Jesus not as a Messiah but as a mere mortal, Christians, Jews, Muslims and atheists alike are united in attempting to answer for his suffering, and find parity in the suffering of living mothers forced to say goodbye to their children, along with others whose lives and families are broken apart by poverty, war and injustice.

Those questions, the wrestling they provoke, and the answers they hopefully produce, demonstrate that, regardless of one's religious or political point of view, the world should be viewed through the eyes of the suffering and that no symbol — religious, nationalist, materialist or individualist — should be allowed to obstruct one's sight line.

Chapter 7

Bodies Hanging in the Trees

The Politics of American Power

If American citizens were to become serious about objectively analyzing the mythical narratives and symbols that influence their lives, in an effort to focus on suffering people, both at home and abroad, there would be a need — a political and moral imperative — to contrast the prevailing myths surrounding American power with its actual nature. American power — its purpose, role in international affairs, and typical methodology of expansion — is treated by political elites from both parties, media heavyweights and the majority of the populace with deferential awe. The assumption that American interests and activities are always benevolent ("spreading freedom") or benign ("we made a mistake") rules over American politics and culture with almost no interruption. This nearly universal treatment of American power is especially important because throughout the twentieth century American power was world power. Its seemingly unlimited financial resources, combined with a monstrous military, placed it head and shoulders above every other country and allowed it to set the agenda and determine the hierarchy for the entire globe. Although many are predicting the end of empire because of the American financial crisis, one must be cautious when forecasting that demise because the financial crisis is indeed global and not exclusive to the United States. In fact, the crisis throughout many European nations is far worse. Therefore, considering that America dictated international affairs throughout the second half of the twentieth century and will continue to play a pivotal role, if not the leadership role, throughout the twenty-first century, anyone who is concerned with the fate of the world and the lives of everyday people must unsettle him or herself from comforting illusions of American benevolence and view American power with a bold willingness to answer tough questions from the bottom up.

The election of Barack Obama captured a promising moment that symbolized the potential for grand reform. However, the people who passionately supported his campaign must relentlessly apply pressure to his administration to ensure that it follows through on his vision of change rather than blindly subscribing to the "great men of history" theory. Before that brand of desperately needed activism can begin, citizens must intelligently look to the past and develop a deep understanding of American power. Otherwise they will continue to fall into the trap of being conscripted into what Gore Vidal calls the "United States of Amnesia," which "wakes up every morning having forgotten what happened the night before."[1] In this hungover condition of perpetual forgetfulness, there is no room for moral growth, intellectual development or spiritual maturation.

Despite the near blackout of alternative voices in the mainstream media and dominant culture, a few important critical perspectives have emerged from the sterile heap of pacified praise and restricted dissent that characterizes newspapers and the shout shows alike. A reliable source of principled, unrestrained dissent has come from the artistic community. This is why, along with small segments of academia, Hollywood and the arts and entertainment community in general has been the target of such scorn and slander for the past couple of decades. Anyone who attempts to unveil the scarred face of American power poses a threat to the establishment and is immediately and insipidly littered with accusations of "anti-Americanism," troop-loathing and other political trash. Bruce Springsteen is no stranger to this ancient but recently popularized weapon of political attack. He has been ridiculously labeled everything from "unpatriotic" to "left-wing loon," despite overwhelming evidence to the contrary on both counts, for "attempting to chart the distance between American ideals and American reality," as he defined it on *60 Minutes*.[2] Although Springsteen has amassed a strong record of public speech and political activism, his most-employed and effective way of promulgating his unique vision of American progressivism is through combining the intellectual and rhetorical tradition of narrative storytelling with the dramatic and emotional tradition of music. By artistically expressing his rage, sadness and disappointment with the exercise of American power and his hopes, dreams and ideals for American possibilities through the stories of characters that closely resemble countless living people, he has created a compelling vision that Americans can use to view their country. However, because his mode of dissent is less strident and more open to interpretation than the films of Michael Moore, the essays of Gore Vidal or the lectures of Noam Chomsky, many fans and critics alike have simply missed the point. Beginning in the 1980s, Bruce Springsteen has built a body of work that powerfully, poetically and poignantly gives the three sources of

American power (its market-driven culture, its self-interested politics and its too often disconnected populace) a critical treatment by viewing them through the eyes of the huddled masses that suffer at its feet.

THE WAR ON IRAQ: A CASE STUDY OF AMERICAN POWER AND SPRINGSTEEN'S ARTISTIC DISSENT

On the subject of war, Springsteen has consistently produced an angry commentary that is both skeptical of power and sympathetic to people. "Born in the U.S.A." pays tribute to the Vietnam vets' suffering. "Souls of the Departed," written in the wake of the first war in Iraq, mourns for a lost soldier and then scathingly makes a connection between the elites who started that war, the elites who rule over the entire country, and the precious blood that is shed not only on foreign battlefields but in neglected segments of rapidly decaying America. Live versions featured a spooky opening combination of a news anchor repeating "The skies over Baghdad have been illuminated" and a whining guitar. Springsteen would angrily sing the first verse and chorus, which tell the story of a young soldier who was assigned to detail the clothes and belongings of all the soldiers who have died and eventually becomes haunted by the sight of their souls rising into the skies like geese. After announcing "this is a prayer for the souls of the departed," the backbeat kicks in with ferocity. Guitars stretch and wail. Drums thunder. It becomes clear that this prayer is not one whispered in mourning but one that is shouted in rage. In the second verse a knife-edged indictment is issued to the elites who demonstrate cruel indifference to the tragedy and death that exists all around them.

> Now Raphael Rodriguez was just seven years old
> Shot down in a schoolyard by some East Compton Cholos
> His mamma cried "My beautiful boy is dead"
> In the hills the self-made men just sighed and shook their heads

As Springsteen's voice grows more impassioned and intimidating, and the music becomes harder with more intensity and rock power, he identifies his surrounding culture and country as the "land of king dollar" where moral silence "passes for honor." The "hatred" and "dirty little lies" go unmentioned, as they have "been written off the books" and into "decent men's eyes." This is a ferocious condemnation of the society and power structure that has produced victims like the exploited and neglected Vietnam veteran in "Born in the U.S.A.," the ignored man dying from AIDS in "Streets of Philadelphia" and the young boy in "Black Cowboys" who was born with the odds stacked against him and would be abandoned by his mother and forgotten by his country. Springsteen's suggested response to this cacophony of trauma and tragedy possesses a moral quality that is beautiful in its simplicity. Speaking from the role of a loving father he laments, "Tonight as I tuck my own son in bed / All I can think of is what if it would've been him instead?"

This basic question should be asked by all people — regardless of the racial, class or sexual-orientation differences that distract us from our wealth of more plentiful and important commonalities — when determining how to politically and morally move forward when learning of another death in Iraq or another shooting in the inner-city. Would our complacency and tepidness continue to prevail if the victim were our child, parent, spouse or friend? Would we treat these life-and-death issues as trivialities if we suddenly found ourselves in a soldier's boots or an Iraqi's shoes?

I remember listening to Springsteen's introduction of "War," from *Live 1975–1985*, for the first time in high school. After describing what it was like to grow up with "war on TV every night" during the Vietnam era, he warns the young people in the audience that "The next time they're going to be looking at you, and you're going to need a lot of information to know what you want to do." Then before launching into a heavy, assault-like version of the classic protest song in which he terrifyingly screams the lyrics, he says, "Blind faith in your leaders can get you killed." Although I was moved by the song and admired the sentiment, I thought that the final statement about the fatal consequences of blind faith was overly dramatic and bordering on paranoid. My naïveté became abundantly clear when that chilling warning was transformed into a truism — a piece of rock 'n' roll political prophecy. On March 20, 2003, when the bombs began to again "illuminate the skies over Baghdad," the Mesopotamian soil began to shake as the homes erected on top of it crumbled while frightened families huddled inside and thousands of men and women my age, wearing my country's uniform, brandishing firearms, invaded Iraq.

It had been clear long before that day that should forever live in infamy that war in Iraq was inevitable. Any faith in the Bush administration's claim that war was a "last option" was crushed when they pushed UN weapon inspectors out of Iraq before they had even approached completion and continued to accuse Saddam Hussein of possessing "stockpiles" of biological, chemical and even nuclear weapons in spite of not finding any evidence to support that now universally debunked pretext. An equally ludicrous claim that was treated as unquestionable truth in the march to war was that the Hussein regime maintained an allegiance and connection to Al-Qaeda and was therefore somehow responsible for the 9/11 attacks. This was contradicted by the 9/11 Commission and several other sources. Experts and former insiders like Scott Ritter (UN weapons inspector in Iraq throughout the 1990s) and Robert Baer (Middle-East CIA field officer during the 1980s, 1990s and the early part of the current decade) repeatedly went on the record in an effort to bring desperately needed truth to the American public and stop the war. However, their efforts, along with the committed activism of thousands of citizens, and the anti-war votes of 23 senators ultimately failed to prevent the death and destruction that continues to unfold in Iraq and the repercussions unfolding back home.

The deceitful record of the Bush administration has been thoroughly documented by many courageous and competent journalists, former insiders and activists. Perhaps the greatest compilation and organization of evidence against the Bush administration has been produced by the Center for Public Integrity, in a report that documents 935 false statements made by Bush administration officials in the interim period between 9/11 and the invasion of Iraq.[3] The complacency of Congress — a body that not only neglected its constitutional mandate to officially declare war but also its duty to hold a long, detailed debate on the subject — has also been rightly and fully condemned by a variety of sources. The Bush administration's deception and congressional cowardice would have been impossible without the full support and cooperation of the American media which essentially functioned as an unpaid marketing agency for the U.S. Defense Department during those unnerving few months when armies mobilized and citizens mostly stood mute. The facts implicating American democracy with failure are staggering for anyone who grew up cherishing free expression, press and assembly.

Every major metropolitan newspaper in the entire country supported the war. Every cable news talk show host, with the exception of MSNBC's Phil Donahue, could not wait to start firing missiles.[4] Donahue, despite having the highest-rated program on the network, got fired for his dissent which, according to an internal memo leaked to the internet, "presented a difficult public face in a time of war when all our competitors are waving the flag."[5] On the radio, Limbaugh and his acolytes were ratcheting up the psychotic rhetoric while on FM the Dixie Chicks were banned from Clear Channel stations for having the audacity to mildly express vague unhappiness with the beloved emperor and god of War resting comfortably in the White House. Typically totalitarian tactics were used against anyone — be it an elected official, artist or journalist — who even hinted at doubt over the administration's claims of Hussein's diabolical plans to destroy the United States. Their patriotism was questioned and they were accused of hating soldiers and sympathizing with terrorists.

It is tempting to reflect on this abysmal record of political mendacity, media manipulation and citizen conformity and merely point fingers at particularly contemptible individuals who spearheaded the savage and scandalous operation. However, one's examination of the war and what continues to make it possible, cannot end there, but it must penetrate every facet of society. It must demolish pretenses that provide comfort to both leadership and public, and jump start a self-critical interrogation of American power, democracy and citizenship.

Democracy and the duties of citizenship require an unobstructed flow of information to function properly. Without a well-informed citizenry, which necessitates a truthful and aggressive press, the American political system will fully revert to its now built-in oligarchic tendencies. Thomas Jefferson's emphasis on the importance of reporting and free inquiry could not have been stronger, for he called "information" the "currency of democracy." Therefore, it becomes very important to examine who distributes that currency and effectively enriches or bankrupts the populace.

The currency is largely controlled by five large corporations (Time Warner, Disney, Bertelsmann, Viacom and News Corporation) whose principal owners and operators wake up every morning with a single-minded agenda: accumulate as much wealth as possible. Their colluding interests ensure that despite competing for ratings, readership and ad revenue, they will cover mainly the same stories and offer opinions that exist within a narrow framework. Media ownership interests collude with the interests of the multinational corporations that supply advertisement money, and in some cases the corporate interest and state interest is one and the same.[6] General Electric, which oversees a vast television empire that includes NBC, MSNBC and CNBC, is also a Pentagon defense contractor. GE equipment and technology is purchased by the Pentagon and utilized throughout Iraq and Afghanistan. Therefore, GE stands to profit from the nation going to war.

As long as journalism is relegated to a marketplace ghetto it will serve that master. The liberal versus conservative media-bias debate distracts citizens from the real problem of corporate ownership and corporate control, which is dependent on other major corporations for success and will therefore paint a picture that is friendly and comforting to wealthy elites. Link this simplistic, shallow and sycophantic media with a Bush administration that was giddily willing to constantly lie and a political team led by the sulfuric Karl Rove and Andy Card who brazenly admitted that the timing of the war was primarily a marketing decision, saying, "From a marketing point of view, you don't introduce new products in August,"[7] and an all too apathetic American people will be easily and passively pushed into an unnecessary war.

This background information is essential for seeing the ghost that haunts the words and music of the title track from Bruce Springsteen's 2007 album *Magic*. Springsteen sings in the first person with a quiet deliberation and an unshakable confidence that belongs to only the most wicked among us. A steady heartbeat provides the foundation for an eerie organ. An unfittingly chaotic mandolin is combined with a funeral fiddle while a distorted echo repeats some of the narrator's most threatening promises. During the final verse the drumbeat slightly picks up, as do the stakes of this gloomy forecast of death, destruction and democratic demise. The evocation of magic and the tricks of a magician perfectly describe the tactics of deception, distortion and distraction that dominate the media and that defined the Bush administration. The quiet melody and whispering vocal attempt to induce the listener into a false sense of comfort by remaining subtle and refusing to sound threatening. However, as the melody drifts along and the singer continues unbothered, even while his promises grow more violent, an ominous cloud begins to poison the atmosphere and darken the landscape. Disaster looms, and there is nothing a journeyman who travels through the land that awaits its wrecking date can do to prevent it. Just as a child in the front row of a magic show cannot stop the masked magician from stunning his faculties with well-learned illusions, American dissenters looking out at a fraudulent President, fainthearted Congress, fellating media and frightened public had no levers of power to pull to reverse the bloody and costly course that their nation was about to embark on.

"Magic" starts out simple and seemingly innocent. The singer tells us he has a "coin in his palm" which he can "make disappear." He can also call your card and, for a trifecta, pull a rabbit out of his ear. He then mysteriously declares "This is what will be." He continues by boasting of his ability to escape any trap and emerge unscathed from even the most constricting cage. He'll slip shackles on his wrist. If chained inside a box and thrown into the river he will "rise singing his song." This perfected ability to avoid accountability and dodge punishment closely resembles the American political system, which is often governed by unaccountable front men like Bush and shadowy operators like Cheney who, because of a compliant media and inattentive public, are able to enact agendas, influence legislation and violate constitutional controls on their power. Credible allegations of distorting the truth in the run up to war, irrefutable evidence of the illegal wiretapping of civilians through a secretive National Security Agency program, and widely broadcast failures of intelligence prior to 9/11 and the federal response to Katrina did not slow the administration down during its eight years of painful rule. The slightest hint of impeachment was treated with open-mouthed horror, as if even toying with the idea was an assault on everything held sacred in American life. The Downing Street Memos, which detailed statements made by Bush about "fixing the intelligence to the policy"; the testimony of ambassador Joseph Wilson, and later that of his wife Valerie Plame, about the falsity of the Bush claim that Iraq was seeking uranium from Africa; and the whistle-blowing of CIA officers and FBI agents all failed to keep the architects of war shackled by the wrists or chained in a box. Every time they rose up like beasts with unshakable confidence and unbreakable concentration, singing the same song: "We had the intelligence," "Post-9/11 world," "We did it for freedom."

Meanwhile, most of the media continued to parrot and most of the public continued to believe. Only criticisms of military strategy and war tactics were given an audience. The tactics of deceit — the illusory tricks of distraction — and every sleight of hand ruled the day. The consequences grew starker, bloodier and bigger. Not only was America losing its reputation, and its treasure, but thousands of its young people were dying, losing limbs or returning with psychic scars that will not easily heal. Hundreds of thousands of Iraqis were losing their lives, families and homes. During the move to war, and for the first couple of years after its launch — including the infamously infuriating day that Bush declared an end to major combat operations under a banner that read "Mission Accomplished" — the media and the public continued to happily go along with business as usual. No amount of inaccurate predictions — "We will be greeted as liberators," "The oil revenue will pay for the war," etc. — or knowledge of a rising death toll could snap the people out of their slumber.

The conjurer in "Magic" grows more devilishly cocky when he predicts that he will bring pain and treachery while his pacified audience will continue to sheepishly grin. The tonality and volume of his voice does not change, and the dry consistency of the melody remains the same.

> I got a shiny saw blade
> All I need's a volunteer
> I'll cut you in half
> While you're smiling ear to ear
> And the freedom that you sought's
> Driftin' like a ghost amongst the trees
> This is what will be, this is what will be

The audience will accept its pain with delight and will casually wave goodbye to its freedom as the wicked magician celebrates his victory. Once he persuades them to abandon principle and intellect in favor of base urges he will gain his final and fateful triumph.

> Now there's a fire down below
> But it's comin' up here
> So leave everything you know
> And carry only what you fear

On the road the sun is sinkin' low
There's bodies hangin' in the trees
This is what will be, this is what will be

As the heartbeat-resembling drumbeat slightly picks up pace, along with the anxiety of concerned observers, the conjurer makes his most threatening promise and his most audacious command. One can tremble at the thought that this order will be accepted, as one looks back on the disheartening history of the war in Iraq which was augmented by an executive branch of government with a cooperative legislative branch convincing the media and public to relinquish the demand for evidence, ignore the burden of proof, abandon moral principles and applaud the invasion of a country that posed no threat and had no connection to the attack on its people.

"The smoking gun will come in the form of a mushroom cloud." "There is no doubt Saddam Hussein is amassing weapons to use against us." "What if we had this chance before 9/11?" "What if . . .?" "What if . . .?" "What if . . .?" until the overwhelming majority of the country was paralyzed with fear, and those that managed to maintain composure were accused of naïveté at best and treason at worst. The fire down below quickly ascended and the trees began to grow ever more crowded with the blood-dripping bodies of fallen soldiers and countless Iraqis who are callously disregarded as "collateral damage." The consequences of falling for illusion and allowing deception to overtake democracy began to hideously reveal themselves, despite the best efforts of many to conceal them behind the magician's curtain.

The track that follows "Magic" on the album of the same name is a gripping protest song entitled "Last to Die." The title is taken from the question that spits out at the listener throughout the chorus: "Who'll be the last to die for a mistake?" This stunning moral interrogation is a modified version of what a young John Kerry, recently returned from Vietnam, posed to Congress in 1971: "How do you ask a man to be the last man to die for a mistake?"[8] Springsteen makes it clear that he is paraphrasing the senator who ran a failed bid for the presidency in 2004 when he concludes the first verse, which precedes the first chorus, with the line "I thought of a voice from long ago." In many ways this voice has vanished from the soul of John Kerry who, despite showing great courage and clarity in his opposition to the Vietnam War, struggled to muster principled criticism of the aggression in Iraq during his presidential campaign. One of the defining moments of that election season was when he shocked his supporters and pleased his detractors by declaring that he would have voted to give Bush the authority to go to war even if he knew weapons of mass destruction would not be found in Iraq.[9] More important than Kerry's personal weakness is the inability of America to morally reckon with itself by recognizing the human consequences of war, which are far more important than the often discussed loss of American treasury, reputation and position.

This need for moral reckoning and compassionate acknowledgment of tragic losses taking place in thousands of American and Iraqi homes is exactly what Springsteen identifies in the powerfully dramatic "Last to Die," which possesses a musical energy, movement and theatrical quality that bombards the senses of one who has just been hypnotized by the eerily quiet and threateningly calm manifesto of a dark conjurer in "Magic." Its opening contrast of soaring strings and crashing guitars summons images of a battle-field and awakens one from the politically indifferent slumber induced by the nefarious magician. When the singer takes his place after a steadily harsh and purposeful drumbeat, among the chaotic attack of scorching guitar bends and lifting strings, he sings in a voice equally characterized by incurable pain and unbending anger. He describes a family on the highway, driving until the "road turns black," and being forced to choose between two dichotomous destinations: "Truth or Consequences." They can face the truth, which is essential to democracy's survival, and undertake the labor that it requires to reverse course and rebuild what lies in the devastated heap of unjust war launched by unaccountable elites, or they can travel on in complacency and continue to suffer the inalterable consequences. The finality and fatality of these consequences are identified in the chorus, which is sung at quicker pace than the verses — a pace and passion that emphasizes the urgency of the singer's search for answers and plea for peace.

> Who'll be the last to die for a mistake
> The last to die for a mistake
> Whose blood will spill, whose heart will break
> Who'll be the last to die, for a mistake

The band blasts through the second verse with the force and quality of a dis-turbingly beautiful yet terrifying, controlled demolition. It is as if they believe with their weapons — guitars, drums, bass — they can destroy the makers of war and the complacency that gives them comfort. Unaffected by the drift-ing voice of conscience, the rider in the narrative confesses to "counting the miles" but failing to "measure the blood we've drawn" while the bodies pile high "outside the door." The bipartisan obsession with progress, at any and all costs, that has characterized American foreign policy is captured poeti-cally and succinctly by Springsteen while he desperately draws attention to its all too often unacknowledged victims. Whether or not great progress has been made in foreign adventures is often arguable. However, it is often the only argument that ever exists. Rarely is a mainline American foreign policy debate targeted on the millions of civilians who were killed in Vietnam.

The 58,000 American servicemen who experienced their last moments in horror on Southeast Asian soil may receive a passing mention, but typically only in the middle of some sanctimony over how unfortunate it is that the United States "lost" that war. Discussion of war in Iraq is frequently framed in the same stultifying and tragically narrow way, while smaller crimes that took place in between those two wars in Latin America (executing coups in Chile and Guatemala, waging proxy wars in El Salvador and Nicaragua) and the Middle East (supporting dictatorial and murderous regimes in Iran and Iraq, ignoring Palestinian suffering) have been wiped clean from the historical slate.

While it is obvious that the Iraqi civilian death toll has not been considered in political discourse, it remains disappointing that Iraq and Afghanistan War vets continue to receive unreliable health care and shifty answers about their various injuries, illnesses and conditions. Twenty percent of returning soldiers with post-traumatic stress disorder (PSTD) do not receive treatment (even when they demand it).[10] Female soldiers continue to get raped in the barracks in large numbers while the attackers essentially operate with immunity, and even physical health care is sorely lacking, as the hideous conditions at Walter Reed in 2007 demonstrated.[11] These terribly tragic scandals of moral failure are rarely mentioned in the media and almost universally ignored in politics. The dominant culture would rather worship the military as a robotic institution of American power on the march than deal with it as a body of real human beings — many of whom are suffering and in need of aid and care.

Throughout American culture "support for the troops" has been used as a bludgeon to pound anti-war dissenters into silence. As undemocratic, deceitful and despicable as that tactic is, it would be mildly tolerable if support was measured in one's ability and desire to bring vital resources, assistance and services to men and women in uniform. In reality, what persists is an abstraction of the soldier, which is rooted in myth and friendly to power. The soldier is seen as a stoic warrior who is uninterested in thinking beyond popular American narratives that serve as justification for war. The soldier mindlessly fights for the flag — not the principles it is intended to represent — seen as a symbol of expansion and conquest. He believes violence is a guaranteed problem solver and that questions and concerns should be saved for the prissy pacifists who are too cowardly to get their hands dirty. Amazingly, he is also the capeless equivalent to Superman: Never injured. Never wanting. Never slowed down by anxiety.

The perfect illustration of this American mythos is the radical reversal in coverage of NFL star-turned-Army Ranger, Pat Tillman. When Tillman first enlisted in the armed services, shortly after 9/11, he was immediately anointed an American hero and after he was killed in Afghanistan the entire political, military and media establishment launched a tributary parade and promised to "never forget" his legacy and sacrifice. The commitment to remember the NFL safety-turned-Army Ranger soon proved hollow as troubling information emerged surrounding his death, which was originally ruled an in-the-line-of-duty killing and later amended to "friendly fire," which also failed to hold up to scrutiny. A whistle-blowing military doctor — whose name was blacked out from the incendiary report — said that Tillman's gunshot wounds indicated that he was shot from less than ten yards away and that the "medical evidence did not match up with the (officially described) scenario."[12] Following that revelation, there has been a complete blackout of media coverage of the mystery that shrouds Tillman's death, even as his family continues to seek answers. This disappearing act is most likely due to the implications of his possible homicide and his unsettling viewpoint on war and power. Not only does his disturbing death reveal something dark about American military culture and bureaucracy, but Tillman himself appears to have been anything but stoic, imperial and unthinkingly violent when closely examined. He strongly opposed the invasion of Iraq, was harshly critical of the Bush administration and planned to meet with Noam Chomsky when he returned to America.[13] Tillman transformed from embodying the abstraction of the soldier — a silent warrior for American power no matter what the aim and agenda — to a symbol of service and justice who shook the highest halls of elites and presented, in his life and death, uncomfortable questions to the dominant culture.

In "Last to Die," Bruce Springsteen reminds Americans that Tillman, and others like him, speak from beyond the grave in a unified call for justice. Their untimely deaths must be recognized, honored and applied to developing a deeper understanding of war, along with a nobler vision of American power. In the final verse, he identifies this duty, issued to us by those who did their duty, and condemns a prevailing indifference that allows for America's moral stagnation.

> A downtown window flushed with light
> Faces of the dead at five
> Our martyr's silent eyes
> Petition the drivers as we pass by

The subsequent chorus reasserts that crucial question, "Who'll be the last to die for a mistake?" and strikes a blow against the abstraction of the soldier. These are not symbols of American might but human beings whose suffering should not be sanitized. Springsteen places their deaths, along with those of civilians, directly at the heart of the Iraq War discussion and the band cooperates with a fury fit for a fighter jet.

"Devils & Dust," released two years earlier on an album of the same name, takes the opposite musical approach. It is quiet, slow and contemplative. However, it too resists abstracting the soldier, presents the suffering and struggling people of war as the crux of the issue, and offers compelling commentary on American power. Also similar to "Last to Die," its clever use of instrumentation creates a mood and quality of conflict. However, unlike the *Magic* track, the conflict most likely implied through countermelodies is not the physical horror playing out in the theater of war but the spiritual unrest and turmoil that manifests behind the curtain and within the soul of the soldier: A young man or woman who has been trained to kill but whose enemy does not wear a uniform; A blossoming citizen, barely old enough to vote, whose every decision and movement may end or save a life. It is impossible to imagine how one must feel carrying that awesomely terrifying burden but Springsteen attempts to get inside the mind of these paradoxically frightened and brave soldiers. He not only seems to pull it off with complexity and empathy but also succeeds at placing the listener in those combat boots. Over a plodding acoustic guitar that steadily builds into nothing — symbolizing the lack of answers to this spiritual inquiry and perhaps the unwinnability of the entire Iraq War — a voice of torment emerges.

> I got my finger on the trigger
> But I don't know who to trust
> When I look into your eyes
> There's just devils and dust
> We're a long, long way from home, Bobbie
> Home's a long, long way from us
> I feel a dirty wind blowing
> Devils and dust

Missing home — the location — and longing for the sense of home — a feeling of belonging — is made clear in the need to acknowledge that he is "a long way from home" yet "Home's a long, long way from us." A companion named "Bobbie" is addressed in what may be an allusion and homage to Bob Dylan, whose similarly phrased "God on Our Side" is as unsettling and unnerving an indictment of the mythology that motivates war that has ever been put to record. The thousands of miles separating the soldier from home and Bobbie may be easier to endure if the comforts, love and humanity of what people associate with the term "home" were to be recognized in the desert air of Iraq, which weighs heavy with the scent and threat of death. The dirty wind blows this air against the young man's face and, along with being unclean from the mortar shells, fumes and gun smoke, it is ominous and owned only by the devils and dust that make unlabored breathing, physical security and peace of mind impossible.

In just a few lines of song a sterile and frightening setting is captured but the explosions and gunfire that characterize it are never mentioned. Instead the soldier only refers to the war for his spirit. He says "I got my finger on the trigger / But I don't know who to trust." Civilians that have never served in combat think of a gun as a fatal weapon that should be respected and only carried when absolutely necessary, which for most people is never. Men and women serving in war depend upon that weapon for survival, and "when absolutely necessary" goes from being never to always. This has a profound effect on the individual. Nathan Lewis, an Iraq War veteran writes in *Warrior Writers: Re-Making Sense* (published by Iraq Veterans Against War) that his time in the Army taught him that a rifle is a "tool of death" and that it does not "spread democracy or peace." In spite of this realization, he confesses "I loved carrying a rifle. After a while it fused into my skin, bones, character, and soul," and then goes on to ask, "Am I evil for that? Am I a violent monster?" After informing the reader that he grew up in an ordinary American home, without conflict or abuse, played little league and continues to "open doors for old ladies," he concludes: "if I am a normal middle-class lad, then something is wrong." Then he wonders aloud, "Why did I know the difference between an M-16 and an AK-47 before I could compare a Hindu to a Muslim, or a sonnet to a Haiku?"[14]

If the gun becomes an extension of the body, character and soul, and takes on grand importance which far outweighs comparative religion or literature for one soldier, it may be personified as a close, personal friend by another. Drew Cameron, another Iraq vet, writes that he named his rifle Nikki after his officers "encouraged us to develop a relationship with our rifles." He describes the weapon as a "companion that defines our effectiveness as a soldier, a methodically trained killer."[15]

Considering that a soldier is trained to kill and that the gun becomes the ultimate symbol, and most valued limb, of a serviceman, it is essential to examine where the gun is pointed, and who may fall victim to its fatal power. The singer in "Devils & Dust" laments "I don't know who to trust" while attentively keeping his finger rested on the trigger of his companion. The lack of trust pervading the entire Iraqi landscape, along with the unavailability of distinctions clearly separating enemy from civilian, instills paranoia within the soldier, never allows him a moment's peace, and has the constant potential to create atrocities. Michael Nowacki, a former infantryman and counterintelligence agent in Iraq, describes the ambiguity of the conflict with candor:

In Iraq, nobody — not your commanders, not Rumsfeld, not Cheney, not

even Bush — can tell you exactly who your enemy is. You only know for
sure if they are caught with weapons or explosives — hard evidence. But
those are few and far between. More common are the cab drivers, the day
laborers, college professors, policemen, guys detained just for walking
down the street, guys who were snitched on. You have names for these
kinds of detainees. You call them dirt farmers or jaywalkers. Their offense?
You refer to it as DWI — Driving While Iraqi.[16]

The propensity to bust people for DWI no doubt made Nowacki's job as
an interrogator, which requires sorting the insurgents from the innocent,
extremely difficult. A mistake could very easily send someone who murdered
his fellow soldiers back to his freedom or more likely, according to Nowacki,
send a harmless Iraqi who lacks even the intention to hurt an American to
a prison where Abu Ghraib tactics of torture may be commonly practiced.
Soldiers on Iraqi streets have to make similar discernments, but not with
one person in a closed room. They must attempt to separate the threatening
from the benign in the middle of crowded chaos. In this predicament, where
it is impossible to tell friend from foe until it is too late, preemptive action
must be taken and, like preemptive war in general, the evidence almost
never justifies the violence, and war crimes against the civilian population
are inevitable. The military officers' tendency to dehumanize anyone who
resembles the enemy certainly does not help matters, ease tempers or calm
nerves. Gore Vidal remembers serving in World War II and hearing countless officers discuss how kamikaze pilots flew into buildings because their
"eyes were too narrow to fly right." Tim O'Brien, James Webb (now Virginia's
junior senator) and Larry Heinemann — all veterans of the Vietnam War
who have produced fine novels inspired by their combat experience —
describe how the Vietnamese were called "gooks," "dinks" or "slopes" almost
without exception. Former Marine Martin Smith writes that during his
training "raghead" and "sand nigger" were the epithets of choice lodged at
Arabs and Muslims.[17]
    As a soldier cautiously walks down an Iraqi street with a "finger on the
trigger," who can be trusted and who should feel the wrath of his rifle pros-
thetic? If the soldier believes her superiors, no Iraqi citizen can be trusted,
and certainly she has witnessed the death of her fellow soldiers at the hands
of Iraqis. Those grisly deaths could emotionally justify the hate and fear
that brews inside her. However, she has also most likely seen goodness in
the Iraqi people, which casts doubt on her officers' bigoted caricature of this
country's populace but only leads to more confusion. The anguish and agony
eventually simplifies into a few self-assurances but even those come with a
spiritually deadly cost. The singer continues in an uneasy chorus:

I got God on my side
I'm just trying to survive
What if what you do to survive
Kills the things you love
Fear's a powerful thing
It can turn your heart black you can trust
It'll take your God filled soul
And fill it with devils and dust

Throughout the entire process of what is loosely called "fighting in Iraq," a soldier walks threatening streets, breaks into houses and mans checkpoints, with survival at the forefront of her mind. The question that is raised so powerfully in "Devils & Dust" is what if what is deemed necessary to continue living makes living less valuable? If human solidarity, communal trust and love, along with ideals of tolerance and judicial ethics, must be destroyed in order for one's survival to remain secure, what kind of life is left? This inquiry is vital both to the individual on the ground in Baghdad and an entire nation at war. Convinced by dishonest leadership and governed by inexorable fear, the American public sacrificed civil liberties, ethnic and immigrant progress, and moral standing after 9/11 to invade a nation that posed no threat. They overlooked increased government surveillance, allowed the torture of detainees and betrayed the Constitution. All of this was done in the name of survival. Fear corroded American faculties and led to a welcoming of practices and policies that were traditionally considered categorically un-American. Hearts were blackened against countless Arab-Americans, and entire nations of people suddenly became vulnerable to increased suspicions from the world's only superpower. Yet much of the American public and leadership maintained that during all of the bombing, spying and torturing the United States enjoyed the blessing and approval of the Christian God.

Theological justification for American foreign policy has a long and sordid history in America. The slaughter of the Native population had a heavy religious tilt because indigenous people were deemed "uncivilized heathens." Manifest Destiny — the belief that America had the God-given right to stretch into the world and bring along their beaming vision of themselves — led to adventures of conquest in Hawaii, Mexico and the Philippines. The tension of the Cold War permeated into American living rooms largely because the Soviet Union was an officially atheist state. This was the motivational factor for President Eisenhower — a secular man himself — to insert the words "under God" into the Pledge of Allegiance.

The Cold War belief that American capitalists fought for God is brilliantly depicted by Norman Mailer in *Harlot's Ghost*, in a scene where a young student in the CIA — Harry Hubbard, the novel's protagonist — asks his instructor, "Why are Communists so awful?" He answers, "It's very Russian to be awful" and goes on to explain that this is because of their resistance to a Westernized Christianity which "not only brought love into the world, but civilization, with all of its dubious benefits." Despite being spiritual, they, and a large portion of their "backward" satellite states, "cling to pre-Christian realms — awe, paranoia, slavish obedience to the leader, divine punishment."[18] One would think that the evil of Stalinist Russia and Mao's China would be enough to galvanize the public to support action against Communism. However, as Mailer correctly identifies, Americans must not only recognize the evil of others but also constantly be reminded of the unflinching goodness of themselves.

This continues right up to the present, even though the religious dichotomy is not as clear as Christianity versus atheism. Dueling monotheisms now rule the day in what political scientist Benjamin Barber labeled "jihad versus McWorld."[19] Barber defined McWorld as corporate control of the globalized political process and economy. However, it is not difficult to see the current of religiosity running through America's worldview, which would be acceptable if it were not a brand of religion that always justifies American power, regardless of the intent or consequences. George Bush claiming he consulted a "higher father" when he decided to invade Iraq, and a military chaplain policy that leaves many non-Christians feeling harassed and miscast, demonstrate the perniciousness of the problem.

Professor of religion at Georgetown and ordained Baptist Minister Michael Eric Dyson summarizes the unfortunately pervasive belief that Americans can always rightfully claim "we got God on our side," similar to the confused soldier in "Devils & Dust":

> Even in sacred circles aggressive forms of militarism are masked in religious metaphors: God seeks to punish those who disagree with America, and God seeks to put down nations that refuse to obey God. Of course, obeying God and agreeing with America are often conflated in the basest version of our civil theology. This can be seen in religious figures like staunch fundamentalist Jerry Falwell and sophisticated conservative evangelical Ralph Reed.[20]

Much of the American religious tradition reveals a maturity marked by deep, deliberative torment such as that expressed by Martin Luther King and William Jennings Bryan over whether America is guided by fairness and justice or whether it is stricken by mad militarism, intense imperialism and wealth worship. In "Devils & Dust" it is clear that despite the soldier's own inner turmoil, he has internalized the "basest version of our civil theology." After the first verse, then following the second verse where dreams of death haunt the soldier while the plodding guitar conflicts with an unnerving synthesizer underneath, and finally during the song's conclusion, the only announcement he can make with confidence is "I got God on my side." This confidence is unshaken even by the confession that his own faith is weakening.

> Now every woman and every man
> They want to take a righteous stand
> Find the love that God wills
> And the faith that He commands
> I've got my finger on the trigger
> And tonight faith just ain't enough
> When I look inside my heart
> There's just devils and dust
>
> Well I've got God on my side . . .

In order to hold on to faith — faith in God, faith in humanity — he must feel and witness what fuels faith — love and righteousness. These two vital aspects of human life may be unwelcome in a deadly, occupying war launched for specious reasons. The public failure of war results in a private spiritual death in the soldier who, if lucky enough to physically survive, must contend with the consequences of killing people, nearly being killed, and watching friends be killed. For future deaths of this kind — both physical and spiritual — to be prevented, America must become self-critical of its pervasive myths surrounding its own power, most especially the one concerning its heavenly mandate. A reliable tool for this job is the soldier's words of suffering and struggle, which challenge American power and the "mythology of the military veterans as stoic saviors of civil society's virtues and values," as Jan Barry writes in *Warrior Writers*.[21]

Springsteen creatively confronts this mythology, and allows the soldier's suffering to speak in "Devils & Dust." He captures the angst, fear and confusion that dominate their service in Iraq, demonstrates the importance of allowing their stories to be told without sanitation, and even makes the point, with love and not venom, that some soldiers may possess an ideology that exacerbates the problems of American power and helps make its ignominy possible. Projects like *Warrior Writers* and Springsteen's songs of soldier narratives serve an important purpose in American culture and will emerge as beacons of moral and political light if the populace is to ever find its way out of the enveloping darkness of apathy and indifference.

Political apathy, which is always accompanied by indifference to suffering and willful ignorance, is what made the entire war in Iraq possible.

It is also the culprit responsible for the persistence of political problems that range from health-care inaccessibility to ecological destruction. Fifty years from now, a middle-aged historian may attempt to explain the Iraq mess by analyzing the mendacity of the Bush administration, studying the cowardice of Congress, and examining the bizarrely uniform compliancy of the media. But the question that would continue to haunt the hypothetical historian would be one regarding Americans. How could almost an entire nation be so easily deceived into applauding a war that targeted a country which by all accounts had no involvement in the attack that took place on its own soil? Polls taken throughout the war revealing that high percentages of Americans believed Hussein possessed weapons of mass destruction and that nearly a third believed such weapons were found only intensify already severe worries. Worse yet, what does it say about the American populace that a president with limited rhetorical ability could transform a significant percentage of citizens into intolerant lunatics who excitedly anticipated the invasion of Iraq and hurled insults, accusations and all manner of bile at critics of the war — even those as benign as the Dixie Chicks? Answers may vary, but none of them say very much about the state of American democracy. The election of Barack Obama offers hope and does symbolize change. But, the fact that it took eight years of wreckage and the most charismatic and articulate candidate since JFK to compel Americans to reverse course — along with a financial crisis and a disorganized campaign from John McCain — is troubling.

The consequences of apathy are destructive, and the war in Iraq is a perfect illustration. However, citizenry indifference also encourages the corruption of the entire political system. Most elected officials, at least to a certain extent, operate according to compelling reasons. If corporate power convinces political power that it stands to gain greatly and has much to lose if it does not placate a big business agenda, the concerns of middle class, working and poor people will be roundly ignored. The only existing check and balance to the corrosive influence of corporate power is the citizenry. When the citizenry fails to pay attention, and is in dereliction of their democratic duty to ensure that their concerns, needs and agenda are respected, political officials will continue to behave as they have for the past few decades — deregulating the financial markets, removing oversight, giving tax breaks to the inordinately wealthy, and ignoring increasing inequality. Without the regulatory power of the citizenry it will also be extremely difficult to prevent State interests from dominating the political process — regardless of how reckless and radical those interests become. Illegal wiretapping, torture and rendition, and the excesses of the Patriot Act are perfect examples. Throughout the eight years of Bush carnage, critics often self-righteously pointed the finger at "them," without measuring the culpability of "us." As long as "us" continues to fail — drowning in a poisonous pool of apathy — "them" will accrue a perfect record of success.

Music often summarizes or defines an idea far better than mere words on paper. When words fail to characterize a concept, music can pick up the slack and offer a more holistic and emotionally truthful version of the story. This is particularly true when attempting to describe the fundamental nature of apathy. Words fail to capture the ebullience it ignorantly shows in the face of compounding consequences. Therefore, the Bruce Springsteen song "Livin' in the Future," which appears on *Magic*, takes on great importance in this context and the artist's corpus because it captures the essence of indifference with a profundity and truth beyond the power of essays and rhetoric. Musically it is one of the most joyful records that Springsteen and the band have recorded in the past two decades. Shouting soulful vocals move the narrative along but what makes the song so memorable is its saxophone-energized, organ-infused, beach-and-club mixed sound of Asbury Park rock 'n' roll. It resembles the fun, party quality found on early Springsteen recordings of "Spirit in the Night," "Rosalita," and "Tenth Avenue Freeze-Out." Upon hearing its opening one is immediately given the indefatigable impulse to dance and sing along. When a drum crash is followed by a loud siren from Clarence Clemons's forceful horn, the expectation of lyrics marked by images of beaches, clubs and beautiful women is clear. This could be the soundtrack for nearly any party, including one thrown in foolishness, stubbornness and selfishness. "Livin' in the Future" may sound like party music, and it may be a musical companion to Springsteen's early dance hall records, but its lyrical content is anything but joyful, and could not be more distinctly opposite in tone and imagery than "I ain't here on business / I'm only here for fun" or "From the coastline to the cities / All the little pretties raised their hands."

"Livin' in the Future" opens on a dark and ominous note that entirely contradicts its playful melody and seems more appropriate for an epic ballad or angry rock song.

> A letter come blowin' in on an ill wind
> Somethin' 'bout me and you
> Never seein' one another again
> Yeah, well I knew it'd come
> Still I was struck deaf and dumb
> Like when we kissed, that taste of blood on your tongue

Despite the forlorn temperament of the singer, and perhaps in spite of the fatalistic imagery and quality of the narrative, the mood established by the song's highly danceable groove and dynamic opening cannot be brought down. The chorus — sung with absolute confidence and happiness, complete with backup vocalists — reveals how this stark contrast of political reality and personal psychology is possible.

> Don't worry Darlin', now baby don't you fret
> We're livin' in the future and none of this has happened yet

The assurance that worrying is not necessary, no matter how bleak the outlook appears, and the blissful ignorance that informs "none of this has happened yet," allows the singer to maintain such glib and gregarious composure throughout disaster. The political picture gains clarity, and the threat of devastation becomes graver, in the second verse.

> Woke up Election Day, skies gunpowder and shades of gray
> Beneath a dirty sun, I whistled my time away
> Then just about sundown
> You come walkin' through town
> Your boot heels clickin'
> Like the barrel of a pistol spinnin' 'round

In obvious allusions to Bush, who was criticized for bringing cowboy ethics and aggression to the White House, and to voter disengagement, the singer reveals that while citizens "whistled their time away," harmful hordes and calamitous cadres of ill-intentioned power mobilized, and their work will soon appear in every town square. However, the narrator of "Livin' in the Future" continues to gleefully dance on without pausing to measure the losses being felt all around him. He repeats the chorus, along with his recommendation of complacency and insistence that nothing dreadful (which would require action) has happened. The images begin to take on apocalyptic proportions — "The earth it gave away, the sea rose toward the sun / My ship Liberty sailed away on a bloody red horizon" . . . — but the singer does not break his concentration on naïve optimism and refuses to allow his determination to sleepwalk through Hell to relent. The final lines of the last verse show the stakes of this casual and self-destructive attitude.

> My faith's been torn asunder, tell me is that rollin' thunder
> Or just the sinkin' sound of somethin' righteous goin' under?

The question is answered with another shamelessly joyful chorus which eventually leads into a brief saxophone solo and a "Na, na, na, na" sing-along that is so tempting even a mortician would be helpless to its bouncy seduction. The voice that carries it belongs to a man who most likely smiled throughout the deception of the Bush administration, the Congress and media depicted in "Magic." He cheered and chuckled at the sight of the conjurer's tricks. He drives by the "faces of the dead" in "Last to Die," and never ponders the question of unjust, unfair and unnecessary death in Iraq. Over 4,000 Americans have died in that war, and even the most conservative estimates of Iraqi civilian deaths are well over 100,000. Yet this man does not know about that, and he does not care to know about it. He has never been introduced to the stirring testimony of soldiers like those who speak in "Devils & Dust" and therefore has never wrestled with its profound moral implications. He has accepted the framework of American power as either benevolent or benign. Sadly, this voice belongs to the American people.

In an introduction to live versions of "Livin' in the Future," Springsteen identified a list of things Americans love about their country — "baseball, cheeseburgers, the Bill of Rights" — and then mournfully remarked that in recent years things like "voter suppression, rendition, illegal wiretapping and the loss of some of our best young men and women in a tragic war" have been added to the list.

Perhaps the most threatening and terrifying aspect of apathy is that its consequences are without limit. Power will not draw a line separating the acceptable from the unacceptable because that job is given to the people. If the people do not draw the line, no line will ever exist and we will watch traditions die, principles perish and a way of life vanish.

The Iraq War illustrates that American power is not always charitable and chivalrous. Although it has been responsible for greatness throughout its history, it is also capable of producing unjustified suffering on a global scale and, like any system of power, it will often follow its own interest without considering the interests of those outside its narrow concentration. Historians will debate the reasons for launching a war on Iraq for decades after its eventual end. However, it has become abundantly clear that these reasons do not include any that were officially sold to the American people. The financial and strategic gains of the Iraq War are also rather obvious. Companies like Halliburton and Bechtel have made hay in the war zone, and future U.S. governments will have an invaluable Middle East site of military operations in the form of massive permanent military bases located throughout Iraq. Detailed motives for invading Iraq may be difficult to nail down with precision but one can be sure that no invasion would have taken place if "Iraq was a Pacific island whose main export was pickles," as Noam Chomsky phrased it.[22] Even though Americans have still failed, by and large, to examine the moral failure of Iraq, they are looking at the years of involvement in that country and seeing very little gains. This leads them to ask questions like "How could this happen?" and "Why did we ever go there?"

As Springsteen courageously and correctly points out in his scathing yet party-inflected treatment of apathy, "Livin' in the Future," questions similar to these would have been better asked years ago before the war began. But they could not break through the cacophony of distortion and deception, and they could never be heard over the multitudes who tirelessly sang a simple, ecstatic refrain: "Na, na, na, na."

BABY ONCE I THOUGHT I KNEW: BUILDING A DEMOCRATIZED COMMUNITY AND DEVELOPING HISTORICAL MEMORY

The timeless lesson transcribed through the joyful musicality and hauntingly apocalyptic lyrics of "Livin' in the Future" is that Americans cannot whistle their time away if they expect the institutions that regulate their lives to work in their favor, or the country to continually improve upon their interests. Systems of power, and those that manage them, need strong incentives and compelling reasons to implement an agenda that is extraneously recommended. The war in Iraq offers a clear, if extreme, example of this principle in action. However, other examples, ranging from the equally extreme — the Vietnam War — to the mundane — changes in tax policy over the last 40 years — are unfortunately easy to find. In order for the system to achieve balance and for examples such as these to become increasingly rare, American power must be redefined by those at the bottom, who could then provide crucial oversight and critical regulation over those at the top. A democratized community that includes broad constituencies of civically involved and politically active citizens could have the power to do just that.

In the late nineteenth century the populist movement managed to organize with enough efficiency and power to establish direct election of senators and other vital steps to expanding American democracy. Throughout the 1920s and '30s, a progressive coalition succeeded in compelling leaders to pass child labor laws, create a government pension system (Social Security), a progressive income tax, and give women the right to vote. The civil rights, anti-war and anti-poverty accomplishments of 1960s and '70s activism are well known, if underappreciated, components that greatly civilized the United States.

Many of the freedoms and policies Americans now take for granted were the product of long and bitter struggles waged by countless unsung heroes who coalesced, even while aware of ethnic and religious differences, to create a powerful community that would question the legitimacy of arbitrary and self-serving exercises of power and demand a more egalitarian approach. The election of Barack Obama proved that, despite the apathy that afflicts many Americans, there still exists the potential for great communal rallying around a common cause. As promising and inspiring as the diversity of the Obama coalition was, building a democratized community cannot be dependent upon instructions from powerful figures of leadership — even those who possess many admirable qualities. The reemergence of actionable community in American civic and political life requires a localized system of management and an operation of savvy and passionate everyday people who, while engaging and pressuring politicians, always maintain a safe distance of skepticism so as not to be unduly influenced.

Before this is likely to occur America must overcome its condition of collective amnesia and dedicate itself to finally developing historical memory. Sanctimonious talk about "moving on" from the universal failures of democracy that made the worst tragedies of the Bush era possible dominates much of the political discourse. It is difficult to look at the catastrophes of Vietnam, Iraq and 9/11 and find anything remotely beneficial. However, the one thing they give us is great windows into the American past and present. Failing to look through the window of Vietnam led to walking through the deadly door of Iraq. As long as Americans ignore the lessons of Iraq, future tragedies will loom large on the horizon. To invoke a now famous cliché, those who fail to learn from history will be doomed to repeat it.

The opening track on Springsteen's *The Rising* is called "Lonesome Day." Although it does not explicitly mention the attacks of 9/11, it has been assumed that the song was inspired by that dreadful day — given its timing and thematic content. The song opens with a violin introduction that quickly builds into a dramatic riff which soon gives way to the singer's tired, but battling voice. He sings of the comfort of false security — "Once I thought I knew / Everything I needed to know about you" — and the agony of unwanted surprise — "But, I didn't really know that much / Joke's on me . . ."

The song moves along with great purpose and drama. Like "Livin' in the Future," the melody contradicts the dark lyrical content. However, in this case the purpose is to inspire hope and offer reason for perseverance. In spite of the horrors of 9/11, which went well beyond any American's imagination, the American people must continue to labor, fight and believe — just as the singer of "Lonesome Day" solemnly vows to do. The imagery seen outside his doorstep resembles the worst attack in American history.

> Hell's brewin' dark sun's on the rise
> This storm'll blow through by and by
> House is on fire, Viper's in the grass
> A little revenge and this too shall pass
> This too shall pass, I'm gonna pray
> Right now all I got's this lonesome day

It appears as if the end of the world has arrived but the singer insists — with a community of vocalists supporting him — "It's all right, it's all right, it's all right, yeah!" The middle break of the song features a violin, guitar and saxophone building on each other in near competition to create an epic moment of transcendence. The rising of the horn, followed by the winding of the violin and guitar provides a perfect soundtrack for overcoming adversity. However, the third verse soon begins and includes a cautionary note from a now possessed singer. The lazy mentality that believes tragedy can be surmounted with such an easy plan of "A little revenge and this too shall pass" is roundly rejected with brevity and clarity.

> Better ask questions before you shoot
> Deceit and betrayal's bitter fruit
> It's hard to swallow, come time to pay
> That taste on your tongue don't easily slip away
> Let kingdom come I'm gonna find my way
> Through this lonesome day

The need to be self-critical even in victimhood and the imperative to exercise moral, spiritual and political discernment is reaffirmed with the simple line "Better ask questions before you shoot." The line comes bellowing through after the saxophone and winding violin do their work, demonstrating that advice like that may be hard to follow, and may require sweat, diligence and tears, but it is essential to progress, recovery and redemption. The singer vows that he will accept whatever fate awaits ("Let kingdom come") as he will continue to find his own way through the now dangerous and mysterious world. He is committed to cultivating his own answers and values and then taking action accordingly, rather than relying on the convenient proclamations of power. He serves as a microcosmic template for the spiritual complexity, historical understanding and moral maturity that is necessary for revitalizing a bold, democratic and influential community of political progressives in the twenty-first century.

Chapter 8

Gonna Be a Long Walk Home

The Politics of Community

My own beliefs, my personal beliefs, came into being during the most traumatic moment in American history: the Great American Depression of the 1930s. I was 17 at the time, and I saw on the sidewalks pots and pans and bedsteads and mattresses. A family had just been evicted and there was an individual cry of despair, multiplied by millions. But that community had a number of people on that very block who were electricians and plumbers and carpenters and they appeared that same evening, the evening of the eviction, and moved these household goods back into the flat where they had been. They turned on the gas; they fixed the plumbing. It was a community in action accomplishing something.

And this is my belief, too: that it's the community in action that accomplishes more than any individual does, no matter how strong he may be.

— Studs Terkel, 2005

The problems and challenges that confront America at this pivotal moment in its short history are vast, and on certain days, when hope fails to emerge from the monstrous shadow cast by understandable cynicism, they appear to form an insurmountable mountain. Legalized bribery and normalized corruption in the political system combined with unchecked greed in the corporate world, all of which are encouraged by heavy strains of apathy among the public, make excesses of power at the state, along with the near omnipotence of big money, difficult to counter.

A spineless media and its cousin — a shallow, materialistic pop culture — exacerbate woes across the board. Anyone who proclaims to possess all of the solutions is either suffering from unconstrained conceit or operating under deeply suspicious intentions. Perspectives from all sides of the multifaceted political debate, which includes not only Republicans and Democrats but also libertarians, democratic socialists, populists and independents, should be seriously considered, as should the experiential-based recommendations of social workers, activists, organizers, teachers, academics and public officials. Although a contentious myriad of ideas may struggle to be heard, one issue on which all Americans should be able to agree is the need to rebuild deteriorating communities throughout the nation and restore a strong sense of community among its people. A democratic community guided by intelligence, civility and clarity, and always remaining steadfast to principles of love, charity and responsibility would not only have the capacity to empower the individuals that work within it but also the potential to reshape this country's politics into one that does not ignore ordinary people but strives to uphold the public interest and common good. Revitalization of physical communities and the inculcation of a political, spiritual and moral community requires that the effort start as early as possible in the lives of America's youth, and that power is localized and concentrated in smaller cities and neighborhoods. Equally important is that communities, from the small but mighty family unit to communal institutions such as schools, all the way upward to the branches of government assigned to regulating and guiding the national community, are either strengthened or expanded. The United States, in its most inspirational and triumphant moments, has been energized to correct injustices or explore new opportunities by a mass of organized people tirelessly thinking, working and fighting for a purpose of greater importance than individual success.

Bruce Springsteen has sung, rallied and campaigned for this grand vision of community throughout the majority of his career as a musician and his adult life as a concerned citizen, practicing what he calls "human politics." His music has addressed the topic of community with a clarity, consistency and complexity not seen from any other living American songwriter. The songwriter also has a Pavlovian propensity to use the very word "community" whenever discussing politics, family or even music. However, this popular term, when not applied to geographically bordered areas or ethnic enclaves, is vague enough to almost lose meaning if one does not carefully define a sustainable and workable concept of community, and in the process remain loyal to the integrity of the vision that undergirds it.

Sociologist David Grazian is quick to point out that "the notion of community represents a romantic and idealized form of social organization that can only be defined and evaluated subjectively, in part because it does not exist independently of the set of collectively agreed-upon symbols of community."[1] If community is simply an invention of people within it who value shared priorities, ideas and symbols, comfort can begin to find all of those working to revitalize it in America because they have the awesome power, but simultaneously frightening responsibility, of shaping its continual invention which, unlike the creation of a tool or electronic system, is never finished.

Any constructed community instills "social capital" in its members, which is necessary for individual growth and societal improvement but is not a blueprint for utopia. In fact, it can lead to its dangerous opposite.

Also sharing the belief that community is invented, Robert Putnam convincingly argues that social capital can produce severely negative outcomes when it is distributed through the strengthening of intra-group relations. An illustrative example of bad social capital is visible with every street gang that prowls impoverished streets hawking debilitating substances and relying on brutal tactics of intimidation and force to maintain authority over their respective territories, all the while feeling an overwhelming sense of belonging to a providing and protective family organization.

The invention of community, along with its potential dark side, makes precision when nailing down a progressive agenda for America's future community absolutely essential. Therefore, taking a close look at the specificity of Springsteen's artistic vision for community, rooted in "human politics" that are fertilized by compassion and courage, and examining the local, political and educational practices that exemplify it is required work for democratic socialists and social capitalists who hope to create a community that not only effectively responds to abuses of power and unfair distribution of institutional resources but is also preventative of future failures of American democracy.

MY FATHER SAID: EDUCATION, CIVIC DUTIES AND THE INSTRUCTION AND INHERITANCE OF VALUES

Bruce Springsteen began to narrow his focus on community and politics in the mid-1980s with the release of *Born in the U.S.A.* and its subsequent tour. Although he participated in benefit shows and advocacy concerts prior to that point (No Nukes and A Night for the Vietnam Veteran being the two most significant efforts), it was not until that stage in his career that he began incorporating a socio-political vision into nearly all of his recordings and performances. Interestingly enough, this elevation of consciousness occurred exactly when he became arguably the most popular rock musician in America — selling millions of copies of *Born in the U.S.A.* and playing in football stadiums for the first time. Perhaps with his increased visibility and cultural influence he felt a greater sense of responsibility, and instead of doing all he could to ensure that he would not lose his superstar status he began to speak politically from the stage, add a serious social component to his lyrics, and work closely with various food banks, political groups and human rights organizations. His embodiment of a communal core that expresses a particular political vision became clear on the Born in the U.S.A. Tour, which served as a counterargument to the cheap optimism of the Reagan years. Springsteen sung of suffering people on the margins of society — the unemployed and victimized by deindustrialization tempted by the potential lucre of crime for lack of better options, and battling feelings of national betrayal. He also spoke sympathetically of Woody Guthrie, telling the story of how "This Land is Your Land" was an "angry song written in response to 'God Bless America,'" before performing his own cover version.

The most important moment of the show — its narrative and performative centerpiece — took place just before the conclusion of the band's first set. After playing a rousing version of "The Promised Land" — a song that captures the hope and dream of both personal happiness and public implementation of "justice for all" — Springsteen would speak, without musical accompaniment, about the necessity and desire of "belonging somewhere to something" and explain that the next song is one "about responsibility." This responsibility would be clarified when he would then announce the presence of a local food bank in the arena, describe their work, and emphatically encourage the audience to either give a donation or volunteer their time to the representatives waiting in the lobby. The importance of the food bank's mission would be summarized by the impassioned singer, unapologetically taking on the role of activist with candor and conviction: "Every year in this country about 20 percent of the food that gets produced is wasted. Meanwhile, in every city in every state, there are people who are not getting enough to eat, and are falling through the cracks of our social system. They have nowhere to go. Sometimes these things feel like they are happening far away. But, they're not. They are happening right here in your hometown."[2]

With those words, the E Street Band would begin to play the opening of "My Hometown" — the melancholy ballad from Born in the U.S.A. which would eventually become a hit single. Its music is defined by a repetitive synthesizer riff that is understated but deliberate enough to ensure audience attention. It is sung in a passionate voice of deep yearning which drifts from unsure nostalgia to unexpected mourning and insecurely lands on unstable hope. It emotively captures the bewildered resentment and sadness that many Americans feel as they helplessly observe their beloved towns and cities go through unwanted changes which cause conditions to worsen and the quality of life to decline. The song's melody is soft and unthreateningly repetitive — musically illustrating how these changes rarely come with an explosion or dramatic event. They typically are the result of a steady erosion of traditions, values and infrastructure, which can be initiated or worsened by public policy. Although the town observer may feel helpless, she may have been presented with a plethora of opportunities to raise a voice in protest and contribute to the strengthening of the town's financial and spiritual base. "My Hometown" ultimately questions the passivity of Americans and offers them a musical moment to reflect on the responsibility that comes with freedom: the responsibility to establish, forge and improve community. Hence Springsteen's call for food bank support before performing the song in the mid-80s. This obligation is strongest when it concerns one's own family and this point is not lost on, and indeed emphasized by, Springsteen. The song begins with a simple and relatable image.

> I was eight years old and running with a dime in my hand
> Into the bus stop to pick up a paper for my old man
> I'd sit on his lap in that big old Buick and steer as we drove through town
> He'd tousle my hair and say son take a good look around
> This is your hometown

The idea of a father reminding his son of his communal origin as he looks around the streets where he was raised, schooled and where he has matured is a dramatic illustration of a familial attempt to instill local pride in a child and also say, "This is where you belong." That belonging need not be tribal or even literal as the child grows older but it should remain within his spirit. The values inculcated, along with the partnership awarded for shaping the community's future, should never be neglected or forgotten. This is a moment of crucial education and it symbolizes the instruction in communal responsibility and civic duty that should take place throughout America.

After providing the listener with two troubling images of a destabilized town in conflict and desperation — one of racially motivated violence and the other concerning "boarded up windows" and disappearing jobs — the singer takes us back to the importance of instruction by demonstrating that it should be cyclical.

> Last night me and Kate we laid in bed
> Talking about getting out
> Packing up our bags maybe heading south
> I'm thirty-five we got a boy of our own now
> Last night I sat him up behind the wheel and said son take a good look
>   around
> This is your hometown

The little boy in the opening verse has become the father of his own boy and he prioritizes the same teaching experience his father gave him. Despite his desire to move, find new opportunities, and pursue different aspirations, he remembers the importance of instructing a child in matters of communal and civic belonging and the weight one must carry in its honor.

Over two decades after the release of "My Hometown," Springsteen wrote and recorded its counterpart. "Long Walk Home" appears on *Magic* and although it was written in response to much larger, national issues of American politics — war in Iraq, abandonment of constitutional liberties, and the betrayal of civil traditions — it contains a message of communally assigned responsibilities and familial education that closely resembles "My Hometown," and offers prescriptive hope for a nation looking to recover after a series of traumas — some self-inflicted.

The final verse culminates this effort and reaffirms lost values.

> My father said "Son, we're lucky in this town
> It's a beautiful place to be born
> It just wraps its arms around you
> Nobody crowds you, nobody goes it alone.
> That flag flying over the courthouse
> Means certain things are set in stone
> Who we are, what we'll do and what we won't."
>
> It's gonna be a long walk home . . .

At the end of a journey to rediscover the community he held dear in his youth, and an attempt to recognize its qualities that once comforted him, a local traveler remembers his father's imparted wisdom of national values, the need for community to respect certain rights while valuing individuality, and the need for it to offer vital support, compassion and, when needed, assistance. The essentiality of education is reasserted through an illustration of the power of memory. Memory is what often creates solutions in times of strife, struggle and suffering. Remembrance allows one to prophetically distinguish between what needs to be preserved and what should be changed. Memories are created through experience but education allows the rememberer to contextualize and categorize them.

This valuable lesson is given by the singer after he creates a particular setting and communal condition. The first verse has the character smelling the grass of his childhood while looking at the town where he was born, just after he is dismissed from a friend or lover's house. He asks this companion "what went wrong," and receives no definitive answer, only the slip of "something" into his palm. This interaction makes it obvious that there are no easy answers to personal or national tragedies and that those who undergo them should not seek solutions in the commands and narratives of others — whether they reside in a house on Main Street, Wall Street or Pennsylvania Avenue. This realization is expressed in the chorus, which implores a loved one with "It's gonna be a long walk home / Hey pretty Darling, don't wait up for me."

Although it is clear that the miles that must be walked are those of the soul, the physical surroundings of this character are described in ordinary detail, which soon takes on depressing meaning.

> In town I passed Sal's grocery
> The barbershop on South Street
> I looked into their faces
> They were all rank strangers to me
> The veterans' hall high up on the hill
> Stood silent and alone
> The diner was shuttered and boarded
> With a sign that just said "gone"

While silently passing the local landmarks of his life he becomes overwhelmed with a peculiar sadness that is the result of unexpected unfamiliarity. These buildings — the barbershop, grocery store, abandoned veterans' hall — that once welcomed the character with love and warmth are meaningless now that the cherished ideals they embodied have been collectively violated. Those that live inside, who at one time were dependable friends and allies in an uncertain world, are now strangers who, because of their betrayal of communal principles and civic responsibilities, have become untrustworthy and unknowable. He remembers the clarity and importance of those values with the recollection of his father and the instruction he eagerly and happily gave. Through that bittersweet reminiscence he again realizes that it will be a long walk to the home that is now so far away — the decency and dignity of communal strength and civic pride.

"Long Walk Home" and "My Hometown" are both about community and how communities — both local and national — should be created and honored. This similarity is noticeably contrasted by their opposing melodies. While "My Hometown" is characterized by melancholy and quiet observation, "Long Walk Home" is the sound of action and the musical embodiment of the movement it describes in its title and demands in its narrative. It opens with a steady strumming of an acoustic guitar set against a foundational backbeat which provides energy and stability. Bending guitar notes and a faint violin drift in the background until the second verse begins with a stronger, more pronounced drumbeat and the crashing accompaniment of an electric guitar. Only brief guitar and saxophone solos give the purposeful vocal-delivery pause. The concentration and focus of the band is on the arc of the narrative and the steps towards a national destination of truth, reconciliation and healing which reside within a carefully constructed community.

Undoubtedly, this community will contain many architectural alterations and newly designed developments. Springsteen is a progressive, and has continually argued through music and activism that America is in dire need of democratically oriented political, social and economic reform that favors social justice and equality. However, he also makes a compelling case for the preservation of civic traditions and community principles that keep the country grounded in the best moments of its history and its citizens imbued with the cultural understanding necessary to seek the survival and duplication of those moments. In this sense, Springsteen's vision can best be described as preservative progressivism. His emphasis on preserving sustaining traditions while progressing towards the political and economic change that democracy and equality require is never more clear than when he deals with family and the instruction and inheritance of values.

This is evident in the respective dialogues that take place in "My Hometown" and "Long Walk Home" which, due to the profound nature of the relationship between father and son, take on grand meaning and great importance. These dialogues, brilliantly portrayed through emotionally stirring musical forms, show that family is crucial not only to the development of the individual but also to the cultivation of community because family is the first community in which an individual can claim membership and partnership. Secretary of State Hillary Clinton famously titled her best-selling book on what local and national policies are needed to ensure the well-being of children *It Takes a Village*. The right-wing (most famously former senators Bob Dole and Rick Santorum) responded with vitriol and insisted, "It takes a family." The preservative progressivism that emerges from Springsteen's best work reveals that both modifications of what is believed to be an African proverb are correct, and that neither the family nor its surrounding institutions can be neglected when attempting to ensure that children will mature to create loving communities based in justice, fairness and equality, and that they will pledge to uphold the democratic traditions that make such a creation possible.

The poignant and reflective narratives of characters battling the angst of uncertainty in "My Hometown" and "Long Walk Home" have the capability to resonate with all listeners because of their emphasis on family. Through two similar but markedly distinct moments of crisis, men of different generations find solace, comfort and, most importantly, hope by returning to family — both physically and spiritually. Family is what allows these struggling Americans to gather strength and summon courage to be loving parents and to make the labored and listless walk home, where every step must feel like a mile. The love, nurture and support of family give them the necessary self-confidence and resilience to move around obstructive measures and surmount obstacles. The instruction in values of service, principles of love and a commitment to truth provides them with the concrete resolution to maintain unbreakable focus on a single destination.

Long before and after a child's education becomes institutionalized, she is dependent upon the words and actions of family for guidance. However, the institutionalization of her education is nearly as important — as it will be her introduction to social life and her first encounter with conflicts characterized by ambiguity and fought by various people of different personalities, ethnicities and sentimentalities. Her observations of how authority behaves, resolves conflicts and respects diversity will contribute to the forming of her ideas on citizenship, the role of independently critical thought, and the necessity for civility. Both democracy and community rest on these concepts and therefore they are difficult to overvalue. Tragically, as the infrastructural capacities of public schools have diminished in recent decades so has the prioritization of cultivating democratically workable versions of these concepts in the minds of the young. American children go to schools where conflicts are typically resolved with anger, where omniscient authority demands unfettered deference and where diversity is given great lip service followed by hollow application. Disputes consistently intensify, demoralized teachers lose control and, in the most extreme cases, firearms become an unlikely school supply. The consequences for youth, whose crime numbers continue to increase as college enrollment numbers drop, and the implications for building a stable, democratic community, are severe.

Although government has been dreadfully slow in their response and the media has insisted on giving any discussion of the problem unhelpful frameworks (e.g. "Will school prayer help?"), there are burgeoning brilliant initiatives being pursued on the local level throughout the country. Several smart and savvy social workers, psychologists and teachers have recognized that all forms of intelligence — most especially emotional and social intelligences — should be addressed in the classroom and education must be about more than the instillation of necessary skills for future employer satisfaction.

The most promising campaign for instructional reform is called the "Resolving Conflict Creatively Program," which has been implemented in more than 350 schools across the country. Linda Lantieri, the co-founder of the RCCP national center, described the program's humble beginning in Brooklyn as "working with teachers, administrators, young people, and parents to foster emotional and social development by focusing on the skills and practices of conflict resolution and diversity education. Our aim was to create caring, safe school communities in a society that seemed to be giving up on children, abandoning them to a climate of perpetual violence."[3]

The program attempts to accomplish this idealistic yet practical goal by instituting a cross-curriculum education that calls for the participation of not only those within the school but the surrounding community as well. It seeks to position itself as a communal catalyst, operating from the base of the school for proactive involvement, direct engagement and heightened aware-ness from students, teachers and townspeople alike. Cooperation rather competition is emphasized in the classroom by implementing activities that stimulate dialogue and reward groups working together for a common aim and purpose. The teacher assumes the role of facilitator rather than lecturer. He or she takes a more democratic approach to the enforcement of rules and regulation, and creates an environment that bolsters discussion, debate and deliberation over appropriate behavior and useful pedagogy. Students who excel in this system become "Young Ambassadors" who not only promote the RCCP program to other school districts but also organize civic activities in the community, such as neighborhood cleanups and service projects.[4]

This entire program, from the changes in curriculum to the extra-curricular element, is implemented with the oversight of a specially organized parental advisory council and the school board. Direct involvement from parents in their children's schooling demonstrably results in improvements of academic performances and decreases in social dysfunction. It also goes to strengthening local ties to civic processes and political policies. Shortsighted cynics who write programs like this off as naïve notions of building a minia-ture utopia within the school should study the indisputable results of RCCP. Of the hundreds of schools that have implemented the program, 70.9 percent report a drop in physical violence, and the overwhelming majority boasts of better academic performances.[5]

In order for the democratic and communal values of mediated conflict resolution, cooperation and empathy to triumph, they must be directly taught to young citizens. While the RCCP excels at instilling desirable models of social behavior, it still leaves the democratization of the intellect unaddressed. The beauty of the father's narrative in "Long Walk Home" lies in the depth of his instruction. He is not only teaching his son to discern between right and wrong on an individual and social basis; he is also building the foundation for a historical memory and political understanding that is vital to the survival of America's best political values. This idea can also be transmitted into the classroom.

For the past few decades, civics education has been systematically elimi-nated from educational curriculum. Unsurprisingly, throughout the same period of time Americans' knowledge of the structural procedure and protocol of public policy-making has drastically declined.[6] The youthful excitement surrounding the Obama campaign, along with increased voter turnout, illustrated a promising sign of hope for political awareness and civic involvement. However, inculcating the desire to participate in the political system is not a job that should be relegated to a charismatic figure that comes along once every 50 years. It should be the result of a committed effort to embed civic principles within the culture through the institutionalization of civics education, the RCCP and various other important programs and activities.

Civics gives young people the tools for effective maintenance of democracy, and these are reason, civility, dissent and debate. "How a bill becomes a law" and the "three branches of government" are required learning for any civics student but those tools will not be imparted until civics education is taken out of the classroom and self-applied to conflicts and questions that influence the lives of young people. After demonstrating high levels of knowledge pertaining to local, state and federal political procedures, a class of students should be given the opportunity to choose a local issue, through the democratic processes of debate and voting, and rally in support or opposition to what is being proposed on that issue by local leadership. Political passions could also be connected with outreach programs to local organizations in need of financial and voluntary assistance.

Episodic community service that is done for extra credit or to pad a college application fails to have significant social impact. However, sustained service that becomes built into the school routine for young people could show them the political stakes of awareness, the social value of engagement, and the personal benefits of communal belonging. A political agenda that incorporates broad community service, volunteerism, educational improvement and the prioritization of family worries and struggles would not only raise the standard of living in America, increase happiness, and lay the foundation for the revitalization of community. It would also strengthen the progressive position on political debates that are often stultified by sensitivity. For example, an organization that has mobilized people to volunteer in local health clinics, hospices and nursing homes would gain great credibility when advocating a universal, publicly funded health-care system. A diverse selection of similar opportunities for combining charitable service with social justice exists for those progressive leaders and activist groups that are willing to rethink their calcified approach to communal outreach and political persuasion, which is soaked in the thick and sterile mud of irrelevancy and disconnection. Leftists should insist on establishing a forceful presence in local communities by positively influencing the lives of their constituents. They should also seek to actively form relationships of mutual assistance with progressive churches, synagogues, and mosques in struggling neighborhoods.

As the right-wing has overseen the demolition of social compacts built within capitalist society, the breakdown of civic traditions, and the increased isolation of the American, it has also attempted to exploit the universal communal instinct by replacing interdependent communities with nationalism and narrowly dogmatic brands of religion. The left has responded with criticism without offering a distinct alternative, which should place at its center an on-the-ground service campaign with schools, local governments and community organizations. Isolated citizens who are dissatisfied with the current vision of community that prevails throughout the country — one of homogenized culture and commerce, self-minded hedonistic private obsessions and non-existent public priorities — would then be more likely to pay attention to progressive political proposals and less likely to be persuaded by slanderous right-wing attacks. An equally significant counter to the "conservative revolution" that began in the 1980s and was thankfully brought to a close in 2008 can only occur with a progressively democratic approach to community enlargement and expansion.

Bruce Springsteen demonstrates a profound understanding of this concept, along with a poetic vision of community, and it is dramatically evident in his acoustic reworking of "Born to Run," as performed on the 1988 Tunnel of Love Express Tour. Musically the song underwent a seismic shift from a loud, confrontational and rousing anthem which used a combined saxophone and guitar riff, multiple solos, powerful piano playing and pounding drums to create the "wall of sound" Springsteen has made famous to a quiet and contemplative ballad which reflected a new maturity emerging from the search-and-question process that the lyrics so romantically describe. The singer is longing for an understanding of love, spiritual satisfaction and emotional transcendence, and he is willing to forfeit stability and risk heartbreak to find it. "Tramps like us, baby we were born to run!" was an epic cry of rebellion made in the wild abandonment of youth. As Springsteen evolved into a different man — older, seeking answers to new questions about freedom, justice and country in addition to the preexisting existential ones — the signature song that in many ways defined his career underwent a compelling transformation.

A wise, beleaguered, but emboldened journeyman standing behind guitar weaponry has not allowed disappointment and disillusionment to end his search. But now it has grown quiet — narrated by a voice that no longer expresses itself in scream but rises from the heart of a humble prayer. Before the prayer begins, its spiritually restless singer provides a homily from the stage.

"This is a song that's changed over the years. When I wrote it I was 24 years old. I was sitting in my bedroom in Long Branch, New Jersey. I think back and it surprises me how much I knew about what I wanted. Because the questions I asked myself in this song, it seems I've been trying to find the answers to ever since. I guess when I wrote the song I thought I was writing about a guy and a girl who wanted to run and keep on running — never come back. But, I realized that after I put all those people in all those cars, I was going to have to figure out some place for them to go. In the end, individual freedom when it is not connected to some community or friends or the world outside, ends up feeling pretty meaningless. I guess that guy and that girl were out there looking for a connection, and that's what I'm doing here tonight. This is a song about two people trying to find their way home."[7]

Beginning with an intentionally indistinct harmonica introduction and then, moved along by the soft strum of an acoustic guitar, the singer's lone voice emerges, not with authority as in the famous rock version of "Born to Run," but with the longing of a storyteller who dreams of being heard. He is "looking for a connection" and with every syllable his body and soul aches into the word to slowly and steadily carry on that search. Poetic pleas for companionship and community take on entirely new meanings:

In the day we sweat it out in the streets of a runaway American dream . . .

Wendy let me in I wanna be your friend
I want to guard your dreams and visions . . .

Will you walk with me out on the wire
'Cause baby I'm just a scared and lonely rider
But I gotta find out how it feels
I want to know if love is wild
Girl I want to know if love is real . . .

I wanna die with you Wendy on the streets tonight
In an everlasting kiss . . .

Together Wendy we'll live with the sadness
I'll love you with all the madness in my soul
Someday girl I don't know when
We're gonna get to that place
Where we really want to go
And we'll walk in the sun
But till then tramps like us
Baby we were born to run

While "trying to find their way home", these searchers, physically entangled and spiritually bound, explore the elements that have sustained individuals through the darkest times and are vital to the creation and survival of any community worth living in — friendship, trust, sacrifice and, ultimately, love. Through that power they undergo a transformation. They begin with a dream that is running away from them — something to be chased but perhaps never obtained, and end with an inescapable entrapment in each other's soul. The singer's wish to die on the street, surrounded by the chaos of America's desperate and abandoned heroes on a "last chance power drive," is not a suicidal pact for physical death but a promise to be reborn into a new man through the magic of love, and the connection they have found, wherein they become not blended into each other but two unique human beings resting on each other under a promise of permanence. This arrangement is best symbolized and expressed with a kiss — two people's bodies existing apart but for a moment interlocked at the lips, and sharing each other's breath. The vow contained in the final verse summarizes their commitment to each other and their resistance to external forces of obstruction and division. The singer's determination is not weakened by his acknowledgment of uncertainty surrounding their dream and he takes his sacred oath: "Someday girl, I don't know when / We're gonna get to that place / Where we really want to go / And we'll walk in the sun / But till then tramps like us /Baby we were born to run."

Doubt as to whether they will reach their redemptive place will always exist. But as long as they continue to search, work and fight for it they will find meaning and moments of joy. This is not a place of isolated happiness or solitary comfort but a community of peace, love and justice. Its attempted cultivation is guided by the belief that "individual freedom when it is not connected to some community or friends or the world outside, ends up feeling pretty meaningless."

America has long allowed individuality to trump sustained community. Individual autonomy over lifestyle and self-expression should be bolstered and defended in any fair society. However, the dominant culture in America has given the market the authority to define individuality. Under the hegemony of the marketplace, individuality becomes a branded identity that subverts a truthful understanding of the self and encourages identification to be chained to commodity rather than creativity. Purchasing power becomes the primary source of self-expression. "You are your after shave" or "You are your cell phone ringtone" becomes the prevailing philosophy.

Springsteen rejects this narrow sightline in "Born to Run" and, more importantly, delineates a vision of onward progression towards the values and practices of love, compassion and companionship. These abilities and actions act as the center for a livable community. However, that center will not hold without the sometimes painful work of the tramps — those who refuse to adjust to the dehumanizing demands of power and matriculate into narcissistic and hedonistic institutions. These principled progressives must take their individual transformation and attempt to project it out onto their surroundings and in doing so doggedly fight for a community that insists on equality and does not allow health care, quality education, precious resources or the respect and dignity that accompany them to be tightly rationed according to wealth. This is a community that encourages individuality, self-reliance and personal responsibility but seeks to level the playing field and ensure equal opportunities for the responsible individual to succeed. This is a community that holds itself to the same standard it applies to others and restlessly pursues peace and sanity, which Studs Terkel identified as the "same thing." This is a community in which "all men are created equal" and "justice for all" are not hollow slogans but ways of life.

The projection required to create this community comes from individuals who have gained the capacity to think for themselves and yet acknowledge the physical, emotional and spiritual need for belonging. It is a projection that may seem universally appealing. But for it to occur it must be political. For it to triumph, progressive politics, organization and activism must be reshaped with shrewder tactics, deeper reaching service and a bigger imagination.

A REASON TO BEGIN AGAIN: PROGRESSIVE POLITICS AND LOCALIZED OUTREACH, SERVICE AND GOVERNANCE

Educational reform, increased volunteerism and civic outreach programs are effective ways to begin the complicated and cog-filled process of forging an American community where "nobody crowds you, and nobody goes it alone" — a home for independent-minded individuals searching for belonging among fellow travelers who believe love, service, justice and democracy should be its cornerstones. These approaches to communal construction are privately edifying and publicly stimulating. However, they could be likened to cosmetic surgery on a quadriplegic with a big nose if they are not accompanied, encouraged and complemented by deep public policy reform that alters the status quo on social infrastructure, inequality, criminal justice and the fundamental nature of politics. The spreading poverty throughout desolate rural outposts and crime-stricken inner-cities where vulnerable people are targeted by the prison industry; the erosion of middle-class stability and security while higher education and health care become less affordable; and the muting of the voice of everyday people by media and political elites throughout the public discourse must be dramatically reversed if a vibrantly breathing incarnation of a democratized community is ever to develop.

Through Bruce Springsteen's powerful, prophetic and poetic critique of American society and the connected work of journalists, scholars and activists it has been established that social suffering and communal concerns are forced to the margins by a political system that is enslaved to the whip of corporate cash. For any community to be expanded it must include a plurality of experiences, witnessed truths and honest perspectives within its project of enlargement. Such a plurality in America would pass the megaphone to a West African immigrant victimized by police gunfire on an impoverished city street; to a gay man dying of AIDS who has been professionally discriminated against and personally castigated; and to victims of wars — those who wear American uniforms and those who wear civilian clothes of foreign citizenship. Efforts by Springsteen and others to give some representation to these stories should be applauded and honored but they can only go so far under the current climate, which presents great difficulty to those seeking reform as these stories are essential to community expansion, and crucial to achieving some victory against the apathy and indifference that conceals the conscience of many Americans. Therefore, two institutions of unmatched communal influence and unparalleled communal power must be entirely changed: the media and the political system.

Media reform centering on deregulation and decentralization would bring a real diversity to America — one that goes beyond slogans on posters hung in high-school halls. Unfortunately, American power has consistently gone the other way by allowing conglomerates to gobble up more and more television stations, newspapers and radio stations. Plurality becomes punctured by a homogenized discussion from a boring and stale selection of pundits. In order to adjust to the flexing of muscles from national media giants, newspapers have increasingly gone local, but in the process have ignored vital state and national issues that deeply affect their own communities, while radio programming has been outsourced and local television is relegated to bake sale announcements and school board meetings. Not only should consolidation be reversed but local media outlets should be enlivened by a fairer approach to media. Localization would increase the opportunities for citizens to get involved with their own programming, and provide greater visibility to writers, artists and activists who come from a variety of backgrounds and traditions. A deconsolidated traditional media that incorporates the important lessons of open participation, and the opportunity for self-generated education provided by the new media — not just its convenience — would not only most likely turn some of its financial problems around but also expand and enlarge the fledgling community of American democracy.

The political system, which operates according to the same elite-dependent model of the media, must undergo similar reform based on parallel lessons if the American community is to be revitalized and reinvigorated. Instead of forcing candidates to compete for money, and thereby enlisting them as kiss-ups for wealthy donors, the American political system should force them to compete for volunteer time and support based on the originality, effectiveness and innovativeness of their ideas — not the ability to pantomime an interest group-written, corporately directed production. Campaign finance reform which would allow candidates who can prove a substantial level of support with petition signatures to equally collect money from a public pool would level the playing field and elevate electoral competition to battles of intelligence and integrity. Federalizing standards for third-party entry into campaigns is also a necessary step. This would not only allow candidates to represent larger and more diverse constituencies with their proposals, because the power difference between a rich man and poor woman would not be so vast, but it would also enable a greater amount of people to run for office. Rather than constantly being subjected to contests between wealthy graduates of elite schools who slap towels in the same country club locker rooms, Americans could be presented with candidates from their own communities and of similar backgrounds.

The combination of media and political campaign reform would produce a prioritization of policy changes designed to achieve equality, fairness and justice throughout American society. Instead of constantly placating and parroting the corporate agenda, political and media institutions would issue policy proposals as varied and interesting as their racially, sexually and economically divergent members. Single-payer health care, educational equality and criminal-justice sanity would certainly be on the agenda, as those who face the consequences of current medical unaffordibility, school funding and judicial policies would suddenly be at the policy-formulating table.

The common strength found in proposals for media reform and visions for political expansion is their emphasis on localized accessibility for everyday people. Prophetic projects for communal enlargement from bottom-up participation, beginning at the local level, not only bring to mind the adage "think globally, act locally," but also the practice of "human politics" by Bruce Springsteen.

Beginning in the 1980s, Springsteen transformed his revue of rock music into a larger campaign for political "vigilance," charitable advocacy and social criticism. The Born in the U.S.A. Tour performance of "My Hometown," along with its dedication to a food bank, is emblematic of this unique service project which expressed "human politics" through the artistic form that continually sustained him and many of his fans — rock 'n' roll music. The food bank effort, accompanied by political speech, continues on through the present in Springsteen concerts. However, his commitment to connecting with local organizations in the cities he plays goes well beyond the admirable support of food drives and homeless shelters. He has turned his music into an institutional force that barnstorms from town to town communicating directly with social workers and legal advocates for a diverse selection of political activist groups, veteran support centers, charities and social organizers. The culmination of this campaign often comes in the form of benefit shows — the already mentioned examples of Vietnam Veterans for America, the Christic Institute (a public interest law firm) and the Asbury Park Guild being a few of the beneficiaries — but Springsteen wages a quieter campaign during every tour to establish a connection with various groups located throughout the country. Often unreported, his effort is intended to give much needed support to worthy causes by "working with an organization that's providing immediate care for people in distress, and also an organization that's trying to have some impact on local policy," as he summarizes the activism. He goes on to say that this outreach also maintains his own artistic integrity and political awareness by giving him a "sense of what is going on in those towns, and the circumstances surrounding the people I imagine in my songs, in the imagined community I create with my music."[8]

Springsteen's deliberate attempt to turn his music into "activity and action" that has a tangible impact on the localities he passes through demonstrates a profound commitment to connecting his imagined community with the physical communities that directly inspire it and to addressing the communal concerns delineated in his imaginary world by taking action in its real counterpart. It also contains a heavy dosage of adrenaline for the American progressive cause, should it be adequately applied to the broader politically organizational effort undertaken by left-of-center advocacy groups. Springsteen's emphasis on localized expression of larger positions is instructional of the template that should guide progressives working to reform American politics, institutions and cultural narratives that frame the understanding and treatment of crucial issues.

Anyone who has made a contribution to, and freely become part of, the membership rolls of a political interest group can testify to the passivity and lack of excitement that characterizes such a well-intentioned but ultimately empty endeavor. Typically upon receipt of a donation, the advocacy group — whether it be Greenpeace, United for Peace and Justice or the ACLU — sends a letter thanking the generous citizen and reminding her why she has spent her money wisely and usefully. She will receive no encouragement to connect with people in her city and no guidance on how to exercise the principles of the organization in her own community. A listing of fellow members within her proximity will not even be provided. She will only be contacted when the organization is seeking another donation or ticket buyers to an annual fundraiser. This entirely undemocratic approach sends a disheartening, perhaps unintentional, but clear message: Your money and only your money is appreciated. Leave the work and driving to us.

This organizational inadequacy and elitism is doubly harmful because it not only makes supporters feel powerless, it also renders the organization itself as ineffectual. Under the current methodology, political advocacy may make a marginal legislation achievement or earn some attention in the media. Those victories should be applauded and continually pursued. However, they will not effect the deep political change that is required to reshape the country — the kind of change that requires the empowerment of progressives in their local communities who could apply a democratic vision to the enlargement of those communities. Springsteen's attempt to make his art and performance into a political force by investing great energy, attention and capital in local policy is indicative of the necessity and effectiveness of communal building efforts at the micro level, which will have important consequences on macro level policy. Unfortunately, Springsteen is not the only person who seems to understand this significance.

Richard Viguerie, a chief organizer for forces of darkness, applied localized participatory politics to an American right-wing movement that was struggling to register as a blip on the radar screen in the 1960s, when American politics was markedly more liberal. The Johnson Administration was ramming the biggest social welfare program since the New Deal — the Great Society — through Congress with little fight or interruption. After Barry Goldwater's trampling, the Republican Party allowed its moderate wing to seize power. Various leftist groups were well-organized on issues ranging from civil rights to foreign policy and were exerting almost unprecedented influence on the political process. With the exception of William F. Buckley and the *National Review*, the right-wing appeared dead on the table, without hope for resuscitation. Only a few election cycles later Ronald Reagan — a right-wing, union-busting, corporate crony with theocratic, homophobic and racist tendencies — was sworn into executive office and presided over a rightward shift that would culminate in the catastrophic Bush/Cheney presidency. Viguerie, although typically uncredited and unpunished, is largely to blame.

Exhausted with the ineffectiveness of national politics, Viguerie shifted focus and by rallying various organizations — Young Americans for Freedom, Christian Voice and the American Conservative Union to name a few — and pioneering direct mail techniques he was able to overtake small Republican groups that would go on to dominate local elections. School and village boards, city and county positions, and often politically ignored offices like mayor, sheriff, council members, judges and district attorneys were the targets of his program. From the pulpits to his database of activists, he found and linked like-minded people to run for these offices or work for candidates already seeking the job. Many of these races could be secured with only a few thousand votes. Therefore, it was very easy for Viguerie's plan to succeed and the results are seen, felt and suffered all over the county.[9] Gore Vidal is one of the few intellectuals to regularly discuss Viguerie's influence and in a recent interview he provided a succinct summary: "He's a very clever political operator, and he said, 'I'm going to go after the very small elections.' And he pulled it off, and that's why we have these weird governments now. He established an entire infrastructure working with the Protestant-Right to put their gang in."[10]

The strength and simple brilliance of Viguerie's tactic lay in its ability to galvanize, energize and mobilize groups of people around conflicts they care most about — namely those taking place right outside their front doors. He started with what mattered most to people — their sense of communal pride and direction — and saw to it that the concern directed toward the local level would rise to state and federal disputes after being provoked into making upward connections by the established political and organizational infrastructure that he created, and Vidal correctly identified. Although Viguerie's vision of community formation is horrific, the organizational and administrative methods that succeeded in constructing it are reliably effective and should be adopted by preservative progressives who would like to revitalize community not around greed, bigotry and jingoism but the common ground of love, civic participation, justice and equality. National policy changes, such as universal health care, labor union empowerment, educational reform and public campaign finance, are essential, but the effort must begin with a localized approach which is similar to Springsteen's inspirational activism, and closely resembles Viguerie's winning strategy.

Certain political campaigns have taken this approach to electoral politics and have had promising results. Jesse Ventura "shocked the world" in 1998 by winning the gubernatorial race in Minnesota after implementing an aggressive grassroots campaign and using the internet — then a politically neglected communication tool — for voter outreach. In the 2004 Democratic primary, then Governor of Vermont Howard Dean rose from an obscure figure who was written off as an asterisk to the "electable" candidates to an exciting frontrunner by utilizing the internet in a direct electronic mail campaign which, in addition to seeking donations also organized supporters according to town and county by establishing "Meetups" for them to network and coordinate demonstrations, letter writing, phone banking and canvassing.[11] Dean's prophetic and nearly unique opposition to the war in Iraq was also crucial to his success in building buzz and injecting some passion into the otherwise lifelessly predictable primary. Dean derailed after the conservative Democratic Leadership Council sabotaged his campaign and the media reported on his infamous scream with more thoroughness and detail than they did his anti-war position or his granting universal health care to children and pregnant women in Vermont. The way his idealistic and reform-oriented campaign was destroyed to make room for the bland, boring and benign candidacy of John Kerry is illustrative of the narrow framework that is imposed on American politics by corrosive corporate control and mendacious media moderation.

Four years later, Barack Obama used the Dean model to soar to authoritative victory in an immensely successful campaign — picking up blood-red states like Indiana and Virginia. He certainly had advantages Dean did not — running against a party at the bottom of its popularity, possessing unmatched charisma and rhetorical abilities, and expressing a message full of the vagueness and ambiguity that Dean avoided to a fault. But his campaign strategy was almost identical. It relied on deep involvement from supporters at the local level, even in small states, and constant communication on the web. Concerts featuring Bruce Springsteen in Ohio and Pennsylvania where those in attendance were not large donors — in fact there was no mandatory donation required for admittance — but those who committed to volunteering a certain number of hours in their local Obama office is indicative of the entire approach to politicking. Although Obama's personal story makes him an eloquent symbol of the best of America, truth emerged from his "Hope" slogan because of his supporters. The man at the podium was pretty thrilling on the campaign trail but the excitement and vision of limitless possibility could be found in the sea of people watching him. They embodied an expansion and enlargement of the community of American democracy that activists, social critics and civic educators have long fantasized about and that Springsteen has made the subject of some of his best songs. African-Americans were donating and volunteering in unprecedented numbers. Young people were finally energizing around politics after years of disappointing passivity. First-time voters were coming out in droves and a significant amount of moderate Republicans were switching alliances. Certainly Obama's unique personality and professional and political gifts were partially responsible for this groundswell of support but one must never discount his experience as a community organizer. The ubiquity of his campaign network, the efficiency of local Obama offices and the relentlessness of their outreach demonstrated what community organizing may look and feel like if it were routinely injected with steroids.

In order for the expansion of democracy to thrive beyond the 2008 electoral season, Obama's supporters must hold him accountable by taking the newfound energy and empowerment gained from his victory and investing it in the improvement of their local communities as well as applying it to pressuring congressional representatives, senatorial leaders and the President himself to uphold the public interest and common good. The common thread that should run through all of this — from activist organization on the ground to legislation signed in the Oval Office — should be a strengthening and revitalization of the American community. This multifaceted project includes, but is not limited to, the expansion of crucial social programs and financial services that will assist families, schools, small towns and urban areas and promote important educational, criminal justice and political policy changes. For organizers this effort should begin with a localized focus that steadily builds into state and national directives. The duality of roles that Springsteen plays on tour — constantly switching from artist to activist and back again — along with the shrewdness of Richard Viguerie's political strategy and the promise of Obama's community-organizing campaign effectiveness should be instructional to progressives attempting to make the appealing electoral promise of sweeping change into a tangible reality.

These three examples of a localized version of politics prove that this idea of community engagement is more than conceptually appealing. It is also politically practical. Perhaps the best application of community service connected to public policy advocacy is the work of Sustainable South Bronx and its founder, Majora Carter. Her mission for environmental justice in the poorest congressional district in the country makes upward connections between the social misery experienced in her community and city, state and national policies. It does so in such a way that her constituents are direct beneficiaries of her work and are therefore willing to explore those issues after being directed by someone who has dramatically improved the quality of living in their neighborhood. Sustainable South Bronx not only works to beautify and detoxify the area by organizing to prevent the installation of new waste facilities and remove already existing ones from the Bronx. It also brings the "green economy" to one of the most economically depressed parts of America. Making the South Bronx sustainable requires manual, technical and intellectual labor that manifests in jobs that cannot be outsourced. This component of the campaign influenced Carter and company to create Bronx Environmental Stewardship Training, which trains people — many of whom have been previously incarcerated — to earn "green collar jobs." What started as an honorable, brilliant but simple effort to improve the health of Bronx children by removing the countless toxins and pollutants from their breathing air has grown into a politically bold initiative that tackles the root problems of Bronx suffering — poverty, unfair distribution of resources, jobs and noxious facilities, and the prison-industrial complex — along with the global concern of climate change. After people pick up their first paycheck or watch their daughter breathe more freely, they will invest trust, respect and devotion in the activists and organizers who made those beneficial changes possible.

Bankable concepts for service-oriented political organization, along with the forgotten but reliable ideas of interdependence, social responsibility and "community in action" may be uniquely appealing during and after the financial collapse which has caused almost unprecedented suffering in the United States. In 2000 Robert Putnam wrote, "Creating (or re-creating) social capital is no simple task. It would be eased by a palpable national crisis, like war or depression or natural disaster, but for better *and* for worse, Americans at the dawn of a new century face no such galvanizing crisis."[12]

Seven years later America's financial system finally broke, proving that greed and selfishness are not reliable models for managing markets or organizing a society. Americans embraced change at the voting booth and displayed a level of involvement and participation not seen in several decades. The crisis loomed large and Americans responded slowly but eventually with a combination of electoral wisdom and political shortsightedness. A heavy and onerous workload remains untouched and calls to be carried by power and the public alike.

Bruce Springsteen's best political songs rarely indict only one element of society. They do not take comfort in easy finger-pointing or self-righteous protest that is removed from the shared responsibilities of democracy. "American Skin (41 Shots)," "The Ghost of Tom Joad," "Souls of the Departed," along with many others, provide a comprehensive examination of American society and the complex and often combustible mixture of socio-political, cultural and popular forces that are responsible for both the failures and triumphs of America's unique brand of shared governance. Although consistently contemptuous of market and political power, these songs emphasize the mutual accountability for a fully functional laboratory of social ills which is doctored with the participation, or at least tacit approval through indifference, of the citizenry. In "American Skin (41 Shots)" the social disharmony engineered through racist legacies rests on the shoulders of policy makers who oversee racial profiling, drug wars and urban decay but also on those of the everyday people who allow stereotypes and presupposition to paralyze beneficial interaction and cross-cultural understanding with fear, distrust and resentment. "The Ghost of Tom Joad" not only condemns the indifference to poverty that prevails among governing institutions but also the apathy that afflicts middle-class and affluent Americans. "Souls of the Departed" is a scathing presentation of profit-utility ethics and aggressive militarism. Its protest is balanced by a complex look at the hypocrisy of which every citizen is, at certain times, guilty. These songs, and especially "My Hometown" and "Long Walk Home," also dramatically demonstrate that American solutions lie in the mutual reciprocity of its community members that must guide an effort of challenging each other to remember its best and worst moments while progressing according to the instruction gained from that history and the stories of people who triumphed and suffered as a result of it.

Springsteen's music may introduce listeners to, or remind them of, an American tradition that is critical of self-minded decision-making processes regulated by narrow concentrations of power. It will also be instructive or reaffirming of the tradition that has provided strength in moments of crisis and is built on a bedrock of values that should be foundational to the creation and nurture of any community — values of love, trust and interdependence. In December of 2008, in the early stages of the financial collapse, a New York social worker described the pain of his routinely professional difficulties:

> As the year has progressed and New York State has chosen to repeatedly victimize its most vulnerable citizens, it has become more difficult to help people meet these needs. I have visited food banks with empty shelves, been told clients were ineligible for help when I knew they were and had to challenge these decisions. I have sat with clients while their applications for public assistance were reviewed by fraud investigators at social services. Our local social services department actually hired fraud investigators at the same time that it was laying off child protective workers, demonstrating conclusively where our values lie and how genuinely mean spirited we are as a people. At the federal level Social Security routinely denies people eligible for benefits in the hopes that they will not reapply. Many people who receive benefits must hire a lawyer before social security will concede that they are indeed eligible. As the resources have become more limited, the level of scrutiny and inhumanity has risen accordingly.[13]

This description of the hostile treatment struggling Americans receive at the hands of the government in one of the nation's most liberal states is disheartening to anyone who would like to see the American community flourish. Distrust, selfishness and mean-spiritedness should not play such a prominent role in the discourse and daily life of Americans at the bottom, who feel victimized and ignored, or at the top, who succumb to paranoia and self-rewarding judgments of those below.

The simple beauty of Springsteen's narrative embedded in the lifting melody of "Long Walk Home" is most abundant in the perfect definition of a sustainable, workable and livable community found in the final verse: a place where "nobody crowds you, and nobody goes it alone." For far too long too many Americans have been made to feel crowded and alone at the same time. If a community is to be forged from the heap of ashes left in the wake of the worst financial situation since the Great Depression, Americans must work to bring themselves back to a period which may have never existed. They must stop idealizing the past and begin idealizing the future, while remaining dedicated to ensuring that the sight of a rain-soaked or sun-dried flag "sets in stone" an irrevocable guarantee of "what we'll do and what we won't." As Springsteen's music, along with the work of Americans whose names many children are taught to remember by rote (Cesar Chavez, Susan B. Anthony, Martin Luther King, etc.) and the struggle of unacknowledged warriors for justice, should remind us — this project of democracy and community rests on the continuance of America's ability to empower the individual but also on the broad establishment of love and service on a sweeping scale that seeks to include all those willing to participate.

THEY MADE THEIR HOME IN THE AMERICAN LAND: DEVELOPING MULTICULTURALISM MORE AUTHENTIC THAN THE MARKET AND MORE SOPHISTICATED THAN POLITICAL CORRECTNESS

Whenever one raises the grand concept of community in America, the ground the speaker walks begins to form potholes, uncovered wells and sinking sand. The level of inclusion in America continues to inspire masses on all continents. Ethnic groups of every sort risked life and limb to reach what they, with hope-filled hearts, called "the land of opportunity." This part of the story is often fondly told by self-aggrandizing nationalists and thoughtful dissenters alike. But it cannot be truthfully told without an unflinching recognition of the socially supported and institutionally imposed exclusion that victimized the "new" Americans — whoever they may have been. The Irish and Italians were persecuted because of anti-Catholic bigotry. Benjamin Franklin warned that if Germans were permitted to enter the country they would refuse to assimilate and "Germanize" everything east of Ohio. Such outlandish fears are unfortunately familiar to followers of the current immigration debate. Latinos are demonized with the same ignorant broad strokes, and certain pundits like Pat Buchanan have furthered their careers by writing such paranoid ravings as *Death of the West*. Asian-Americans and Jews were also treated with the same hostility and cruelty for decades. For a nation that prides itself on diversity, much of its multiculturalism was uneasily earned or forcefully prevented with a gavel or gun. Indigenous peoples faced brutality in varying forms — physical extermination, psychological abuse and imposed cultural death — and still suffer today as a result. From that point on, America became a nation of immigrants. Its cultural richness is largely due to its open borders. The unbelievably diverse selection of religion, music, food and fashion that Americans enjoy would not exist if the United States was an exclusively Anglo-Saxon country.

Bruce Springsteen has written several songs about immigrants — most of them are found on *The Ghost of Tom Joad* and *Devils & Dust* and most have melancholy melodies that carry heartbreaking tales of sadness and struggle. "Galveston Bay" tells the story of a Vietnamese immigrant who kills two Texans to protect himself against a homicidal hate crime attempted by bigots hoping to send him the message "America for the Americans." "Matamoras Banks" describes, in reverse order, the journey of a Mexican who dies of thirst while crossing the border in search of a better life.

Springsteen's most recent immigrant song is markedly different from those that came before. Written for and recorded with the Sessions Band, "American Land" is moved by a pounding Irish-dance beat and accentuated by swinging folk fiddles, a supporting horn riff and a delightful blend of the banjo, piano and penny whistle. Before the first word is sung it is clear that it is an acknowledgment and celebration of the contributions that various ethnic groups have made to American life. Were it not for Irish folk music, Appalachian Americans would have had great difficulty creating country music. Three African-Americans sing gospel-flavored backup vocals and remind anyone who has slept through all of American history that African rhythms and vocal styling were essential to the establishment of jazz, blues, gospel, rock 'n' roll and hip-hop. The smorgasbord of musical style and influence presented in this song, and by the Sessions Band in general, serves the multitude of traditions that make America great.

"American Land" tells a story that is familiar. It begins with the voice of a wide-eyed, optimistic foreigner planning to make his home in the land where "so many travel." He speaks of a magical place where "women wear silk and satin down to their knees," "beer flows through faucets," and there is a "treasure for the taking, for any hard working man." Halfway through the song, the narrator's voice changes into that of a seasoned social observer who celebrates the courage of the various peoples who "Come across the waters a thousand miles from home / With nothing in their bellies but the fire down below." This observer also painfully laments how America is not magical, and that the costs of trying to make it are often severely high.

> They died building the railroads worked to bones and skin
> They died in the fields and factories names scattered in the wind
> They died to get here a hundred years ago they're still dyin' now
> The hands that built the country we're always trying to keep down

The bloody history of immigrant struggle, during which immigrants gave a life's worth of tears and sweat and asked only for equal respect and opportunity (which has often been violently denied) in return, is summarized in one line of song: "The hands that built the country we're always trying to keep down." Cathedrals and colleges built with immigrant hands, food farmed with immigrant backs bent, and culture cultivated by immigrant minds and spirits ensured America's majesty, excitement and joy, which is why "American Land" never loses its danceable melody and celebratory tone. However, it also makes sure to wrestle with both the accomplishments and suffering of America's multicultural and multicolored populace. "They're still dyin' now" recognizes that for many the struggle for decency and dignity continues.

Marketplace-dominated culture attempts to co-opt this ongoing narrative with slick, quick ad machines which operate continually to please all potential customers and constituents through a campaign that removes human qualities, including ethnicity and ancestry, from the equation and replaces them with false needs for fashionable consumption. Although the so-called "War on Christmas," invented by shamelessly divisive right-wing talking heads, is laughable, it is illustrative of the cynicism that corrodes much of the multicultural conversation. Corporations insist on "Happy Holidays" not to honor Jewish, Islamic, Hindu and Buddhist traditions but to coat marketing campaigns in neutral, inoffensive language. Many white pundits respond with hyperbolic and lunatic ranting about an underground campaign to kill Christmas, and hope it will succeed at distracting their white listeners from issues of importance by turning their attention to those damned, uppity minorities. There is no real recognition of cultural contribution by non-white, non-Christian ethnic groups, and no attempt to appreciate and alleviate their struggle. This formula is used to deal with several other issues, from foreign language instruction to the immigrant debate itself. Liberal institutions, most notably higher education, respond to this by enforcing a superficial and suppressive political correctness which restricts speech but does not do much else. Meanwhile, both the corporation and its cousin called the university, along with public schools and most churches, offer endless praise for "multiculturalism" with consistently hollow application.

Philosophy instructor, Carmelite priest and writer Edward R. Ward presents a clairvoyant view of the reality behind all the "sociological cheap talk" in *In Days of Old: Some Thoughts on Language* by examining the predominant beliefs about the ubiquity of foreign languages and surrounding issues.

> The pleasant talk amid the lack of commitment to language-learning and to the study of differing cultures serves to mask what is absolutely crucial: life is configured so that power is housed where the majority says that it should be — in the hands of those already in authority and in the majority. In turn, arrangements of power allow people to have their way over other people, who do not have as much power as they have. The world turns on these "schemes of interpretation." The outward face is that things are fine between and among various groups.

Ward goes on to observe that, "if Spanish and few other languages are perceived to be everywhere, and if both dominant and subordinate people encounter them daily, how can the citizenry say that it is not multicultural?" He addresses such self-comforting assurances as preposterous because "cultures are extolled, but not invested in. Issues requiring serious study are breezily dismissed as unnecessarily time consuming and not entertaining enough."[14]

The educational system, which offers a "tourist approach" to diversity, demonstrates this "pleasant talk" and "lack of commitment" most clearly. At the lower level, schools give scattered lessons on black history in February or the United Farm Workers during a rushed reading of Steinbeck and then forget about their implications for the rest of the year. At the higher level, affirmative action is implemented and ghettoized minority studies programs are part of the course catalogue. Egregious back-patting takes place in countless seminars and "world banquets," while marketing campaigns never fail to include some mention of either "diversity" or "multiculturalism." But the unjustifiably exorbitant and consistent increases in tuition ensure that only a certain class of people will climb the ivory tower. Climbers continue to be mostly white and increasingly upper class.

The failure to be authentically multicultural, along with the cynicism that surrounds its half-hearted attempt, does great damage to the project of expanding, enlarging and enriching the American community. Barack Obama's election was a powerful strike against the status quo on this score and it was the result of a detailed history of activism that preceded it. However, the activism will have to continue if a truly diverse and multicultural American community is to flourish. It may be difficult not to dance to Springsteen's "American Land," but it should become just as difficult not to remember the truth of its lyrical content — that social costs will diminish and cultural benefits will multiply if Americans commit themselves to understanding the suffering of the eclectic mix of peoples that fill the American community and respond with service to their country, which prioritizes dissent, and service to those peoples. It is also essential for justice and ethical consistency that multiculturalism goes beyond ethnicity and includes gay and lesbian Americans who continue to face social prejudice and institutional discrimination, especially in the 31 states where they are not protected from firing based on sexual orientation and in the 41 states where they cannot marry — as well as Americans of non-Christian or secular viewpoints.

The creation of an inclusive, just and compassionate community is wrapped up in a tradition of patriotism that runs through Frederick Douglass to Martin Luther King to the countless unnamed workers who struggle without fame or favor, both in the past and present. When Springsteen offers pecuniary, physical and promotional support to a food bank, he gives a lesson in this patriotism. This lesson is taught again when someone teaches a child to read, wipes the brow of a dying woman, helps a blind man cast a vote, or joins an organized effort to oppose the structurally solidified injustices and inequities that afflict America. All of these activities are done in the name of establishing a community where people feel loved, respected and supported. A country is not its symbol and arbitrator of power — whether it be George W. Bush or Barack Obama — and it is not the policies dictated by that arbitrator. A country is the people who form its history, create its cultural traditions, and determine the sweep of its promise. If a nation dare call itself just, it must receive its people, especially the newly arrived, with hospitality and inclusion.

Springsteen summarized it best when he explained the intention and process behind writing "Land of Hope and Dreams" — a powerful locomotive of a spiritual rocker about reaching a place where "all this darkness" is "past."

> I played with the refrain from "This Train," the old folk spiritual. Instead of a chorus of exclusion, "This train don't carry no gamblers," I wanted my refrain to be inclusive: "This train carries . . ." everybody.[15]

Chapter 9

Is There Anybody Alive Out There?

The Politics of a Bruce Springsteen Performance

Existential freedom is a mode of being-in-the-world which resists
dread and despair. It embodies an ecstatic celebration of human
existence without affirming the prevailing reality.

— Cornel West

One of the most quotable statements made during Bruce Springsteen's career is his four-part definition of any live performance he makes with a band, most notably the E Street Band: "Part circus, part spiritual meeting, part political rally, part dance hall." It is difficult to find a better description of what rock music should be about, a more laudable goal of creation for a performance, and even perhaps a more comprehensive survey of what it should mean to be a free person. The chaotic circus that often characterizes life is recognizable to anyone who has outgrown the crib. Party rituals, which encompass friendship, sex and escapism are required for any well-balanced person to find occasional moments of happiness. Politics is fundamentally a struggle for power and political rallies attempt to make a contribution to the shaping, exercising and concentrating of that power while representing the struggle of the powerless to gain some collective opportunity to influence institutions that guide and regulate their lives. The spiritual is the common search for transcendence — an attempt to find that which provides meaning, joy and hope in a life that is often troubled by confusion and pain. The fact that Springsteen walks into each concert with the aim (which would be absurd if he did not usually succeed) to create such a well-rounded spectacle of transcendent, challenging and comforting music is of particular interest to anyone who finds any value in his body of work because it is in the live setting that it most potently thrives.

Springsteen's danceable rhythms, escapist lyrics and party sounds possess a uniquely infectious energy which spreads through the stadium with excitement like a contagion. The fantastical tales of his early career, because they are rarely played, have a nearly magical aura when actually performed which causes dedicated fans to spread the word ("He played Incident") and from that point on make references to the envious catch ("I was there for Incident in Philadelphia"). Political protest songs are performed with a greater urgency that results from the increased stakes of the live performance. In order to demand attention to the anti-war narrative of "Last to Die" or poverty lamentation of "The Ghost of Tom Joad," Springsteen and company must overcome the countless distractions that inevitably appear in a room with 25,000 people. Spiritual moments are dramatized by the ritualistic capacity created by audience participation and it becomes clear why Springsteen chose to use the word "meeting" when describing this portion of the show; the crowd contains a crucial element to the performance's strength. Regardless of the song and its purpose, it often takes on new meaning, effectuality and accessibility when played at a Springsteen concert.

A version, albeit a narrow one, of Springsteen's vision of community also emerges before, during and after the show. Fans exhibit a mutually reciprocal understanding, kindness and in-the-know dialoguing that can be called cultish by some less dedicated attendees or warmly charming by others.

In these respects, and others, the Springsteen concert is the culmination of almost all the ideas expressed in his work and the elevation of its musical quality, artistic fidelity, and political and spiritual urgency.

A SPIRITUAL CIRCUS: ATTEMPTS AT TRANSCENDENCE DURING A BRUCE SPRINGSTEEN SHOW

Whenever one pays money to see a band perform live, one is hoping to gain some richness in experience. It may be mere entertainment. It could be pleasant nostalgia or it might be a moment of transportation from the mundane routine of the ordinary to an extraordinary plane where troubles are temporarily forgotten, adrenaline is accelerated, and ecstasy arrives. This form of unique joy elevates the concert performance from mere entertainment to something beyond that which is so easily rendered "entertaining". It becomes memorable for its power, dynamic energy and lasting effect.

Transcendence of this sort is usually thought to be limited to religious revivals, classical artistic exhibitions, and theatrical readings of poetry. However, rock music does have this capability. One need only watch early footage of Elvis shaking his hips and belting out lyrics sorely lacking in content to find sufficient proof. The lack of lyrical substance on Elvis's early rock records did not weaken their strength. He performed them with such ferocity, sexual dynamism and unfettered power that scores of women would cry, faint or convulsively shake, while their male companions would feel helpless against the urge to shout and dance. Images such as these reveal the transcendent capacity built into rock music and demonstrate that even if it can be viewed as mere pop culture, or even low culture by some, it has built a track record of moving, shaking, uplifting and unsettling people.

The Bruce Springsteen concert most often reaches rock 'n' roll's emotional peak when theatrical songs featuring tales of fantasy are performed for the benefit of the audience's imagination or dramatic and ritualistic spiritual anthems are played with captivating sincerity and energy. The pure power of the performance is not enough on its own to accomplish transcendence. Unlike those Elvis numbers, lyrical depth is a vital component. "Rosalita" and the all too rare "Thundercrack" are exceptions to this formula, but those songs could just as easily be categorized under the escapist dance-hall portion of the show.

The circus element is best expressed through songs like "Incident on 57th Street" and "Jungleland" which contain musical movements of compelling drama, along with romantic lyrical tales of triumph or tragedy. This commanding combination of sound and substance produces a fantastical scene on the stage which permeates into the audience — especially on performances of "Jungleland," given that the crowd's participation is demanded on the "down in Jungleland" shout, which precedes the musical lift that raises the mood of the song and room. The key to the performance of these songs, along with others such as "Spirit in the Night," "Kitty's Back," and "New York City Serenade," is that they stimulate, both sonically and narratively, the imagination of the listener — just as a circus does with clowns, beasts and freaks, if Springsteen's comparative category is to be taken literally.

These songs, with the possible exception of "Jungleland," take on a mystical quality when performed, because of their rarity. When an excited fan hears the opening piano notes to "Incident on 57th Street," the sheer surprise of the moment is transformational — changing the concert from ordinary to legendary. The epic rarities also become fodder for lengthy conversations on Springsteen internet discussion boards, and the shows during which they appeared become prizes for bootleg collectors everywhere. The songs that possess this aura of magic and mystery were all written and recorded during the earliest portions of Springsteen's career when his songs were much more musically innovative, unpredictable and combinative (blending blues, jazz, soul and traditional rock). *Darkness on the Edge of Town* represents the shift in Springsteen's songwriting to more traditional structures, as he felt they were more complementary to the lyrical themes he began pursuing at the time — political commentary, along with psychological and sociological observation on working-class struggles. Therefore, when "Kitty's Back" is played live it is almost as if a different Springsteen, one no longer active, emerges on the stage and through that emergence the audience is given a momentary and experiential glimpse into a past performance personality and musical style. This is essential to the circus portion of the show because it puts the most committed members of the audience in a state of disbelief, i.e. "After all of the shows I've been to, am I finally seeing this?" A ghostly quality drifts through the arena as Springsteen revisits a part of his career and artistic vision that is rooted in the past, has been replaced by something altogether different, and is clearly not coming back. While nostalgia and mystery characterize these performances, so does a longing for an ideal. Their stories detail down-and-out characters desperately seeking a solution to their social isolation and personal misery. "New York City Serenade" describes an urban paradise founded on values of bravery, integrity and honesty. Not to appear naïve, Springsteen introduced the song in the 1970s by declaring "This is what New York should be like." The conflict and struggle of "Jungleland" is also set in the Big Apple but it is about a man who recognizes the city's flaws and fights for a moment of transcendence. However, the real drama is in the music, which not only provides emphasis of the narratives but far eclipses their emotional arches with imaginative beauty, grace and power. The chase for an ideal is documented through fantasy and serves to balance the stories of suffering that dominate the political portion of the show. They go beyond mere dance by intrinsically recognizing the disappointment and dread that is often at the center of life through the character's urge to escape it, which is played out dynamically in the music — the saxophone solo on "Jungleland," the musical interlude in the middle of "Kitty's Back," the closing chant of "New York City Serenade." When these songs theatrically conclude, leaving the audience breathless, the mysterious wind that brought them back to the building drifts out the window just as fast as it blew in. It is not to be contained but only momentarily experienced through a mighty gust.

The closest Springsteen came to completely summoning that ghostly wind and revisiting this style of fantastical music was on his tour with the Sessions Band in 2006 which, although underrated, was a high moment of his entire career. The eccentric rhythms and wild playing that defined those shows more closely resembled Springsteen's early '70s musicianship than anything else he has done before or since. Its bigness was also similar, boasting a full horn section, a mini-choir of backup singers and multiple fiddlers. However, those shows were far too rooted in the political devastation of the Bush era to ever verge on fantasy, even though a circus element strongly remained. By aiming to pay tribute to Pete Seeger, the show consisted of anti-war ballads, civil rights anthems and folk era protest that unlike "Incident on 57th Street" or "Spirit in the Night" directly referenced troubled times. Far from being exclusively political, the Sessions show was also deeply spiritual. "This Little Light of Mine," "O Mary Don't You Weep," and "Jacob's Ladder" bristled with revival quality and energy, which filled people with the spirit to stand and shout. "When the Saints Go Marching In" and Springsteen's own "My City of Ruins" maintained a quiet, meditative gospel that called for deep reflection and consideration on how one lives a spiritual life in a modern world too often conflicted with trauma and catastrophe. The historical resonance of these performances, which were indebted to Pete Seeger, legions of folk and gospel writers and players and those who made these songs the soundtrack of their struggle for justice, gave them a unique profundity and authenticity that reminded people of the constancy of battling tragic circumstances and unjust order.

When the E Street Band enters spiritual-meeting mode it does so with its own history. It may not be as textured and longstanding as that of folk and gospel music but it does possess great importance to their fans, and contemporary relevancy. It also, like any spiritual program, is highly ritualized and ritualistic. Fans chant with fists in the air to "Badlands" without being directed or instructed. They sing in synchronicity and gesture in unity with "The Promised Land" and "The Rising." Spirituality is emphasized not only through the musical strength and audience participation in these songs but also their lyrical content, which centers on faith — faith in God and certainly faith in humanity as a shared experience that allows people to courageously face losses of dignity, abortions of justice and conditions of horror. It does not eliminate pain but allows one to labor through it by enhancing the preexisting faculties and qualities shared by all peoples: compassion, solidarity and tenacity. Through this commonly shared, artistically performed and mutually expressed faith a unique form of prayer emerges. This special prayer most closely resembles what French philosopher Jean-Luc Nancy, with help from poet Michael Deguy and social theorist Theodor Adorno, calls "prayer demythified." Similar to the Derridean concept of prayer, "prayer demythified" is not specifically addressed but it is considered in itself, according to its own value. Nancy concedes that a term that presents prayer as a concept without myth is oxymoronic. However, this oxymoron contains power derived from a "tension to be maintained."

Constant tension results from the unlikely construction of prayer demythified's bridge, joining skepticism and belief — secular doubts and religious forms. The ecumenical engineering feat is established when an individual, or in this case a gathered community, ritualistically expresses a hopeful and faithful desire for some end without directly seeking that end. For example, when Springsteen sings, joined by a chorus of fans, that he would like to "Take a knife and cut this pain from my heart" before firmly stating belief in "the promised land," he is leading people to join him in a call to simply express this faith, along with a shared desire to see the faith actualized. But Springsteen at no point posits, nor does the audience accept, the idea that the prayer will tangibly affect the desired actualization. "Land of Hope and Dreams" contains a similar demythologized prayer in its refrain which speaks of an open train that carries whores and gamblers, fools and kings alike. The same observation can be made about "My City of Ruins" which directly mentions God but does not seek God's assistance in rejuvenating the financially devastated and spiritually deadened city. It only expresses desire for divine assistance in serving the communal need for strength, love and hope.

Nancy's treatment and endorsement of this form of prayer is useful and helpful to those who find solace in Springsteen's spiritual performances, and recognize beauty, truth and power in his sophisticated prayer:

> Prayer does not supplicate to obtain — and thus it is that "prayer demy-thologized" is, in Adorno's terms, "freed from the magic of the result." Prayer does not ask in order that its request be granted, nor does it produce that result. To have one's prayers answered — that is the expectation, as self-interested as it is illusory, of religion, which consequently is doomed to content itself with imaginary satisfactions (if I am not healed, it is because an even higher good has been granted me . . .). But to be lifted up (for that is the word, and that is its sense), that is the true efficacy of the word that rises, that is to say, that simply turns from the being-posited, given, toward the real in that it gives itself and is given, presented.[1]

Nancy makes a similar point when he explains that prayer is "adoration" in its essence. It is not primarily a "request in order to receive response." It is address, homage, recognition, veneration and "simply the movement of transcendence." Those who seek and obtain transcendence at a Springsteen show do so for this very reason, in addition to the undeniable power in the music. The planned, oft-repeated moments of ritualistic gesture and sing-along, and the spontaneous reactions to surprises are categorized as communal prayers for the creation of a world that, although hoped for in unity, is understood to have little chance of ever existing. These moments transport the listener from the mundane and common to the dreamed-of and imagined for a few precious minutes. They also reaffirm some of Springsteen's most important political values: community, participant democracy and inclusion. They are not dependent on adherence to a particular dogma, nor do they offer slick and quick marketplace comforts of constant consumption and mad materialism. They only demand that people join together in the projection of edifying values and allow those values to have some impact on their individual lives, while connecting their individuated struggles with a sense of purpose larger than one's self.

Springsteen himself has called his career a "community in the making." Lending a democratic quality to his art, he elaborated, "It's not just my creation. I wanted it to be our creation. Once you set that in motion, it's a large community of people gathered around a core set of values. Within that there's a wide range of beliefs, but you still gather in one tent at a particular moment to have some common experience, and that's why I go there too."[2]

This spiritual meeting of a large community is addressed, recognized and venerated at every turn of phrase and with every instrumental note of the Springsteen prayer. However, there are moments when the divergence of those "wide range of beliefs" are tackled and more disagreeable ideas of economic and social justice, political leadership and war and peace become the subject of the Springsteen concert — moments when Springsteen, like Frederick Douglass, insists that people must "pray with their feet."

"THE MUSIC HAS GOTTA BE RIGHTEOUS": POLITICS AND PARTYING

The community of Bruce Springsteen fans is a tight group of people who behave under the auspices of mutually understood codes of conduct before, during and after a Springsteen concert. A separation can be detected among the casual fans and the committed ones by making observations on the level of adherence to the code of conduct, as well as knowledge of Springsteen performance ritual and history. Knowledge of history is a pretty straightforward concept when dealing with Springsteen's music or any other topic. The code of conduct unique to Springsteen fans encourages the expression of certain values which prioritize respect for the artist, solidarity among fan groups and individual sacrifice of small gains so that the group may obtain enhanced enjoyment. For example, in general admission sections, Springsteen fans are adamant about reserving a person's spot when she uses the washroom, and will respond with admonition against those who sneak up to be closer to the stage during that fan's absence. Prior to a show I attended in Cincinnati, while still in high school, a group of fans I met in the parking lot were impressed that a person of such youth would be as passionate about Springsteen's music as I was — in other words, they were excited at the possibility that I was one of them, despite a significant generational gap.

After conversing with me for about 20 minutes, they huddled in resemblance to a football team and broke up to announce their intention of trading two of their tickets with my pair, so that I could sit in the tenth row as opposed to in the back of the building. My half-hearted attempts at refusal were sternly rejected on the grounds that they had "seen a Springsteen show up close several times, and you haven't."

Anecdotes such as these exemplify the vision of community that Springsteen makes the subject of a musical campaign and while he attempts to unify fans on stage by strengthening that communal energy he also creates challenging moments of division during his live performance. This is the political rally portion of the show — the moments when Springsteen presents his idea of how that community can be projected onto a national screen. It momentarily separates the Springsteen community of committed fans according to political allegiance, and also widens the divide between the committed and casual. Sociologist Lawrence Grossberg explains that fandom is based on "giving a certain significance or weight to popular culture, while ordinary audience behavior is based on the pleasure and enjoyment of it."[3] Nothing highlights this contrast as colorfully as an artist's expression of political viewpoints, and Springsteen is far from an exception.

The tension that exists between any live performer, especially Springsteen, and his less devoted fans is a result of set-list disputes. Springsteen typically is interested in spotlighting new material and showcasing his contemporary voice, while many fans, who may not even know that a new album exists, expect to watch a greatest hits exhibition that does not reach beyond the well-known classics from Springsteen's musical catalogue.

It is precisely during these moments, in the throes of this tension and through Springsteen's clever exploitation of casual-fan wishes for pure nostalgia that a political rally unexpectedly takes shape in the middle of a concert. The complementary sequencing of songs, which combines old and new, is where most Springsteen shows reach their peak and where his progressive vision of politics and challenging critique of the status quo explode with clarity and creativity. By linking new songs that have a strong political view with older songs that have a similar message or vaguer meaning, Springsteen redefines or emphasizes certain parts of his most beloved hits, which challenges fans to rediscover them and consider them in entirely new ways.

The conceptual and performative bedrock of the Springsteen and E Street Band show during the 1999–2000 Reunion Tour was a five-pack sequencing of songs that remained intact throughout the tour and can be viewed on the *Bruce Springsteen and the E Street Band: Live in New York City* DVD. It begins with "Youngstown," intensifies with "Murder Incorporated," and without pause erupts into "Badlands," before shifting gears to "Out in the Street" and "Tenth Avenue Freeze-Out."

"Youngstown" typically followed a quiet ballad and, after a few moments of silence, its opening crash would shake the arena like a thunderbolt. Springsteen's howling, gravel-throated voice, inhabited by a misused and abused steelworker, screams the opening lines with infuriated ferocity — painfully holding out notes and stretching his lungs to the limit. The anger and dread of this character was made palpable throughout the arena, and if there were any doubters who missed the rage of this performance, its closing guitar solo by Nils Lofgren clashing against the mighty drums of Max Weinberg presents an irrefutable closing argument. The building of drama with the song's conclusion rises to a new level when the beat quickly changes, and with it Springsteen plays the muscular guitar riff of "Murder Incorporated" and sings its discontented story without losing a hint of the outrage of "Youngstown." Lyrically, the connection is clear — deindustrialization has created joblessness and hopelessness that produces sickening urban decay which, in the place of working-class employment, houses crime, violence and drug dependency. Musically the story begins slowly with a steelworker's bitter lament and theatrically builds power until the anger and disgust explode into "Murder Incorporated." An indictment of the ruling class who neglected working people and inner-cities and thereby created an untamable monster is issued with all the elements, force and fury that rock 'n' roll can summon.

By this time the audience is on its feet. Most of them were not familiar with "Youngstown," but Lofgren's captivating guitar solo followed by "Murder Incorporated"'s raw and gritty power has injected the crowd with adrenaline. The stakes are raised, politically and musically, when "Murder Incorporated" effortlessly plays into the Springsteen classic and fan favorite, "Badlands." Coming on the heels of such assault and battery against the political and corporate elite, this old warhorse finds new life by shifting form and carrying entirely new meaning. Its anthemic quality of existential empowerment against psychically depressing conditions gains specificity because it can be viewed as a response to the political failure and social misery described in its preceding songs. Lines such as "Poor man wanna be rich, rich man wanna be king / And a king ain't satisfied till he rules everything," take on greater importance. The last line of the final verse, "I wanna spit in the face of these badlands," becomes a confrontational pledge of resistance to institutional and individual forces arrayed against the unnecessarily suffering person. Its musical dynamism demonstrates the power that oppositional faith carries and that resistance can produce. A booming drumbeat provides a foundation to Springsteen and Van Zandt's committed and deliberate vocals, an emotional intense guitar solo by the bandleader, and the soaring saxophone of Clarence Clemons. The only thing that remains before the song's triumphant finale when the pledge of resistance is made is an audience chant, which although not containing words, underscores cooperative intention. Simple "ooh, ooh, ooh, ooh, ooh"s echo through the arena, dramatizing the participatory part of Springsteen's political rally and necessitating communal inclusion and organization in resistance. When the song seems to end, Weinberg continues to sporadically beat on his drums and crash his cymbals while the guitarists chaotically clash and the organ calls out to be heard amidst the sonic wreck. These disparate elements are joined by the audience's continued chant. Taking his cue from the audience, leader becomes follower, and demands the band to bring "Badlands" back into its mode of melodic fury. The familiar piano riff starts anew, the song kicks in, and the crowd does not relent. Ritualistic fists are pumped in the air and it becomes clear that should this political rally be internalized, its energy should move through adversity and its call should resound through false endings. If one accepts the pledge of resistance there should be no getting out.

With that the political rally ends. It will be revisited later in the show, but it has been put to rest momentarily. Springsteen's sequencing of a signature anthem with obscure protest songs encourages the audience to make crucial connections between their individual principles and public policy that creates castigation and struggle both in and far outside their neighborhoods. The ability and willingness to make these connections varies from individual to individual but Springsteen's insistence on challenging his audience secures his artistic integrity and reveals his loyalty to the pursuit and projection of his own American, progressive, and at times divisive, vision. Similar rallies were organized on the Magic Tour when Springsteen paired "Magic" with "Reason to Believe" and, later in the set, "The Rising" with "Last to Die," which was followed by "Long Walk Home." The Sessions Band show boasted a tremendous trio of "Mrs. McGrath" (an Irish anti-war song), "How Can a Poor Man Stand Such Times and Live," and "Jacob's Ladder." However, the Reunion Tour five-pack represents a stunning combination of Springsteen concert elements that has not appeared with such complementary strength since.

When "Badlands" ends, the band almost instantly plays the jubilant opening notes of "Out in the Street." The song immediately changes the mood of the show with its organically fun, bouncy and danceable character. Springsteen shares the vocals with his band mates before prompting the crowd to join him in another chant containing nothing but "ohs." The ebullient tribute to leisure and party allows the audience to escape from unpleasant and unjust world conditions and embrace momentary joy. It also allows Springsteen to play his charismatic entertainer role — dancing, mugging for the camera and singing with a carefree spirit that is infectious. Twelve minutes earlier the arena was enveloped in the black, poisonous cloud that hovers over a Youngstown steelworker who was exploited by his employer and forgotten by his political representation. Now, the cloud has temporarily drifted away to reveal a giant dance hall built to be enjoyed by thousands of people. The hall continues to shake when the suspenseful opening notes of "Tenth Avenue Freeze-Out" fill the room. Springsteen leads the audience in yet another "oh" chant — this time substituting it for the horn section that plays on the album version — and reminds them that constant participation is required. The soulful serenade of the first two verses and choruses raises the party's temperature just before a sudden drop when the musical bridge arrives and Springsteen sings "I'm all alone . . . and I can't go home." The music breaks down and plays softly enough for Springsteen's vocal to dominate the room.

After soulfully leading sing-alongs of "It's Alright" and "Take Me to the River," he begins to describe his need to find a "river of love," "a river of sexual healing," and a "river of faith." He does so in the cadence of a Southern black preacher, which he most likely learned from blues and soul black-club singers who shout in that style, rather than his own religious upbringing (Catholic priests are rarely known to holler and whoop). He explains that a searcher can never arrive at this river alone but must have "help" and "companionship." This leads perfectly into the introduction of his helpful companions — the E Street Band. Although this may seem like a hyperbolic shtick created for the amusement of fans, one must remember how rock 'n' roll, by the songwriter's own admission, gave him purpose, a sense of belonging and saved his sanity. Springsteen has, without break or announcement, converted the dance hall to a revival and brought the audience back to that spiritual meeting where they find communion and transcendence. From "Youngstown" to "Tenth Avenue Freeze-Out" and within approximately 40 minutes of music Springsteen has fulfilled all his promised roles and transformed a sports arena into a political rally, dance hall and spiritual meeting. And for those skeptical few who weren't paying close enough attention, he emphatically announces in the middle of the "Tenth Avenue" rap "I'm not bullshittin' back here."

Sociologist David Grazian argues in his study of the Chicago blues scene, *Blue Chicago*, that authenticity is "little more than an idealized representation of reality" and a "figment of our collective imagination." However, he does go on to argue that it remains a social fact, due to its importance as an "organizing principle for evaluating our experiences in everyday life." Performance, Grazian goes on to say, is an attempt at inventing authenticity and by its very nature is typically inauthentic.[4] However, what Grazian may fail to acknowledge is that for many musicians their performances are significantly the result of experiences in their everyday lives.

In junior high school, a youthful Bruce Springsteen was harshly reprimanded by school nuns for drawing a picture of Jesus Christ being crucified on an electric guitar. Several years after being accused of sacrilege, rock 'n' roll provided him with the meaning and purpose promised by religion. The image of the Christian Messiah martyring himself on a Fender has remained deep within Springsteen's consciousness. During the performance of "Light of Day," also available on the *Live in New York City* DVD, Springsteen lays down on the floor, arms outstretched as if they are nailed down to his guitar. The redemptive power of rock 'n' roll — to which he has given his life and paid tribute to in an art class sketch, is illustrated by this choreographed Christological pose. It is a moment such as this that performance and authenticity beautifully collide.

It is important to note in any discussion of Springsteen's live performances that concerts with the E Street Band or the Sessions Band are not the only ones that house the drama inherent in the various roles Springsteen has assigned to the show. His two solo tours, one in the mid-1990s in support of *The Ghost of Tom Joad* and the other to showcase *Devils & Dust* in 2005, were profoundly political, deeply moving and highly entertaining. Springsteen played some of his best shows in his entire career on those tours. He also revealed the more introspective and intellectual side of his songwriting throughout those tours and gave many of his fans an opportunity to reconnect with his songs in such a way that opened the door for new interpretation. The acoustic and intimate performance side of Springsteen is just as important as the side he shows with dynamic bands behind him. The much maligned Other Band Tour of 1992–93, contrary to wide belief, was not akin to a power outage of Springsteen's musical facilities. More so than any other tour, it showed Springsteen at his most soulful. Complete with a mini-choir of gospel backup singers and an African-American rhythm section, these performances heavily relied upon the elements of soul music to fulfill the same roles of any Springsteen show: spiritual meeting, circus, dance hall and political rally. These musical roles represent different personas that Springsteen embodies and projects while on stage and these personas are most divergently displayed during public performances other than his own concerts. No better comparison of divergent performative personalities that exist within Springsteen can be made than the one between "We Are One: The Obama Inaugural Celebration" and Super Bowl 43, which took place just weeks after the new President was sworn in.

Springsteen rejected offers to play the Super Bowl for 20 years before finally agreeing to perform at halftime during number 43. His refusal to appear at the big game most likely mirrored his reasons for declining million-dollar offers from car companies asking to use his songs in commercials: It was corporately branded, and therefore not only robbed the songs of their intended context but also diluted them of artistic integrity. "Born in the U.S.A." did not belong in Chevy commercials, just as it had no place smashed between ads for Cialis and Budweiser during a segment sponsored by Bridgestone. On the other hand, other bands, such as U2, found a way to make their halftime performances both entertaining and emotionally resonant. U2 performed "Beautiful Day" and "Where the Streets Have No Name" as a stirring tribute to the victims of the 9/11 terrorist attacks. It did not seem hucksterish or cheap, despite its corporate and commercial branding. However, U2 is better suited for theatrical grandeur than Springsteen and their respective ticketed shows prove it. Springsteen's resistance to the most highly watched extravaganza on television seemed wise for these reasons, along with several others.

Changes in the music industry and buying demographics, according to Springsteen, changed all of that. "We have an album to promote, Dummy," was his response to Bob Costas after being asked "Why now?" This obviously facetious and flippant answer contains a heavy kernel of truth but only represents half the story, considering that during those years Springsteen rejected offers he also had albums to promote. In an interview with the *New York Times* he elaborated by identifying key shifts in the music industry that have left performers his age with either really big ways to promote their albums or really small ways. The middle-sized venues and formats are no longer viable options. The mainstream mega status of the 1980s is something that Springsteen will never enjoy again, nor will his music find a large young audience, but it seems to be something he still, with certain projects, longs for. Therefore, he has embraced promotional campaigns and marketing tactics that some of his peers, most especially Neil Young, have neglected due to a greater acceptance of their subdued, but still lauded, musical role in popular culture (Neil Young sings on "Fork in the Road": "I'm a big rock star / My sales have tanked / I still got you / Thanks"). Lacking Young's security and strength in balancing fame and obscurity, Springsteen agreed to perform at the Super Bowl in 2009 to promote the most pop-sensible album of his career on the biggest stage of them all. By doing so, he demonstrated that despite consistent political activism, anti-mainstream projects like folk tributes and quiet Western albums, he still maintains significant commercial crassness and is prepared to use it when he sees fit. Commercial crassness most complements his performance personality of charismatic entertainer, which is most prominently displayed when his own shows enter dance hall mode.

Springsteen attempted to convert the entire football stadium into a dance hall during the 12 minutes he was allotted to perform. He promised a party, and reached into the history of his catalogue to deliver. Opening with "Tenth Avenue Freeze-Out," playing an unforgivably edited "Born to Run," and ending with "Glory Days," the set stayed in one tempo and one pitch for its entirety. Springsteen's duet with Little Steven on "Glory Days" was the highlight as it was laced with tongue-in-cheek humor, self-deprecation and terrific interplay between Bruce and Van Zandt. The most cringe-worthy moment was a 60-second version of "Working on a Dream" crowbarred between "Born to Run" and "Glory Days." Springsteen brought out a full, robe-clad gospel choir to sing backup vocals on a song about the physical, intellectual and spiritual labor required to make hope a reality, and gave them about a half-minute to close out the song in one of the most awkward transitions to ever occur during a live Springsteen performance. The choice to rush the only new song in the set was a bit bizarre, especially considering Springsteen's "We have an album to promote, Dummy" justification for agreeing to do the Super Bowl in the first place. The performance was fun, amusing and energetic, and it demonstrated that Springsteen still possesses energy and charisma that most performers half his age would kill for. It also, unfortunately, revealed what a Springsteen concert would be like if it was exclusively a dance hall: enjoyable but forgettable. Escapism without context, without an acknowledgment of the conditions that motivate withdrawal, is not relevant or memorable once the escape ends. The Super Bowl performance, while effectively showcasing Springsteen and the E Street Band's musical abilities and entertainment prowess, fell into the trap of meaningless escapism and failed to highlight any of Springsteen's larger artistic vision.

Two weeks earlier "We Are One," a concert celebrating the inauguration of Barack Obama was held at the foot of the Lincoln Memorial. Springsteen opened the show with a straightforward acoustic version of "The Rising" and before he would take the stage again, acts as diverse as Will.I.Am, John Mellencamp and Garth Brooks would perform for the thousands gathered in the nation's capital, among them President Obama himself. Just before the closing number, Springsteen reemerged onto the stage, this time accompanied by Pete Seeger, the 90-year-old folk music legend, and Tao Seeger, Pete's grandson. Springsteen stepped up to the microphone and with a wide smile said, "Lead us, Pete." This prompted the living monument to musical and activist history to give out his own instructions: "You sing it with us." The three troubadours, each representing a different generation, then began Woody Guthrie's classic tribute to democracy and solidarity, "This Land is Your Land" by strumming their guitars and lifting their voices, surrounded by a multicolored, multicultural and multi-aged choir. After the first two verses, which are familiar to most Americans, Pete Seeger strongly spoke the two formerly "lost" verses and Springsteen shouted each line in urgent and impassioned repetition:

> In the squares of the city, in the shadow of a steeple
> By the relief office, I'd seen my people
> As they stood there hungry, I stood there asking
> Is this land made for you and me?

As I went walking I saw a sign there
And on the sign it said "No Trespassing"
But on the other side it didn't say nothing,
That side was made for you and me.

The call and response between Seeger and Springsteen, with audible audience participation, represented Springsteen at his populist and prophetic best. Pete Seeger was there with his voice and guitar and his sweat and tears when black men were shot with firehoses. He was there to amplify his voice and swing his arms to hold back the blood flowing from Southeast Asia. He was there when Martin Luther King stood at the same steps of the same memorial and invited the world to share his dream. Springsteen's invitation for Pete Seeger to join in a celebratory moment of American triumph against the forces of hate, violence and injustice that he had dedicated his life to opposing was a beautiful illustration of reverence for history, regard for heroes and reaffirmation of a progressive political vision that is larger than any single moment and any symbol of power, even the one who was being honored. Instead of simply applauding the President-elect whom he campaigned for, Springsteen seized the opportunity to realign himself with the suffering and transform the stage and event into something bigger than an Obama celebration. By shifting the spotlight onto Pete Seeger, who so poetically led his grandson and Springsteen in the recitation of Guthrie's radical commitment to freedom and justice, Springsteen created a moment that was instructional of the struggle. The struggle for equality and dignity has a long history, and it does not end with the election of Barack Obama, even if he symbolizes hope and promise. It is wrapped up in the idea of comfort for the suffering and opportunity for the ordinary. Pete Seeger tirelessly devoted himself to telling that story and Springsteen allowed him to tell it once more in front of the largest audience in his career, and for the would-be leader of the free world. Seeger and Springsteen did not hesitate to make Obama an audience member and instead of singing for him, sang to him. This was done in a reminder that the poor and dispossessed must never be forgotten, and that wealth cannot be acquiesced to and substituted for competence and fairness when determining the direction of public policy. It solidified Springsteen's status as a visionary artist who may support certain politicians but remains most loyal to undying principles.

It also dramatized his ability to transform the stage into something of his unique creation. Just as he creates a dance hall, circus or spiritual meeting in the middle of a basketball arena, he too can reorient the celebration of one man's election to the presidency into a rally for an entire nation's progress and promise. This is the art of transformation and the creation of transcendence. This is Springsteen's greatest gift as a performer.

THE CROSS OF MY CALLING: THE MANY MEANINGS OF "THE RISING"

"The Rising," written as a "bookend to 'Into the Fire,'" as Springsteen described it, is not only one of his best songs but also one of his most transformational. This is particularly interesting because a major theme of "The Rising" is transformation. The song was written at a very specific moment in history and was inspired by a very specific tragedy: The attacks of September 11, 2001. But through the course of historical development in U.S. and international affairs, in addition to different responses received by live audiences, the anthem has grown into three different incarnations, each with a unique meaning.

On the album of the same name, "The Rising" appears immediately after "You're Missing," the most mundanely mournful song on the album. Following it is the meditation on loss and visions of the afterlife, "Paradise." Its sequencing, on a highly conceptual album, underscores its most basic themes: death, loss and the possibility for redemptive transformation. "The Rising" begins as a grieving tribute to the sacrifice of the rescuers on 9/11.

> Can't see nothin' in front of me
> Can't see nothin' coming up behind
> I make my way through this darkness
> I can't feel nothing but this chain that binds me
> Lost track of how far I've gone
> How far I've gone, how high I've climbed
> On my back's a sixty pound stone
> On my shoulder a half mile line
>
> Come on up for the rising
> Com on up, lay your hands in mine
> Come on up for the rising
> Come on up for the rising tonight

The weight that these heroes carry is intensified, and nailed to their back by a dominant sense of duty. On VH1 Storytellers, Springsteen described their setting as a "netherworld . . . a place that is familiar but transformed into something unknown and unknowable." As they rush the stairs, fully prepared to lose their lives, they find strength, love and pride in themselves, their mission and their calling: "Come on up for the rising!"

It sustains them through deep fears and dark probabilities that most people avoid at every cost. The verses tell the story with bluesy-rock inflection before the chorus reassigns the song's purpose and the life-ending moment its characters are entering into something more dramatic, beautiful and uplifting. It is the gospel. The physical ascent of these brave young men and women is not only celebrated for its physical courage but also its spiritual purity. The sacrifice for others and commitment to communal good that is endorsed in the philosophy of Confucius and political music of Springsteen is most amazingly displayed by the selflessness of those who embrace the "chain that binds them."

The song's refrain later becomes something of greater and higher value. It describes the journey experienced in the few moments where a man lives on a plane between life and death. He is surrounded by sacred things, envisions his most dearly loved ones, and has a final dream of life.

> I see you Mary in the garden
> In the garden of a thousand sighs
> There's holy pictures of our children
> Dancin' in a sky filled with light
> May I feel your arms around me
> May I feel your blood mix with mine
> A dream of life comes to me
> Like a catfish dancin' on the end of the line
>
> Sky of blackness and sorrow (a dream of life)
> Sky of love, sky of tears (a dream of life)
> Sky of glory and sadness (a dream of life)
> Sky of mercy, sky of fear (a dream of life)
> Sky of memory and shadow (a dream of life)
> Your burnin' wind fills my arms tonight
> Sky of longing and emptiness (a dream of life)
> Sky of fullness, sky of blessed life (a dream of life)
>
> Come on up for the rising
> Come on up, lay your hands in mine
> Come on up for the rising
> Come on up for the rising tonight

The musical treatment of this vision of life and death is almost uncomfortably evocative. The tension that is created in one's final moments, especially when they come too soon, is played out when the singer's straightforward and rough vocal delivery conflicts with lifting strings, which are contrasted by half notes of the guitar. The song continually builds and builds and builds. The second verse is strengthened by a pounding beat which is augmented by a blues slide guitar. The redemptive gospel of the choruses is emphasized by backup singers. A chant of "li, li, li, li, li, li, li" demands not only attention but participation, and the commitment to honor sacrifice by, at least morally and spiritually, standing with those that make it. All of this building dramatically stops when the singer begins describing his final vision of life on earth. Suddenly, everything has stopped and he is momentarily suspended. Then the building resumes with the description of the sky, which represents much more than atmosphere, and the character is undergoing transportation. The song's abrupt ending gives mystery to the conclusion of the journey and establishes distance between us and those that make it. There is a place where they go that is beyond the speculative power of the intellect.

"The Rising" opened up most shows on its tour, which began in 2002 and continued into 2003. This placement provided a thesis statement for the night's performance by laying out all the themes that it would address. It was meant to be heard as a meditation on loss and a grieving tribute to sacrificial heroes. "Come on up for the rising" was a call for unity in that tribute, and an exploration of the opportunities that were laid bare after the brutal destruction of 9/11. The idea was that participation, involvement and staking a claim to a national identity based on positive principles, which were personified by those that were sacrificed on 9/11, could shape America's future and take a form far greater and more substantive than placing flags on car radio antennas.

Within two years of the release of "The Rising," America started a war without justification, demeaned its foundational principles by stripping away civil liberties, and oversaw the demonization and degradation of dissent. On the Devils & Dust Tour, which took place in 2005 after blood was shed on the battlefield and scenes of horror multiplied throughout America, "The Rising" was performed as a centerpiece to the show, in a sad and tearful acoustic arrangement. The gospel possibilities that originally existed had become muted. "The Rising" had become a mournful ballad of regret, of broken promises and blown opportunities.

Regret had intensified into anger on the Magic Tour when the song returned to its full-band, rock incarnation but was performed as a predecessor to "Last to Die." Instead of opening the show and laying out themes to be commonly explored throughout the night it served only as a momentary glimpse into what might have been before being crushed by another tragedy — this one solely of America's making. Springsteen explained that the entire show built to the moment where "The Rising" became "Last to Die." Perhaps, because those moments musically mirrored the nation's decline from togetherness and opportunity for growth to institutional failure, political mendacity and citizenship demented, the gospel built within the song became nearly invisible.

That is until it reemerged with a profound new energy during the Obama campaign in 2008. Springsteen performed the song at campaign rallies and at inaugural celebrations. Through live performance, and inspired by public developments, the song took on yet another incarnation. In the midst of new constituencies of Americans taking a participatory role in the political process, a development which had the potential to expand the community of democracy and the believable possibility of reform represented in the candidate but more importantly in the masses mobilized around him, "The Rising" became a hopeful call for renewal, resurgence and recovery of lost principles, promises and purpose. Its gospel, which dramatized redemption and transformation, finally defeated its blues-inflected rock spirit which characterized catastrophe. Come on up for the rising indeed.

The transformation of "The Rising" reveals that the importance of Springsteen's live performances cannot be overstated. They breathe new life into his songs and allow them to become fully alive with new meanings and applications. This reimagining of his music results from the power that Springsteen's performance gains when he is surrounded by the "large community of people gathered around a core set of values." He called his career "community in the making." The truth in that description calls out like the wild roar of a saxophone most deafeningly when the music Springsteen makes is remade, over and over again, in the company of thousands of community members.

Chapter 10

The Dope's that
There's Still Hope

The Politics of Renewal

"The Rising," better than most Springsteen songs — better than most songs for that matter — captures the essence of hope. Its relentless search for a flicker of light in a sea of darkness, for a rumor of recovery in a cacophony of destruction, instructively demonstrates the defining elements of the hope that can only come from renewal and redemption. It must never lose sight of the adversity and stacked odds that stand against it and it must always remain loyally committed to the work that simultaneously makes hope possible and attempts to transform hope into reality. Even the title, "The Rising," is indicative of what it means to cultivate hope and be hopeful. It not only awakens thoughts of redemption and renewal, it also summarizes the endlessly true component of hope. Hope is the desire, labor and struggle to come out of something, transcend it, and ultimately rise above it. Without a deep understanding of suffering and setback and what causes it, any hope that emerges adds up to no more than a meaningless sentiment — an optimism founded on the shifting sands of naïveté. "The Rising" also translates to upward movement. One must be committed to climbing on crumbling stone against gale force winds and through the rain in order to actualize hope. All the while during this upward travel one needs to take into account what lies below and what remains at the periphery. The progress made solidifies and energizes hope, which many times manifests itself in the measurement taken of the small or great distance conquered and the miles still unexplored. The raising of consciousness, the awareness of history and future mystery, and the commitment to dedicated labor — in these senses, and others, "hope" is a verb, and the noun "hope" is not possible without the verb. Hope is the producer and product of these political and psychological processes because it gives and receives meaning, joy and resolve. It is rising, and it is the rising.

BLOOD BROTHERS IN THE STORMY NIGHT: THE SEARCH FOR HOPE

There cannot be much doubt that hope is tied to memory and mystery. Memories of happiness, memories of suffering and memories that inspire either contribute to hope or demand that it assert its presence. Mystery is the unknown laced with both excitement and terror. History offers clues to how the mystery may play out but one can never be sure, and therefore hope is a practicing faith — a commitment to onward movement even while understanding that it may lead nowhere. Past examples, embedded in memory, of hard-won success — personally, socially, politically — remind people to continue to struggle even in the face of insurmountable obstacles. While these aspects are essential to hope, they are purely conceptual and highly limited in their utility. Hope cannot be gained merely from thinking about history and speculating over the future. It is rooted in experience, most often a common experience made possible with shared values among a cherished community. The conceptual and experiential join together to create hope and have a lasting effect that is forceful and infectious.

These elements combine beautifully in the Bruce Springsteen anthem "No Surrender." Springsteen originally decided to cut it from the album on which it appears, *Born in the U.S.A.*, because he felt that it was too optimistic and unable to fit comfortably with the maturity present in the songs he had been writing. Steven Van Zandt convinced him to allow the song to survive by arguing that the power of friendship is one of the most important parts of the rock 'n' roll story. A studied listening of the song proves that not only does the consigliore sometimes know more than the boss but also that "No Surrender" is far from immature. It presents an intellectually sophisticated, emotionally authentic and politically applicable vision of what it means to be hopeful, and how that difficult state of being is earned.

The power of friendship is a good place to begin when considering renewal and how to obtain a better future. Hope rarely travels alone, and those who attempt to break that habit will not get very far because the consequences of isolation, as well as the benefits of community, have been thoroughly documented and demonstrated. Any leader who inspires hope can testify to the veracity of the need for companionship and solidarity. Martin Luther King and Harvey Milk had the leadership qualities necessary to lead movements for justice but without the thousands, sometimes millions, of unknowns who make up the movement their names would have no historical value. These were movements that opposed the authoritatively enforced order which cloaked both blacks and homosexuals in inferiority and inhumanity. Organizing a campaign of resistance requires the independence that allows for critical thinking and self-generated values which reject those that have been decreed by political or market power. However, it also means that one must have those values of resistance reinforced by a community banded together. It is difficult to move against the grain alone, just as it is tough to challenge practitioners of dominance, whether grand or petty, without communal support. Thoughts of resistance become actionable once the tools to perform an action are built in the company of friends. "No Surrender" dramatizes this transformation by returning to a familiar scene: the high school classroom.

> We busted out of class had to get away from those fools
> We learned more from a three minute record than we ever learned in
>   school
> Tonight I hear the neighborhood drummer sound
> I can feel my heart begin to pound
> You say you're tired and you just want to close your eyes and follow your
>   dreams down

The thunder of the drums and the depth of the chant that begins this anthem are reminiscent of a military call for action. They carry the blood and spirit of those who fight against having their identity defined for them within a cage. This is the sound of that cage door bursting open in a wild show of strength that begins the pursuit to stake out an independent existence which cannot be demeaned or corrupted by external bodies of cynicism and self-congratulatory ignorance. From the opening until the closing, "No Surrender," never loses pace or steam. It rolls on with the power that comes from confident defiance. The narrow, hopeless doctrine that is forced on this dreamer and his classmates every day is to be rejected and those who preach it are to be dismissed as fools. He has found something on the radio that cannot be watered down nor taken for granted. It is a community of possibility and promise, a vision of hope and an opportunity for life. It may not be as instructional as school in the technical sense but, unlike what is passed around in the sterile classroom, it opens the space for one to forge an individual identity that reaffirms the value of one's own life. This is the priceless lesson learned on that three-minute record — that it "ain't no sin to be glad you're alive," as Springsteen would classify it on "Badlands." Rock 'n' roll is responsible for removing this singer from the stultifying quarters where he has been unfairly assigned to serve a sentence for no crime he has committed. Bob Dylan declared that hearing Elvis for the first time was "like busting out of jail," and so he began his life of art, poetry and inspiration. Once one begins to imagine a life — a world — outside of those quarters, freedom and justice become possible. Civil rights activists had to imagine residing in a place where they were not belittled by authoritative proxy but in fact respected for their race, gender or sexual orientation. The echoing of that familiar sound from the radio — the drum — enlivens and excites the singer who, after "busting out of class" both physically and spiritually, is prepared to enter the world with a vision of possibility and a plan for rising above the stasis that is demanded of him. However, the plan is impossible in solitude. "No Surrender" never breaks from pluralistic language and depends on the "we" to carry it through its highest ambitions. The companion is addressed at the end of the first verse by reiterating his fatigue with playing a poorly designed game with idiotic rules; his inability to fit in with the established order. The time has come where these restless and faithful individuals have no choice but to "follow their dreams down." No specific destination is given in that command because one is not needed. These dreams will be followed wherever they go because to not pursue them would be akin to spiritual suicide. Guided by their solidarity, their newly found consciousness of the dominant narrative's inadequacies, and the belief that they can make their own claim, they swear a hopeful vow of resistance, commitment and fulfillment, thereby demonstrating that thinking is acting and that an opinion is an action. It is often the first action necessary for improving private and public conditions.

> We made a promise we swore we'd always remember
> No retreat no surrender
> Like soldiers in the winter's night with a vow to defend
> No retreat, no surrender

This simple, mutually reciprocal promise verbalizes their commitment to resist and fight against culturally assigned limitations while continually grasping for their own territory and treasure. Much like the words "I do" in a marital vow, these words act in their own right. They create something, and seek to preserve it. This is done in recognition of the tumultuous and unpredictable difficulties that organize against that preservation. "Soldiers in the winter's night" is certainly not a hopeful image. These men may be wounded, battling against bitter cold, thick snow and sheets of ice while worried over an enemy attack. But hope remains, and almost grows out of stubbornness: "No retreat, no surrender." If the sight and thought of this torturous hell cannot make us turn around, what will?

The only possible answer to that question is one's own failure — the failure to maintain resolve under such ghastly struggle and the failure to press on against an avalanche of belittlement, despair and discouragement. Submitting under these kinds of circumstances — facing lynching parties in the Jim Crow south, being under constant threat from homophobic police in San Francisco, or simply continually being berated by the dominant culture — is entirely understandable. But once one summons the courage to think independently and the willingness to rebel against the arbitrarily formulated narrative used to bludgeon difference and dissent, an energy is set in motion that cannot be stopped. That energy picks up speed with hope, and dies without it. The rebels in "No Surrender" flirt with submission for a fleeting moment before gratefully returning to the sources of hope that have never let them down.

> Now young faces grow sad and old and hearts of fire grow cold
> We swore blood brothers against the wind
> I'm ready to grow young again
> And hear your sister's voice calling us home across the open yards
> Well maybe we could cut someplace of our own
> With these drums and these guitars

As they grow older and face an increasingly heavy burden, passions burn out, will weakens and bodies weary. However, they are not content to simply drift off into the distance as time races forward as if they were some shadowed horse riders who are unwilling to trek through the upcoming storm. They are armed with guitars — a unique weaponry that symbolizes and exercises their creative power. They possess the ability to make their own space of safety and stability founded on something that uniquely belongs to them, which cannot be commodified and is not consumed. It is created. They spotlight their presence in the world, reaffirm their identity and amplify their voice through music which possesses an edifying utility that not only strengthens the self but also inspires the other. The lifeblood of music running through their veins allows them to hold on to a dear part of their youth — not in a shallow, immature, botox-injected fear of aging — but in a commitment to honor their ambitions and ideals of justice, dignity and self-fulfillment. German poet Friedrich von Schiller implored readers to always "keep true to the dreams of youth." Much in the same way Mark Twain distinguished the "old" from the "ancient" by the ease with which they still dream of a better future. In contemporary America these dreams are often cheaply replaced by a nightmarish perversion of the American Dream — commodities, consumption, wealth and status. The baby boomers that brought an end to the Vietnam War and envisioned a society of peace and equality but who would later applaud the invasion of Iraq and preach free-market fundamentalism are a painfully perfect illustration of this process of corruption.

The temptations of the dominant culture and the mainstream are difficult to resist. But activists and concerned citizens who would like to see what is mainstream become uniformly condemned and what is considered radical become mainstream must remain loyal to their own vision, creativity and, most importantly, both in politics and "No Surrender," communities of solidarity and support.

The vow of "blood brothers" that is made "in the stormy night" in the next chorus is of vital importance in this story of these men's resistance. It gives them the hope that is absolutely vital to their struggle. Their friendship is what they can depend on when everything else is faulty, leaking and caving in. The ache to "grow young again" through each other's shared creativity and companionship is expressed with simple beauty in the memory of "your sister's voice calling us home across the open yards." The comforting sound of familiarity coming from the voice of a loved one is what often marks one's days and makes them worth living and remembering. Running towards the warmth of home across open yards which are undeveloped and unfenced and thereby able to offer the liberation that arises from the limitless possibility of fertile soil, these men are connected with a community that is built on the infrastructure of hope. The civil rights movement had the black church, the NAACP and SNCC. The gay rights movement in the 1970s had Castro Street in San Francisco. Without these physical places where people feel safe, supported and loved, these movements do not exist. This is why it is essential that the left focus on community-building across the nation. Community is often the only place where people can find hope. A solitary individual feels powerless to move against the big government working in collusion with big money and big media. If that individual is linked with the like-minded to take on projects of social change and political reform, he will invest in activism because he will feel that the load is carried communally.

The final verse of "No Surrender" not only emphasizes this point but also emotively shows that the motivational factor for any hope durable enough to fuel social change cannot be anger. It must be love.

> Now on the street tonight the lights grow dim
> The walls of my room are closing in
> There's a war outside still raging
> You say it ain't ours anymore to win
> I want to sleep beneath peaceful skies in my lover's bed
> With a wide open country in my eyes
> And these romantic dreams in my head

Isolation has the danger of physically and spiritually imprisoning this relentless idealist. But the loving and assuring words of a companion emancipate him from a sterile and grim room. The war considered paramount to the outside world — that which battles for status at the feet of politically embedded and culturally enshrined idols of power — is not relevant to their lives and therefore it is acceptable, in fact recommendable, that he desert the battlefield. It is their responsibility to create conditions of peace. Personally, that comes in the company of each other. The love between them silences the machinery and marching of the war theater and provides them with the confidence and dignity to spread those conditions far beyond their own home by working tirelessly for justice, equality and a democracy where people have the opportunities to create just as they do, and the freedom to love just as they do.

"No Surrender" ends triumphantly with drums ferociously pounding as if it were powering the vehicle driving its protagonist out of class and out of a darkened, narrow room. Keyboards provide an atmospheric tranquility that balances the destruction of the drums while guitars wind through the spaces between the sensibility and light steps of the young men running home at their sister's invitation. The singers emphatically repeat "No retreat, no surrender," before returning to the "ooh, ooh, ooh" chant that is sung in unified resolve. Even if peaceful skies are not brought across a country in conflict, and love and justice do not temper the stormy night, these men have found the strength to continue the fight. They've pledged their resistance against the restrictive order and promised to decide for themselves the terms of their own happiness and the governance of their own community. They have found that their love cannot be defeated, and through that ongoing victory, among many defeats, they find hope.

KEEP PUSHING TILL IT'S UNDERSTOOD: "LOVE IN THE AGE OF BUSH" AND ACTIVISM IN THE AGE OF OBAMA

After recording the songs that would eventually appear on the 2007 album *Magic*, Springsteen began tinkering around with a new melody for a song that would eventually appear on 2009's *Working on a Dream*. It is a straightforward rocker with a one-two beat and jangly acoustic guitar providing its foundational rhythm. The vocal is deliberate, without much inflection, almost as if the message being communicated is so important that the listener should not be distracted by any stylistic flare or fancy effects. This is a face-to-face conversation in the middle of an intervention. The intervener is an artist and the bottomed-out addict in desperate need of recovery is an old friend called America.

The lyrics to this emphatically simple call for sanity were classified as a "meditation on love in the age of Bush" by their author. The most repeated phrase of the song is also its title: "What Love Can Do." In the era of tyrannical intentions and ruthless execution on account of government, thoughtless and heartless greed from corporate power, and a slumbering citizenry, Springsteen turns to the undying vitality of love as a way out — a means to not only escape the wasteland but also revive it with democratic virtues and values. It storyboards a scene of apocalyptic proportions and sneaks a silver lining into it that borders a promise of biblical weight. Without an introductory moment to soften the blow, the singer begins in the song's opening instant.

> There's a pillar in the temple where I carved your name
> There's a soul sitting sad and blue
> Now the remedies you've taken are all in vain
> Let me show you what love can do
> Let me show you what love can do

Disease spreads throughout the body (politic) as medicinal solutions are empty. Later, we learn that "truth lay shattered," "memory lay corrupted," and the "city lay dry." The future could not look bleaker but somehow the singer possesses an unapologetic certitude that is oddly compelling. Love has equipped him with a hope confident enough to withstand the elements, financial ruin and a ravaged home front.

Springsteen chose to deeply meditate on "love in the age of Bush" rather than anger because anger burns fast and fleetingly. It provides momentary motivation but does not have the transformative and redemptive power of love. Love enables people to establish community, instill empathy and demand justice because once one loves people, one cannot bear to see them undergo pain, be treated unfairly or have their humanity challenged. Once when Rosa Parks was asked why she refused to move from her seat on the bus, she said she thought of Emmet Till and could not get up.

Emmet Till was a 14-year-old boy who was brutally beaten and lynched in Mississippi for daring to flirt with a white woman in 1955. Parks's love for this boy, although she did not know him, gave her the rock solid resolve to remain stationary and unmovable, despite the insistence of everyone on the bus and an entire society waiting outside.

If one loves gay people one cannot stand to see them fired from their workplace for bigoted reasons nor can one tolerate the sight of them being mocked on television by people who value the word "marriage" more than the happiness of homosexuals. Love for poor people cannot accept Katrina, preventable deaths caused by unavailable health care, functional illiteracy as the result of disgraceful school systems, or a life lost to drugs or gang violence because the victim believed he had no other opportunities or was in the wrong place at the wrong time. This kind of love, that which demands justice, has the capability of redeeming a lost nation because it can reshape values and reorient priorities. It is the most reliable source of hope in moments of painful struggle. Studs Terkel's story from the Great Depression (quoted at the beginning of Chapter 8), which describes how his community rallied to preserve the dignity and quality of life for an evicted family, is exemplary of this human truth. This demonstration of human compassion and communal pride not only gave the recipients hope but also the young Terkel, because he dramatically learned of the power of "community in action," as he called it. His educational moment provided the opportunity to hope and he seized it by committing to a life of hope in the throes of so much pain and darkness. One of Terkel's finest achievements as a writer and oral historian is his tribute to hope, and those who keep it in the face of overwhelming difficulty, *Hope Dies Last*. In this American classic, Terkel amplifies the voices of courageous people who are on the move against powerful forces, searching for a better world — both personally and politically. Terkel's study of perseverance and how it is preserved emphasizes the nurturing quality of community and activism but also demonstrates that not only is hope a belief, it is also something to be believed in.[1]

Springsteen makes this point with great musical drama in the ever-exciting "Badlands." In addition to being a pledge of resistance, this anthem is also a witness to the transformation one undergoes once a commitment to hope is made. The end of the second verse proclaims, "I believe in the hope, and I pray that someday / It may raise me above these Badlands." Classifying hope in such a way encourages people to believe in a belief. Hope sneaks through a crack in the wall of obstruction through love, community and progress but it must be embraced and strapped on tightly like a life vest. Many people, paralyzed by cynicism or buried by apathy, cannot take advantage of opportunity, allow it to vanish and, through that process of perpetual defeat, make their reduced expectations into a self-fulfilling prophecy.

The Obama campaign presented Americans with a moment to believe in hope. Obama packaged it, branded it and sold it as a slogan. However, after months of the primary had passed, citizens could see that something deeper was developing and that the slogan had substantive value. People were practicing the hope and acting as if they could make it a reality and make the flip side of the slogan-bearing placard true: Change. This too became a self-fulfilling prophecy as the "Hope and Change" campaign not only created hope but also brought change. This change was not simply the shift of power that occurred as a result of the election but also a cultural change which momentarily restored faith in the American ideas of democracy and unity. Young Americans who voted and volunteered felt it, and so did

African-Americans who were able to map a major step closer to equality. This progress, which transpired throughout the campaign and culminated on Election Day, energized its hopeful ushers and gave essential fuel to their faith.

The amazing utility of hope is that it allows people to size up current conditions, intelligently look beyond them without naïveté, and act as if the change they seek will undoubtedly come to fruition if they continue to work, fight and believe. People act as if they are entitled to the life, liberty and pursuit of happiness they envision, despite daily discouragement. Civil rights activists acted as if they had equality under the law when they sat down in "white only" restaurants. The Serbian youth movement Otpor!, which led the struggle to overthrow totalitarian war criminal Slobodan Milosevic, acted as if they had succeeded when they led thousands of people chanting "He is finished" and "Serbia has arisen" before Milosevic was removed from power. Both of these examples, along with popular uprisings against U.S.-backed homicidal dictators Suharto in Indonesia, Ferdinand Marcos in the Philippines and Nicolae Ceausescu in Romania, prove that the utility of hope — its enabling of people to act *as if* — cannot be dismissed as overly optimistic or deluded. It is real and its accomplishments have literally changed the world. It is little wonder that Harvey Milk famously declared to acolytes, "You got to give them hope." Moments later he said, with a courage and prescience most people cannot understand, "If a bullet enters my brain, let that bullet destroy every closet door."[2]

These examples of movements for justice are extreme articulations of Springsteen's notion in "Badlands" that "We'll keep pushing till it's understood and these Badlands start treating us good." Inspirational stories of this kind are scattered throughout history and are both applicable and instructive to how progressives should proceed in the era of Obama, especially considering they have a potential ally in the most powerful office in the nation.

Political sociologists Frances Fox Piven and Richard A. Cloward dedicated their respective careers in writing, teaching and organizing to emphasizing and encouraging the power of activism, whether it was through organized movements or disruptive protests. They begin their persuasive process by delineating exactly how almost every single progressive action of political change in American history was made possible by popular demand and social unrest.[3] Although a progressive democrat, Franklin Delano Roosevelt appeased public calls for pensions, social assistance programs and financial regulation because he feared the consequences of ignoring popular protest. Large contingencies of senior citizens were tirelessly seeking retirement benefits. Veterans refused to settle for anything less than a significant increase in compensation and services and poor people were rallying around candidates and causes. Huey Long became the nation's first openly socialist governor in Louisiana and Upton Sinclair, the radically progressive author, barely lost a gubernatorial race in California. Thirty years later President Lyndon Johnson rammed through as much "Great Society" legislation as quickly as he could because he felt that activist demands in the streets had provided him with a "window of opportunity" to launch a "war on poverty" that he himself supported. Tragically, President Bush got away with nearly everything he proposed and planned, with one important exception. His attempt to privatize social security, which would have dismantled it, was aborted by an obstructionist Congress, including many Republicans, because of a groundswell of public activism demanding it be opposed. In a very organized effort, citizens of various backgrounds and beliefs applied pressure on their Congressional representatives and protested appearances by the then President so that his benefit-destroying plan of privatization would be shot down before it got off the ground. This important example not only shows what may have been possible had an organized citizenry been as present on other issues throughout the Bush years. It also demonstrates exactly how substantial activism can control right-wing presidencies and cajole those that are left-leaning.

With that as a guide, progressives should proceed in the age of Obama with more activism, organization and protest, not less. President Obama issued the grand promise of change throughout his campaign, which was grounded in specific policy positions. In order for his victory to mean as much as Reagan's or Bush's, he must be held accountable to his word. A well-organized public constituency, preferably consisting of the same people who got him elected, should enlist in the political, communal and civic enterprises necessary to ensure that promises are kept and public needs, even those unarticulated on the trail, are served due to popular pressure coming down on the White House. A citizenry exercise of political agency can see that the President not only meets his own conditions for effecting change but also those which continually uphold the public interest and common good. American history and contemporary politics prove that hope is hard work and that capitalizing on it poses an even greater difficulty than acquiring it. However, the consequences to the maintenance and movement of a democracy of failing to punch in and perform the tasks it assigns are calamitous and catastrophic. The optimistically apathetic need look no further than recent years, which produced unjust war, unmitigated disaster in New Orleans and economic wreckage for evidence of what happens when fear and greed are allowed to step on hope and community.

Bruce Springsteen pays powerful tribute to the connection between hope, the duties of citizenship and political progress on the title track of *Working on a Dream*. He premiered it during an Obama campaign rally and used it as the theme for his next album (released shortly after Obama's inauguration) and subsequent tour. The music is big and the vocals soar. Otherwise clashing keyboards, horns, guitars and drums come together in harmony to create a whimsical melody which is light on its feet but still packs a punch. It would have been a perfect set closer for Elvis and his early 1970s band, which was complemented by full orchestration and carried by Presley's booming, operatic voice that could make anyone believe in anything — no matter how sweet, starry-eyed and idealistic. "American Trilogy" and "If I Can Dream" would have seemed silly coming from anyone else but Elvis transformed them into potent prayers of hope which were as real as the dreams and tears behind them. With Elvis unavailable to cover and dramatize "Working on a Dream," listeners must depend solely on Springsteen and company who, although rough around the edges, give the pop song an uplifting quality which is balanced only by its surprisingly measured lyrics, characterized perfectly by the third verse and chorus.

> Rain pourin' down I swing my hammer
> My hands are rough from working on a dream
> I'm working on a dream
>
> I'm working on a dream
> Though it can feel so far away
> I'm working on a dream
> And our love will make it real someday

The image of a man swinging a hammer, followed by a description of his beat-up hands, reveals how the labor of hope begins to appear in physical manifestations which in turn symbolize emotional fatigue and spiritual scars. These psychological and bodily wounds are acknowledged throughout a lyrical tone that is hopeful but never content. Working on a dream is an unforgivably continual process which does not take pity on its laborer. It demands relentless devotion, even in the face of discouraging odds and heartbreaking setback. Acknowledgment of adversity, recognition of suffering and reliance on love come together in this anthem of sustained effort, not confident complacency, in the aftermath of a promising election victory.

The Obama win can be rightfully seen as the emergence of light after eight years of darkness. However, that light will burn out as filthily and unceremoniously as a cigarette on a dirty curb if the American people fail to fulfill their duties in the office of citizen. It is a uniquely present and unalterably timeless paradox. The fight to believe in and create hope is long and painful but ultimately meaningless if those who win it are unwilling to enter the next battle, which is fought on a deadlier field for higher stakes, to use hope as tool and weapon to open a fertile space of territory that allows for renewal and redemption. Hope is impossible without laborious dedication and useless without a vow to never surrender in the commitment to work on a dream.

MEET YOU FURTHER ON UP THE ROAD: CORMAC MCCARTHY AND "THE PROMISED LAND"

One of the most gripping, terrifying, beautiful and profound American novels written in the past 25 years is *The Road* by Cormac McCarthy. Its simplicity of plot is counterbalanced by enriching philosophical and moral complexity which offers a luminous, disturbing and transcendent reading experience. The story follows a middle-aged father and his pre-teen son as they attempt to survive in a post-apocalyptic, scorched Earth. They scavenge for small pieces of food in a world that has been cracked and poured over with darkness. Plant life is a rare luxury and animals are scarce. The social terrain is rougher than its natural counterpart. Gangs of cannibals roam the open land hunting for their next victim while other homicidal thugs murder, pillage and enslave pregnant women. Thomas Hobbes meets Revelation in this brutally unkind state of the planet, except there is absolutely no hope for a savior. No one is waiting for a Messiah. Every person unlucky enough to be alive must reconcile with the ugly reality that this wasteland is their home, and that progress and improvement are extremely unlikely. Given this setting and these conditions, which have a Dostoevskian nature as they become a central character in the narrative, it is difficult to imagine *The Road* being anything but grim, bleak and depressing. However, a piece of hope emerges from the black sea like a solitary, creaky wooden lifeboat floating miles away — at once unattainable, yet entirely visible. That hope begins in a miniscule crevice — the endearing bond shared by father and son — then radiates into the entire novel and eventually into the reader's consciousness. The love they share is the only resource that gives them strength, hope and reason for living. It functions as a protective device against the grittiness and meanness of the world they are forced to inhabit, and a seal of mutual guardianship that, although primarily the father's domain, extends both ways. Their pure devotion to each other is best expressed through the son's act of compassion. Although the father risks his life and sacrifices everything for his child's well-being, it is the little boy's love and service to him, untarnished by the slightest impurity, that comes to be most representative of their relationship and the hope it embodies and projects. Huddled by a hand-built fire in the bitter cold on a lonely and hungry morning, the father and son prepare to eat what little food that remains in their worn-down sack.

He sorted through the cans and went back and they sat by the fire and ate

the last of their crackers and a tin of sausage. In a pocket of his knapsack
he'd found a last half packet of cocoa and he fixed it for the boy and then
poured his own cup with hot water and sat blowing at the rim.

You promised not to do that, the boy said.

What?

You know what, Papa.

He poured the hot water back into the pan and took the boy's cup and
poured some of the cocoa into his own and handed it back.

I have to watch you all the time, the boy said.

I know.

If you break little promises you'll break big ones. That's what you said.

I know. But I won't.[4]

Under these lifeless and joyless conditions, it would be perfectly understandable for the father to split his cocoa — a small, yet rare ingredient for
pleasure — from the beginning of the meal. It would be even more expected
for the boy to accept his father's gift and relish in the opportunity to enjoy a
full glass of chocolate-flavored drink. Neither of them will have it. The father
insists on selfless sacrifice, offering all delight to his beloved child, and the
son reacts with anger and disappointment. He admonishes his father for
breaking a promise he made to also enjoy life whenever possible, which
sadly is not often, and allow some happiness and pleasantness to disrupt the
monotony of dread that envelops him. The prevalence of love, sacrifice and
compassion in a chaotic, harsh and hellacious world can be read as a miracle
of goodness. But it can also be interpreted as the emergence of a morality
that is innate within most sane, non-sociopathic members of the human
race. Basic love and kindness, especially given towards immediate family,
has sustained people in the darkest times and provided balancing humility
in the best. It is a human instinct that is muted by fear-politics of division
and bigotry, and discouraged by an unregulated, competitive capitalistic
system devoid of a sufficient social compact. However, this instinct will
appear, perhaps only for a moment, throughout the harshest torture or the
most mundane injustice. The beleaguered father and son, fighting for every
breath in the middle of Armageddon, make a commitment to this virtuous
instinct of courageous service to the other and come to utilize it as a means
of survival. It is articulated with beautiful simplicity by the man and boy as
"carrying the fire." The father instructs his son that they "are carrying the
fire" and should only trust those who willingly share that burden. Fire is of
unequaled importance in their world. It allows them to cook and eat, and
therefore continue living. It gives warmth in the freezing winter nights which
kill many who cannot find shelter by nightfall. It also provides light in a land
washed with darkness and dominated by the "ponderous counterspectacle of

things ceasing to be. The sweeping waste, hydroptic and coldly secular."

Those who "carry the fire" — preserving warmth, light and hope on a deadened planet — are those who allow "goodness to find them" and others. When the child is forced to separate from his loving and beloved protector he confirms that an unknown and helpful man, who has a little boy of his own, is "one of the good guys" by asking him a single question: "Are you carrying the fire?" Unsure how to answer, the man stumbles for a moment before instinctually and intuitively giving an assuring, "Yes we are." His intrinsic goodness enables him to speak in a common language with one who is also intrinsically and devotedly good. Their mutual understanding grants an extension to the boy's life and gives the reader a lesson in the power of hope, which can only emerge under the guise of love, solidarity and compassion. It survives in the hands of those who, despite pouring rains and human forces of extinguishment, stake their lives, their meaning and purpose, on carrying the fire.

A character that comes to an epiphany that he is carrying the fire and is transformed by that realization tells his story and sounds his triumphantly hopeful cry in Springsteen's "The Promised Land." A conflicted young man is driving through the stale desert air, surrounded by vast swarms of nothing. His attempts to find satisfaction in the routine and ordinary are without result. Even the radio, which enlivened the young men in "No Surrender," is "just killing time." He explains that his compromise to follow the letter of the order passed on to him from his family and leaders is corrosive to his vitality and integrity. The restless pursuit of the American Dream, as conveniently and narrowly defined by those in power, leaves him physically and spiritually exhausted. Demoralization gathers intensity as he realizes that under his current lifestyle this fatigue will not dissipate but only strengthen with each passing day. The existential crisis this young man is battling is summarized with ruthless honesty that is both self-critical and contemptuous of his socio-political surroundings.

> I've done my best to live the right way
> I get up every morning and go to work each day
> But your eyes go blind and your blood runs cold
> Sometimes I feel so weak I just want to explode
> Explode and tear this whole town apart
> Take a knife and cut this pain from my heart
> Find somebody itching for something to start

The multitude of forces arrayed against this individual, although unspecified, overwhelms his faculties and emotions with enough power to induce fantasies of mutually assured destruction between him and the structure he struggles against. He is angry, resentful and depressed. The desires he painfully expresses seem unlikely to go anywhere, and so does he. He'll have to live with the pain dragging him down and may find temporary solace in the arms of someone else who is "itching for something to start" but will not be able to achieve the inner redemption so desperately needed. A friend or lover can encourage that process, but only the self can initiate and complete it.

The images in the third verse do not improve. They are even darker and deadlier. The disaster and trauma they bring is unavoidable and irreversible. However, the angle from which one perceives these images, which represent transformative events, has shifted. The song has now become a celebration of beautiful destruction. The destruction that wipes out this man's former self — the weak, joyless and detached cynic — and creates space for a journeyman empowered by hope, bravery and a renewed sense of possibility.

> There's a dark cloud rising from the desert floor
> I packed my bags and I'm heading straight into the storm
> Gonna be a twister to blow everything down
> That ain't got the faith to stand its ground
> Blow away the dreams that tear you apart
> Blow away the dreams that break your heart
> Blow away the lies that leave you nothing but lost and brokenhearted

It can take more courage to come to terms with one's self and challenge the orthodoxies and status quo subjugating one's promise and capabilities than to charge head first into a monstrous tornado. This character has summoned that courage and celebrates the opportunity to annihilate the restrictive dreams shackled to him. He is prepared to raise his arms for truth against the shallow and spiritually murderous lies that have paralyzed him in years past. The realization that he can "carry the fire" for self-determination, justice and truth transforms him into a giant able to withstand the wind and brush away the debris created and tossed about by a dangerous storm. His faith is his shield and shelter, and the selfish or indifferent who lack it, will be lifted off into the void — beaten, discarded and unremembered. The faith that comes from the raising of consciousness and the willingness to embark on the spiritual and political work it requires is a weapon against personal depression and public tyranny. Countless examples from history, many already described, confirm that laborious hope, built on a foundation of solidarity, community and love, can blow back the worst perversions of dreams and defeat the worst lies. Those strong enough to possess it must work to share it.

The music of "The Promised Land" is the perfect embodiment of the classic Springsteen formula — blues verses and gospel choruses. The lifting piano, confrontational beat and organ of deliverance make the singer's final condition joyfully and unapologetically clear. However, the song is at its most potently powerful when it dramatizes his redemptive transformation. Its middle break begins with a soft-spoken, slow guitar solo that is played with tears in each note. Slow, but deliberate, movement away from angst and sadness is mapped by a saxophone that is not soaring but looking onward to a destination that is made home with a triumphant harmonica solo. The harmonica, with its high notes quickly climbing on top of each other, is akin to a biblical moment of miraculous healing. The lame can walk and the blind can see. Except this newly found vision and progression is not the gift of a generous God; it is the product of tenacious and tempestuous examination of self and society, and a commitment to reversing what is unwanted, unwise and unjust.

The vocals are ferocious. This singer is singing for his life. If he is carrying the fire, he has used it to build a flamethrower and everything in his path is targeted for arson. Residents that welcome the fire will become allies and those that cannot will be neglected and condemned. Hope is demolishing the fearful and empowering the faithful with a workably joyful creed of liberation:

> The dogs on Main Street howl
> 'Cause they understand
> If I could take one moment into my hands
> Mister I ain't a boy, no I'm a man
> And I believe in a promised land

This is one man claiming hope against the thoughtless, empathy-deficient centers of power that attempt to impose the limits of their own selfish vision on him. This is one man shouting his promise to make his own identity and life, and to ensure that it contributes to ". . . and justice for all." This is rock 'n' roll. This is the beauty and mystery of democracy in practice.

Conclusion

L egendary playwright Arthur Miller was asked by Charlie Rose, "What do the greatest playwrights share in common?" Miller, who from *Death of a Salesmen* to *Broken Glass* proved that he earned his place on the pedestal to which Rose referred, answered with intense confidence: "What the big ones have in common is a fierce moral sensibility, which is unquenchable. They are all burning with some anger at the way the world is. The little ones make a peace with it, and the big ones cannot make a peace."[1] Although of special interest to aspiring playwrights everywhere, this exchange can easily be broadened to apply to all artists, regardless of what medium or genre they live in.

In addition to mastery of craft or unique talent, perhaps no better criterion exists for judging great artists. The Arthur Miller-standard is a tough filter that mercilessly separates the great from the good and the good from the bad. Bruce Springsteen runs through the Miller-gauntlet unscathed and emerges as a great artist of his era and genre who will be remembered long after he is gone as an esteemed practitioner of rock 'n' roll who could make people dance, but also as an activist, prophetic provocateur and philosopher.

The fierce moral sensibility that burns inside Springsteen spreads into his body of work, which commits to understanding the socio-political issues of his time through the stories of suffering people. It also insists on interpreting psychological issues of identity and self-determination as questions of freedom. These two elements combined make for a perfect soundtrack for democracy which, if anything meaningful, is a system of governance and philosophy of culture that allows people to determine the shaping of their own future and promises respectful representation to citizens of every type. Springsteen's grappling with these fundamental but often ignored and forgotten concepts of autonomy and responsibility is stripped down to its raw core on the life-affirming song from *Devils & Dust*, "Leah." The second verse, similar to the final verse of "Born to Run," provides a challenging yet inspiring summation:

> I walk this road, with a hammer and a fiery lantern
> With this hand I've built, and with this I've burned
> I wanna live in the same house, beneath the same roof
> Sleep in the same bed, search for the same proof
> As Leah

Leah provides the same essential service as Wendy in "Born to Run" — companionship, support and allegiance through the tough weather surrounding any journey of self-discovery, commitment to high calling and independently determined purpose. However, this is not simply discovery. A useful distinction can be made between a discovery and a decision. A decision must occur after a discovery is made, and oftentimes a wise decision cannot be made until the process of discovery is complete. In "The Promised Land" the protagonist undergoes changes that result from a discovery that is enlivening, emboldening and empowering. In "Leah" a similar but perhaps older and more seasoned character makes a clear decision, long after the realization of a discovery. His decision and priorities are delineated with straightforward eloquence in the first verse, which instructs listeners that he wants to build a house on "higher ground" and find a world where "love's the only sound." To do this he is prepared to "shoulder a load" and thereby indicates a sophisticated understanding of the relationship between hope, progress and labor while remaining dedicated to the vital energy and service of love. That alone is enough to make for compelling lyrical content but the most profound passage comes in the first two lines of the second verse when the singer identifies a "hammer" and a "fiery lantern" in each hand — objects that symbolize his ability to build and burn.

Bruce Springsteen explained this lyric in unusually explicit terms, saying that it speaks to the basic blessing and curse of humanity: "That we all hold the tools for our own triumph and destruction." It is obvious by judging from the first verse that the triumph possible is not merely one of financial success and increase in status but also one of spiritual maturity, ethical consistency and emotional satisfaction. The destruction goes far beyond physical threat but applies to those very areas which are uniquely human.

The music of "Leah" is simple and repetitive. A guitar strums a riff that feels unfinished — it builds, rises, gathers tension before failing to culminate and then begins again. Light percussion shuffles on top of it continuously and after each verse faint backup singing runs through a soft "li, li, li, li, li, li, li, li" chorus that also fails to reach a crescendo. The only break in the pattern comes after the second verse, when a brief trumpet solo can be heard in the distance. Like some street musician demanding attention in a shadowed alley off a busy street, it is difficult to make out each note and it comes and goes in an instant. However, just for a moment, it manages to break through the noise and deafen those within earshot with its majestic beauty. Its power gathers, and although it may momentarily vanish, it threatens to return just as the burden and joy of freedom — the capacity to build and destroy — can be temporarily ignored but never wholly avoided. The third verse offers a final glimpse into the spirit and steps of this determined character.

> I got somethin' in my heart, I been waitin' to give
> I got a life I wanna start, one I been waitin' to live
> No more waitin', tonight I feel the light I say the prayer
> I open the door, I climb the stairs . . .

Emerging from the darkness, he makes his move, thereby turning his discovery into a decision and transforming his decision into action. He does not cower from the moral responsibilities of freedom but embraces them and prays that he serves it well and that it serves him well. Hopeful and joyful, he basks in the light of his maturity and autonomy. After a final "li, li, li, li, li, li, li" chorus the song fades out beyond our ability to hear it and with that the protagonist escapes our line of vision. No further mention of Leah is made and the repetitive shuffling pattern of the song is not disturbed. His movement continues onward without our company and the spotlight shifts onto the listener. He is gone but we are not. It is our duty, just as it was his, to consider our independence, give it meaning and act with purpose, all the while considering the freedom and responsibility we inherit. The effect of this inheritance is maximized in a democracy which gives the citizen unique capabilities to endorse, monitor or condemn the actions of power and to assist in the guardianship and service of others. Democracy maximizes the consequences of those uniquely human tools of "triumph and destruction."

These questions of triumph and destruction have been stripped of their spiritual, moral and philosophical bearings in modern American politics. It has become acceptable to debate the usage of torture in polite and civil society because people are paralyzed by overblown fears of physical destruction from terrorists. For far too long financial triumph, founded on greed and heedless self-interest, was allowed to dominate the nation's politics, business practices and culture. The collapse and crisis of 2008 brought the destruction, which inevitably ensues from such an unregulated system, home. Understandably, most citizens reacted with fright over looming threats of bankruptcy, unemployment or foreclosure. Damage to their bank accounts, livelihoods and familial stability is part of the wreckage that was created by decades of politicized bribery which had publicly elected officials placating the avarice of private tyrannies. The Obama administration is scrambling to forge a recovery, Republicans are attempting to emerge with some identifiable vision in their opposition, and talking heads are doing their usual griping. Amidst all the fallout, the principal players still fail to elevate the discourse above base instincts and fears. Without an acknowledgment and examination of the spiritual, moral and philosophical failures that produced the crisis, and the stakes that belong to those domains, the crisis will become cyclical, destined to repeat itself years from now in some new form, and the country will not experience the real growth, progress and maturity that were seen during and after the Great Depression. The crisis will go beyond one of finance and mutate into a crisis of humanity.

William Faulkner addressed a similar crisis of humanity during his acceptance speech for the Nobel Prize in Literature in 1949. The brief, but profound and unfortunately relevant speech is worth quoting at length.

> Our tragedy today is a general and universal physical fear so long sustained by now that we can even bear it. There are no longer problems of the spirit. There is only the question: When will I be blown up? Because of this, the young man or woman writing today has forgotten the problems of the human heart in conflict with itself which alone can make good writing because only that is worth writing about, worth the agony and the sweat.
>
> He must learn them again. He must teach himself that the basest of all things is to be afraid; and, teaching himself that, forget it forever, leaving no room in his workshop for anything but the old verities and truths of the heart, the old universal truths lacking which any story is ephemeral and doomed — love and honor and pity and pride and compassion and sacrifice. Until he does so, he labors under a curse. He writes not of love but of lust, of defeats in which nobody loses anything of value, of victories without hope and, worst of all, without pity or compassion. His griefs grieve on no universal bones, leaving no scars. He writes not of the heart but of the glands.[2]

The author's words cut through every cloud of smoke and slice apart every layer of fabric placed in front of the truth. Faulkner narrows the focus with stunning clairvoyance onto what sets humans apart, making us uniquely free, autonomous and responsible. Issues of the heart and spirit — loneliness, love, despair and jubilation — must be recognized in the public sphere through political policy-making and community-building. However, this is not typically the jurisdiction of politicians as they must manage by crisis and govern with cold pragmatism. Therefore, this great burden falls on the shoulder of the artist. Art is one of humanity's truly renewable resources. It is one of the few things we can keep going back to for joy, truth and trauma — should trauma need to be induced. It strives, and in its high moments succeeds, in motivating great and often self-critical reflection on the very issues Faulkner so eloquently described: love, honor, pity, pride and sacrifice. These are the topics dreadfully absent from public consideration and painfully calling out to be injected into the discussion.

Art also has the potential to be politically disruptive — shaking up the status quo, awakening people from their indifference to suffering and injustice, and discomfiting the powerful who depend on societal conformity and apathy. It can influence its followers but also enable the artist to project a courageous example of freedom, independence and self-expression in the face of unsympathetic authority or misunderstanding audiences. In doing so, it can fill in the gaps of the hierarchy of historical fact by interjecting a counter-narrative or additional narrative into the dialogue of democracy, which has unlimited potential but is often subverted by a narrowly imposed framework. From Da Vinci to Dostoevsky to Dylan, artists inspirationally prove that the "self-willed individual can affect his environment, and his times, in ways that we cannot even calculate," as Peter Guralnick summarized when measuring the power of Elvis Presley.[3]

Bruce Springsteen fits into this tradition, expands it and serves it well. This is his greatest contribution to his environment and time, and his most significant service to the progression of his country and people. He has channeled the liberating energy of rock 'n' roll into music that not only accomplishes something true within his craft but also instills physical joy and rejuvenation. In this sense, when analyzing Springsteen's music, "Rosalita" and "Thundercrack" are just as important as "Born in the U.S.A." and "American Skin (41 Shots)." However, a serious pause must be taken when dancing to observe the emergence of a poetic, progressive vision throughout Springsteen's work. This is a vision of justice, a vision of love, a vision of community and a vision of truth. Other modern artists, including Bob Dylan, Neil Young, John Mellencamp, Steve Earle and others who work with the same tools as Springsteen, exemplify the best of the artistic tradition and calling. Their work deserves the same respect and reverence as Springsteen's and this book is not written to encourage rock fans to ignore them when looking for great music or politically, spiritually and morally provocative lyrical content.

This book is an invitation to reimagine American politics, citizenship and life through an engagement with one remarkably "self-willed" artist. Such an engagement opens up the idea of possibility in American politics and leads listeners on a walk through the underside of America and a tour through the margins of the dispossessed, forgotten and depressed who have been neglected by concentrations of power. More importantly, it also enables one to find energy and empowerment in a newly invested, mature and hard-won hope. This engagement also presents an alternative to the materialistic and narcissistic mode of living and thinking recommended by the dominant society, by demonstrating that an activist and artist can not only survive but thrive when committed to a higher calling.

The ultimate value of Springsteen's work, which goes beyond its illumination of suffering people and its useful truths for organizers on the left, is what Faulkner in his Nobel acceptance speech defined as the "privilege to help man endure by lifting his heart, by reminding him of the courage and honor and hope and pride and compassion and pity and sacrifice which have been the glory of his past." He went on to say that "the poet's voice need not merely be the record of man, it can be one of the props, the pillars to help him endure and prevail."

In other words, "Someday, I don't know when, we're gonna get to that place / Where we really want to go, and we'll walk in the sun / But till then tramps like us, baby we were born to run."

Acknowledgments

Given the length at which I write about community and solidarity in this book, it would be hypocritical and dishonest of me not to thank all the people who helped make this book possible. First of all I would like to thank David Barker at Continuum Books, who had enough faith in this project, and its previously unpublished author, to advocate for its publication. I am also grateful for all of his assistance through not only my writing process but also my multiple questions regarding several other matters, many of which were the result of my personal neurosis. I extend another thank you to him for his support during a scary moment when this book's publication was threatened by something beyond our control. David — thank you for your faith and support.

No amount of gratitude is sufficient to express my thanks to Jan Stabile at Bruce Springsteen's management for her generosity, understanding and assistance with obtaining copyright lyric reprint permissions. I owe her a big one, and should she ever wish to collect the debt, I will gladly pay it forward. Thank you, Jan.

At several points I write about the value of education in this book. Therefore, I would like to thank the educators who encouraged me to think for myself while helping me sharpen the tools required for expressing those thoughts: David Thurn at Trinity Lutheran Elementary in Lansing, Illinois, Kim Praser and Sandy Gnippe at Thornton Fractional South High School in Lansing, and Professors Marvin Katilius-Boydstun, Michael "Chester" Costello and Tim Weldon at the University of St. Francis in Joliet, Illinois, where I earned my bachelor's degree in Political Science. I'd especially like to thank Professors Julie Victa and Salim Diab at USF for their challenging instruction and enduring friendship, which I will always treasure. I would also like to acknowledge the entire University of St. Francis community, along with its President, Dr. Michael Vinciguerra, for their continued commitment to instilling within students, faculty and staff the tradition of love, service and excellence. Besides being an alumnus, I have no affiliation with the university. However, it is my Harvard and second home.

Thank you to my dear friends Nick Cerovac, Chris Foster and Paul Skallas for their humor, camaraderie and encouragement. Father Edward R. Ward deserves my steadfast love and gratitude for his friendship, guidance and influence on my thoughts and work. Ed — when I read your work and listen to your thoughts I am never once tempted to say, "Somebody ring the damn bell." I humbly hope that you afford me the same admiration. I hope even more that no one ever rings the damn bell on our friendship. I extend an enormous thank you to Roger Sullivan, who not only stimulated my intellect in his classroom but continues to do so in the various bars and restaurants that now host our ongoing dialogue. More importantly, his friendship, love and support is a most cherished gift in my life. Bruuuuuce Moeller, Uncle "Gee," has been one of the most treasured members of my family. I love him very much and always feel happier when he is around.

Thank you so much to Sarah, whose love, tenderness and support has added great beauty and grace to my life. Her work is a real-life example of the values Bruce Springsteen sings about. Sarah: You're "tougher than the rest," and I love you very much.

It is impossible for me to adequately express my gratitude to my parents, Pearl and Lou Masciotra. Their love has, in large part, made me what I am. The value of my father's support, of all kinds, cannot be measured. I love and respect him. Mom and Dad: You deserve co-writing credits on this and every other accomplishment in my life.

Above everyone else, I would like to thank Nicholas Bruich, my grandfather, who died on November 9, 2002. He taught me more about dignity, strength and love than I can ever understand. It is my greatest hope that this book, along with everything else I do, honors his memory.

David Masciotra
June 1, 2009

Notes

INTRODUCTION

1 CBS News. "Springsteen: Silence is Unpatriotic." CBS, http://www.cbsnews.com/stories/2007/10/04/60minutes/main3330463.shtml

CHAPTER 1

The following sources were of immeasurable value and assistance when writing this chapter:

Eric Alterman, *It Ain't No Sin to be Glad You're Alive: The Promise of Bruce Springsteen* (New York: Little, Brown and Company, 1999).

Robert Reich, *Supercapitalism: The Transformation of Business, Democracy, and Everyday Life* (New York: Alfred A. Knopf, 2007).

Kurt Loder, "Bruce Springsteen: The Rolling Stone Interview," *Rolling Stone* (December 6, 1984): 18–22, 70.

Joseph Dalton, "Bruce Springsteen: Made in the USA," *Rolling Stone* (October 10, 1985): 20–8, 78–80.

James Henke, "Springsteen: The Rolling Stone Interview," *Rolling Stone* (August 6, 1992): 38–44, 70.

Jann S. Wenner, "Springsteen: We've Been Misled," *Rolling Stone* (September 22, 2004): http://www.rollingstone.com/news/story/6477832/weve_been_misled

The Jeffrey Birnbaum quote is found in Bill Moyers, "The Fight of Our Lives," in James Lardner and David A. Smith (eds.), *Inequality Matters: The Growing Economic Divide in America and Its Poisonous Consequences* (New York: The New Press, 2005).

CHAPTER 2

1 TNS Global, "TNS Media Intelligence Reports U.S. Advertising Expenditures Increased 4.1 Percent in 2006," Taylor Nelson Sofres Global Market Research, http://www.tns-mi.com/news/03132007.htm

2 Dr. Jim Nelson's observation that "every mental health disorder in the country is getting worse" was expressed during a private conversation. The American Sociological Association study on friendship that he referenced is Matthew E. Brashears, Miller McPherson and Lynn Smith-Lovin, "Social Isolation in America: Changes in Core Discussion Networks over Two Decades," *American Sociological Association* (June 2006): http://www.asanet.org/galleries/default-file/June06ASRFeature.pdf

3 The scholarship and analysis of Kathleen Hall Jamieson is particularly useful on the topic of public relations and advertising in politics. See Kathleen Hall Jamieson and Karlyn Kohrs Campbell, *The Interplay of Influence: News, Advertising, Politics, and the Mass Media* (New York: Wadsworth Publishing, 2000).

4 David D. Kirkpatrick, "In Alito, G.O.P. Reaps Harvest Planted in '82," *New York Times* (January 20, 2006): http://www.nytimes.com/2006/01/30/politics/politicsspecial1/30alito.html

5 For a thorough and thought-provoking summary of media history and media consolidation see Robert W. McChesney, *Rich Media, Poor Democracy: Communication Politics in Dubious Times* (New York: The New Press, 2000).

6 By far the best biography of Elvis Presley is the two-part series written by Peter Guralnick. The heartbreaking story of his tragic death and demise is told in the second book: *Careless Love: The Unmaking of Elvis Presley* (New York: Back Bay Books, 1999).

7 For a well-researched and well-written description of Clear Channel's monopolizing effect on American radio see Jeff Sharlet, "Big World: How Clear Channel Programs America," *Harper's Magazine* (December 2003): 37–45.

8 For a much more thorough, researched and deeply penetrating analysis of Hopper's portrayal of American isolation and loneliness see the book that inspired my own thoughts on the subject: Gordon Theisen, *Staying Up Much Too Late: Edward Hopper's Nighthawks and the Dark Side of the American Psyche* (New York: St. Martin's Press, 2006).

9 Cornel West, *Democracy Matters: Winning the Fight Against Imperialism* (New York: Penguin Books, 2004): 26–7.

10 The Arthur Miller quote is found in *The Atheism Tapes*. DVD. Directed by Jonathan Miller, 2005; Alive Mind, 2008.

11 For a detailed definition of the term "superpatriotism," along with a history of its political development, see Michael Parenti, *Superpatriotism* (San Francisco: City Lights Publishers, 2004).

12 Mark Seltzer, *Serial Killers: Death and Life in America's Wound Culture* (New York: Routledge, 1998): 135.

CHAPTER 3

1 Jim Cullen, *Born in the U.S.A.: Bruce Springsteen and the American Tradition* (New York: HarperCollins, 1997): 116.
2 For an excellent summary and analysis of Karl Marx's alienated labor theory consult Bertell Ollman, *Alienation: Marx's Conception of Man in Capitalist Society* (Cambridge, England: Cambridge University Press, 1971).
3 The philosophical observation on repetition is actually made by Cliff, the protagonist in Jim Harrison's funny and insightful novel *The English Major* (New York: Grove Press, 2008).
4 Robert B. Reich, "Totally Spent," *New York Times* (February 13, 2008): http://www.nytimes.com/2008/02/13/opinion/13reich.html
5 "Americans Work Longest, Most Productive in World," *News Limited* (September 3, 2007): http://www.news.com.au/business/story/0,23636,22352457-462,00.html
6 Don Monkerud, "Americans Work Harder and Go Without," *Common Dreams News Center* (July 28, 2001): http://www.commondreams.org/views01/0728-02.htm
7 Tom Hodgkinson's books, both well worth reading, are *How to Be Idle: A Loafer's Manifesto* (New York: Harper Perennial, 2007) and *The Freedom Manifesto* (New York: Harper Perennial, 2007).
8 "Americans to Forego 421 Million Vacation Days," *Journal of Employee Assistance* (July 2005): http://findarticles.com/p/articles/mi_m0PLP/is_3_35/ai_n17210404/
9 "American Workers Take Fewer Vacation Days than Needed," *Voice of America News* (August 11, 2005): http://www.voanews.com/english/archive/2005-08/2005-08-11-voa56.cfm

CHAPTER 4

1 A useful summary of the Diallo case, along with the reaction to Springsteen's "American Skin (41 Shots)," can be found in Samuele F.S. Pardini, "Bruce Springsteen's 'American Skin,'" in June Skinner Sawyers (ed.), *Racing in the Street: The Bruce Springsteen Reader* (New York: Penguin Books, 2004): 329–36.
2 Bruce Springsteen, *Songs* (New York: Harper Collins, 2003): 298.
3 Ibid.
4 Robert Hilburn, "Under the Boss' Skin," *Los Angeles Times* (April 1, 2001): http://articles.latimes.com/2001/apr/01/entertainment/ca-45336
5 Excellent sources on contemporary white flight are Kyle Crowder, "Racial Stratification in the Actuation of Mobility Expectations: Microlevel Impacts of Racially Restrictive Housing Markets," *Social Forces* (Volume 79, Number 4, June 2001): 1377–96; Kevin Michael Kruse, *White Flight: Atlanta and the Making of Modern Conservatism* (Princeton: Princeton University Press,

2005); Danielle Gordon, "'White Flight' Taking Off in Chicago Suburbs," *Chicago Reporter*: http://www.chicagoreporter.com/index.php/c/Cover_Stories/d/%E2%80%98White_Flight%E2%80%99_Taking_Off_in_Chicago_Suburbs

6 Barry Glassner, *The Culture of Fear: Why Americans Are Afraid of the Wrong Things* (New York: Basic Books, 1999): 107–29.

7 Ibid.

8 The New York hiring study is by Devah Pager and Bruce Western and entitled "Discrimination in Low-Wage Labor Markets: Evidence from an Experimental Audit Study in New York City," Princeton University (2005): http://paa2005.princeton.edu/download.aspx?submissionId=50874. For the Milwaukee study see Devah Pager, "The Mark of a Criminal Record," *American Journal of Sociology* (Volume 108, Number 5, March 2003): 937–75: http://www.northwestern.edu/ipr/publications/papers/2003/pagerajs.pdf

9 Although this quote is taken from *Tavis Smiley*, PBS, February 8, 2006 (transcript available at http://www.pbs.org/kcet/tavissmiley/archive/200602/20060208_dyson.html), an invaluable summary and analysis of Hurricane Katrina, along with its political and sociological implications, can be found in Michael Eric Dyson, *Come Hell or High Water: Hurricane Katrina and the Color of Disaster* (New York: Basic Civitas Books, 2006). Also see Douglas Brinkley, *The Great Deluge: Hurricane Katrina, New Orleans, and the Mississippi Gulf Coast* (New York: Harper Perennial, 2007).

10 A terrific summary of findings on the lack of psychiatric care for returning soldiers can be read at Chris Adams, "VA Comes Up Short for Iraq Vets," *Seattle Times* (February 11, 2007): http://seattletimes.nwsource.com/html/nationworld/2003566773_vets11.html

11 Dana Priest and Anne Hall, "Soldiers Face Neglect, Frustration at Army's Top Medical Facility," *Washington Post* (February 18, 2007): http://www.washingtonpost.com/wp-dyn/content/article/2007/02/17/AR2007021701172.html

12 Helen Benedict, "Why Soldiers Rape," *In These Times* (August 13, 2008): http://www.inthesetimes.com/article/3848/

13 Chomsky tells the story during an interview that appears in Noam Chomsky, *Power and Terror* (New York: Seven Stories Press, 2003): 24–5.

14 Billy Graham retracted the statement about AIDS being God's punishment for homosexuality after public outrage and media controversy became too much to ignore. A brief summary is available at http://www.aegis.com/news/ads/1993/ad 931840.html

15 Information regarding workplace protection, or lack thereof, for gay Americans is available at http://www.lambdalegal.org/issues/employment-and-rights-in-the-workplace.html

16 Gore Vidal, *Point to Point Navigation* (New York: Doubleday, 2006): 81–2.

CHAPTER 5

1 For an excellent analysis of the differences and tensions within hip-hop see Michael Eric Dyson, *Know What I Mean?: Reflections on Hip Hop* (New York: Basic Civitas Books, 2007).

2 A well-written and well-researched account of the Giuliani myth can be read at Kevin Baker, "A Fate Worse than Bush: Giuliani and the Politics of Personality," *Harper's Magazine* (August 2007): 31–9.

3 Barry Glassner, *The Culture of Fear: Why Americans Are Afraid of the Wrong Things* (New York: Basic Books, 1999).

4 Cara Buckley, "Young New Yorkers Make a Brand New Start of it, on the Cheap," *New York Times* (May 25, 2008): http://www.nytimes.com/2008/05/25/nyregion/25scrimp.html

5 Jessica Kaye and Richard J. Brewer (eds.), *Meeting Across the River: Stories Inspired by the Bruce Springsteen Song* (New York: Bloomsbury, 2005).

6 Tavis Smiley, *Accountable: Making America as Good as Its Promise* (New York: Atria Books, 2009): 19–20.

7 An excellent summary of the World Health Organization's conclusions about the U.S. health-care system is provided by the University of Maine. See Bureau of Labor Education, University of Maine, "The US Health Care System: Best in the World or Just the Most Expensive?" University of Maine (Summer 2001): http://dll.umaine.edu/ble/U.S.%20HCweb.pdf

8 Michael Mandel and Joseph Weber, "What's Really Propping up the Economy," *Business Week* (September 25, 2006): http://www.businessweek.com/magazine/content/06_39/b4002001.htm

9 Eric Petersen and Kim Hunt, "Casino Impacts and Externalities in Illinois and Northwestern Indiana Communities." Paper presented at the annual meeting of the *American Sociological Association* (August 12, 2005): http://www.allacademic.com/meta/p22894_index.html

10 David Wessel, "Lack of Well-Educated Workers Has Lots of Roots, No Quick Fix," *Wall Street Journal* (April 19, 2007): A-2.

11 Information regarding college tuition and college aid was obtained from Tamara Draut, "The Growing College Gap," in James Lardner and David A. Smith (eds.), *Inequality Matters* (New York: The New Press, 2005): 89–102.

12 Robert King Merton, *On Social Structure and Science* (Chicago: University of Chicago Press, 1996): 155–62.

13 Cornel West and Sylvia Ann Hewlett, "Parents and National Survival," in Cornel West (ed.), *The Cornel West Reader* (New York: Basic Civitas Books, 1999): 334.

14 The story of the Italian-American mafia's beginnings can be read in detail at Mike Dash, *The First Family: Terror, Extortion, and the Birth of the American Mafia* (New York: Simon and Schuster, 2009).

15 Jeff Coen and Gary Marx, "Informant Offered Rare Look inside Gang," *Chicago*

Tribune (July 27, 2008): http://archives.chicagotribune.com/2008/jul/27/nation/chi-latin-kings-28-jul28

16 Leela Yellesetty, "Not Your Average Police Drama," *Socialist Worker* (January 18, 2008): http://socialistworker.org/2008/01/18/not-average-police-drama

17 Statement of H.J. Anslinger, from House Resolution 6385 Hearings, April 27–May 4, 1937: http://www.druglibrary.org/SCHAFFER/hemp/taxact/anslng1.htm

18 For some esteemed observers' commentary on the failed war on drugs see Misha Glenny, "The Lost War," *Washington Post* (August 19, 2007): B01; "The War on Drugs is Lost," a National Review Symposium, *National Review* (July 1, 1996): http://www.nationalreview.com/12feb96/drug.html; Ben Wallace-Wells, "How America Lost the War on Drugs," *Rolling Stone* (December 13, 2007): http://www.rollingstone.com/news/story/17438347/how_america_lost_the_war_on_drugs

19 For information on racial disparities in illegal drug prosecution and incarceration see Phillip Beatty, Amanda Petteruti and Jason Ziedenberg, "The Vortex: The Concentrated Racial Impact of Drug Imprisonment and the Characteristics of Punitive Counties," *Justice Policy Institute* (December 4, 2007): http://www.justicepolicy.org/images/upload/07-12_REP_Vortex_AC-DP.pdf. Also see "Punishment and Prejudice: Racial Disparities in the Criminal Justice System," *Human Rights Watch Report* (Volume 12, Number 2, May 2000): http://www.hrw.org/reports/2000/usa/

20 N.C. Aizenman, "New High in US Prison Numbers," *Washington Post* (February 29, 2008): http://www.washingtonpost.com/wp-dyn/content/story/2008/02/28/ST2008022803016.html

21 For an excellent summary of the "prison-industrial complex" see Eric Schlosser, "The Prison-Industrial Complex," *Atlantic Monthly* (December 1998): http://www.theatlantic.com/doc/199812/prisons

22 Sydney M. Willhelm, *Who Needs the Negro?* (New York: Anchor Books, 1971).

23 Kenneth Meeks, "Racism and Reality in *NYPD Blue*," in GlennYeffeth (ed.), *What Would Sipowicz Do?: Race, Rights and Redemption in NYPD Blue* (Dallas: Benbella Books, 2004): 47–55.

24 Paul Street, "No More Excuses," *Z Magazine* (June 16, 2008): http://www.zmag.org/znet/viewArticle/17919

25 Bruce Springsteen, *Songs* (New York: Harper Collins, 2003): 262.

CHAPTER 6

1 The full text of Kennedy's address to the Greater Houston Ministerial Association, along with an audio clip, is available at http://www.americanrhetoric.com/speeches/jfkhoustonministers.html

2 The exact quote is found in Augustine's *A Treatise on Grace and Free Will*. However, an excellent analysis of Augustine's philosophy, including the statement

quoted, can be found in Phillip Cary, *Inner Grace: Augustine in the Traditions of Plato and Paul* (New York: Oxford University Press U.S., 2008).

3 A Derrida lecture on prayer is quoted in its entirety in Yvonne Sherwood and Kevin Hart, *Derrida and Religion: Other Testaments* (New York: Routledge, 2005): 28–31.

4 The full text of Graham's 9/11 speech, along with an audio clip, is available at http://www.americanrhetoric.com/speeches/billygraham911memorial.htm

5 Confucius, *The Analects* (Chapter 6, Verse 20 in the traditional text).

6 Confucius, *The Analects* (Chapter 11, Verse 11 in the traditional text).

7 Herbert Fingarette, *Confucius: The Secular as Sacred* (Long Grove, Illinois: Waveland Press, 1998): 16.

8 Ibid.: 17.

9 Ibid.: 35.

10 Ibid.: 64–5.

CHAPTER 7

1 Vidal is fond of using the term "United States of Amnesia" and elaborating on its meaning during television appearances. He used that phrase as a subtitle of a recent collection of essays. See Gore Vidal, *Imperial America: Reflections on the United States of Amnesia* (New York: Nation Books, 2005).

2 Bill O'Reilly uses the term "left-wing loon" in his absurd "talking points memo on Bruce Springsteen." It can be viewed at http://www.youtube. com/watch?v=C4puSv4ABEo. Bruce Springsteen's quote is available at CBS News. "Springsteen: Silence is Unpatriotic." CBS, http://www.cbsnews.com/ stories/2007/10/04/60minutes/main3330463.shtml

3 For details on the Center for Public Integrity study see Charles Lewis and Mark Reading-Smith, "False Pretenses," *The Center for Public Integrity* (January 23, 2008): http://projects.publicintegrity.org/WarCard/

4 There are several excellent sources that document the media's servility to the Bush agenda during the march to war. On the web there is Steve Rendall, "Wrong on Iraq? Not Everyone," *Fairness and Accuracy in Reporting* (March/ April 2006): http://www.fair.org/index.php?page=2847; the *New York Times* analyzes the "Fox Effect" on cable news: Jim Rutenberg, "Cable's War Coverage Suggest a New 'Fox Effect' on Cable News," *New York Times* (April 16, 2003): http://www.nytimes.com/2003/04/16/international/worldspecial/16FOX.html. For informative texts see Eric Boehlert, *Lapdogs: How the Press Rolled Over for Bush* (New York: Free Press, 2006) and Norman Solomon, *War Made Easy: How Presidents and Pundits Keep Spinning Us to Death* (Hoboken, New Jersey: John Wiley and Sons, 2007).

5 Rick Ellis, "The Surrender of MSNBC," AllYourTV.com (February 25, 2003): http://www.allyourtv.com/0203season/news/02252003donahue.html

6 As already cited, for a vastly instructional source on the function of the American

media see Robert W. McChesney, *Rich Media, Poor Democracy: Communication Politics in Dubious Times* (New York: The New Press, 2000).

7 William Schneider, "Marketing Iraq: Why Now?" CNN.com (September 12, 2002): http://archives.cnn.com/2002/ALLPOLITICS/09/12/schneider.iraq/

8 John Kerry's full 1971 congressional testimony is available at "John Kerry's 1971 Congressional Testimony," *National Review Online*: http://www.nationalreview.com/document/kerry200404231047.asp

9 "Kerry Stands by 'Yes' Vote on Iraq War," CNN.com (August 9, 2004): http://www.cnn.com/2004/ALLPOLITICS/08/09/kerry.iraq/

10 Terri Tanielian and Lisa H. Jaycox (eds.), "Invisible Wounds of War: Psychological and Cognitive Injuries, Their Consequences, and Services to Assist Recovery," *RAND Corporation*: http://www.rand.org/pubs/monographs/MG720.1/

11 Dana Priest and Anne Hall, "Soldiers Face Neglect, Frustration at Army's Top Medical Facility," *Washington Post* (February 18, 2007): http://www.washingtonpost.com/wp-dyn/content/article/2007/02/17/AR2007021701172.html

12 Martha Mendoza, "AP: New Details on Tillman's Death," *USA Today* (July 27, 2007): http://www.usatoday.com/news/nation/2007-07-26-tillman-friendly-fire_N.htm

13 David Zirin, "Pat Tillman, Our Hero," *The Nation* (October 6, 2005): http://www.thenation.com/doc/20051024/zirin

14 Nathan Lewis, "Me and My Rifle," in Lovella Calica (ed.), *Warrior Writers: Re-Making Sense* (Barre, Vermont: Iraq Veterans Against War, 2008): 24–5.

15 Drew Cameron, "Living Without Nikki," in Lovella Calica (ed.), *Warrior Writers: Re-Making Sense* (Barre, Vermont: Iraq Veterans Against War, 2008): 80–1.

16 Michael Nowacki, "An Interrogation Primer," in Lovella Calica (ed.), *Warrior Writers: Re-Making Sense* (Barre, Vermont: Iraq Veterans Against War, 2008): 91.

17 Gore Vidal writes about his World War II experience in Gore Vidal, *Point to Point Navigation* (New York: Doubleday, 2006). For excellent novels about the Vietnam War see Tim O'Brien, *The Things They Carried* (New York: Broadway Books, 1998); Jim Webb, *Fields of Fire* (New York: Bantam Books, 1978); and Larry Heinemann, *Paco's Story* (New York: Vintage Books, 1986). For Martin Smith's reflections see Martin Smith, "Structured Cruelty: Learning to be a Lean, Mean Killing Machine," in Lovella Calica (ed.), *Warrior Writers: Re-Making Sense* (Barre, Vermont: Iraq Veterans Against War, 2008): 32–8.

18 Norman Mailer, *Harlot's Ghost* (New York: Random House, 1991): 168–9.

19 Benjamin Barber, *Jihad vs. McWorld: Terrorism's Challenge to Democracy* (New York: Ballantine Books, 2001).

20 Michael Eric Dyson, *Know What I Mean?: Reflections on Hip Hop* (New York: Basic Civitas Books, 2007): 95.

21 Jan Barry, "Introduction," in Lovella Calica (ed.), *Warrior Writers: Re-Making Sense* (Barre, Vermont: Iraq Veterans Against War, 2008): 1–2.

22 Noam Chomsky, *Interventions* (San Francisco: City Lights Books, 2007): 162.

CHAPTER 8

1 David Grazian, *Blue Chicago: The Search for Authenticity in Urban Blues Clubs* (Chicago: University of Chicago Press, 2003): 24.

2 At the risk of inviting the RIAA or whoever prosecutes bootleg live recording ownership to my home, I will confess that this Springsteen quote is taken from a live show recorded in Kansas City on November 19, 1984.

3 Linda Lantieri and Janet Patti, *Waging Peace in Our Schools* (Boston: Beacon Press, 1996): xv.

4 Ibid.: 121.

5 All information pertaining to the RCCP program, regarding its parental involvement, civic activism and success, is available at Linda Lantieri and Janet Patti, *Waging Peace in Our Schools* (Boston: Beacon Press, 1996).

6 Morris Berman, *Dark Ages America: The Final Phase of Empire* (New York: W.W. Norton and Company, 2006): 5.

7 This speech can be viewed on *Bruce Springsteen: The Complete Video Anthology 1978–2000*. DVD. Sony Music, 2001.

8 Will Percy, "Rock and Read: Will Percy Interviews Bruce Springsteen," in June Skinner Sawyers (ed.), *Racing in the Street: The Bruce Springsteen Reader* (New York: Penguin Books, 2004): 318.

9 A useful source for learning about Viguerie's operation is Lee Edwards, *The Conservative Revolution: The Movement that Remade America* (New York: The Free Press, 2000).

10 The Gore Vidal quote is from an interview and talk he gave in Los Angeles on November 6, 2004. It was recorded by the L.A. Sound Posse and can be found at http://www.radio4all.net/index.php?op=program-info&program_id =13224&nav=&

11 For an excellent source on the effectiveness and empowerment of the Dean campaign see Zephyr Teachout and Thomas Streets (eds.), *Mousepads, Shoe Leather, and Hope: Lessons from the Howard Dean Campaign for the Future of Internet Politics* (Boulder, Colorado: Paradigm Publishers, 2007).

12 Robert D. Putnam, *Bowling Alone: The Collapse and Revival of American Community* (New York: Simon and Schuster, 2000): 402.

13 Jake T. Snake, "You Know Who We Really Hate?" *Whiskey Fire* (December 28, 2008): http://whiskeyfire.typepad.com/whiskey_fire/2008/12/you-know-who-we-really-hate.html

14 Ward's invaluable insights can be found in Edward R. Ward, *In Days of Old: Some Thoughts about Language* (Dyer, Indiana: Nail Them Up Press, 2006): 22–3. Due to limited availability, Edward Ward, a close friend of mine, has asked those interested in obtaining a copy of this text to e-mail him at ERWard66@hotmail. com

15 Bruce Springsteen, *Songs* (New York: HarperCollins, 2003): 296.

CHAPTER 9

1 Jean-Luc Nancy, *Dis-Enclosure: The Deconstruction of Christianity* (New York: Fordham University Press, 2008): 137.
2 Jon Pareles, "The Rock Laureate," *New York Times* (January 28, 2009): http://www.nytimes.com/2009/02/01/arts/music/01pare.html
3 Lawrence Grossberg is quoted in Daniel Cavicchi's sociological study of Bruce Springsteen's fans. See Daniel Cavicchi, *Tramps Like Us: Music and Meaning Among Springsteen Fans* (New York: Oxford University Press U.S., 1998): 89.
4 David Grazian, *Blue Chicago: The Search for Authenticity in Urban Blues Clubs* (Chicago: University of Chicago Press, 2003): 12–16.

CHAPTER 10

1 Studs Terkel, *Hope Dies Last* (New York: The New Press, 2005).
2 The full text of Harvey Milk's "Hope Speech" can be found in Mark Blasius and Shane Phelan (eds.), *We Are Everywhere: A Historical Sourcebook in Gay and Lesbian Politics* (New York: Routledge, 1997): 451–3.
3 Two texts are particularly useful for understanding Piven and Cloward's historically fact-based theories on activism: Frances Fox Piven and Richard A. Cloward, *Poor People's Movements: How They Succeed, How They Fail* (New York: Pantheon Books, 1997) and Frances Fox Piven, *Challenging Authority: How Ordinary People Change America* (New York: Rowman and Littlefield, 2006).
4 Cormac McCarthy, *The Road* (New York: Vintage Books, 2006): 34.

CONCLUSION

1 Arthur Miller. Interview. *The Charlie Rose Show* (July 3, 1992).
2 William Van O'Connor, *The Tangled Fire of William Faulkner* (Minneapolis: University of Minnesota Press, 2009): 147–8.
3 Peter Guralnick is quoted in Greil Marcus, *Dead Elvis* (Cambridge, Massachusetts: Harvard University Press, 1991): 61.

Index